OBEDIENCE
CLASS
INSTRUCTION
FOR
DOGS

OBEDIENCE CLASS INSTRUCTION FOR DOGS

THE TRAINER'S MANUAL
Revised Edition

Winifred Gibson Strickland

MACMILLAN PUBLISHING CO., INC.
New York

ACKNOWLEDGMENTS

Grateful acknowledgment is made to the American Kennel Club for permitting me to reprint their Obedience Regulations in this book, and to quote from them a few times. Also, my thanks and appreciation to Ross Carson for his photographs.

Macmillan Publishing Co., Inc.
866 Third Avenue, New York, N.Y. 10022

Library of Congress Cataloging in Publication Data
Strickland, Winifred Gibson.
Obedience class instruction for dogs.
Includes index.
1. Dogs—Obedience trials. 2. Dogs—Training.
I. Title.
SF425.7.S77   1978   636.7'08'86   77-12988
ISBN 0-02-615010-7

First Revised Edition 1978

Printed in the United States of America

CONTENTS

FOREWORD

It was in February, 1948, that I first met Winifred Strickland. She and her husband had come to Williamsport, Pennsylvania, to buy a four-month-old German Shepherd puppy from my sister. The way she looked as she came through the gate, a small person in a ruby-red coat and hood edged with black fur, and the way she spoke with a soft New England accent won my heart immediately. As she rode away with a handsome, clumsy puppy, we seemed to sense that she was meant to own him. He was a puppy of soft, gentle temperament who could have been ruined in the wrong hands. In hers, and known as Topper, he became famous nationally and abroad. With him at her side, this petite, attractive young woman marched into the obedience world—a world that has changed because of her entrance. Because of her own perfect grooming, she lends dignity to the show ring when she competes there; her low-pitched voice proves to all who watch that one need not and should not use harsh, loud tones in training and showing; her skill in handling, to which her dogs respond with an equal skill in performance, produces a poetry of motion in the ring which adds an intangible sparkle to her work.

Over the years since that winter day in 1948, Winifred has won ninety-one obedience titles—thirty-eight Companion Dog degrees, thirty-one Companion Dog Excellent degrees, eighteen Utility Dog degrees, and four Tracking Dog degrees. Three of her German Shepherds have won the title of Top Obedience Dog in the United States for five consecutive years. First was Topper—Margelen's Chieftain—UDT—who won the title in 1950, 1951, and 1952. Second to win the same title was her Hussan vom Haus Kilmark, UDT. Hussan was runner-up in 1952 and 1954, and Top Obedience Dog in the United States in 1953. In 1954, her Alf vom Kroppelberg, UDT—Arry—came on the Obedience scene to make the greatest record ever made in this country. Arry won all his titles, including Tracking, in five months and three weeks with an average score of 199 points out of a possible 200. In that year, the year that Hussan was runner-up, he gained the title of Top Obedience Dog in the United States. Between them, Hussan and Arry won twenty-two perfect 200-point scores; other dogs in her hands have increased the total to forty.

Winifred has been a member of the German Shepherd Dog Club of America for thirty years; she has judged Obedience since 1952 and has bred German Shepherds for fifteen years. Her goal in breeding is to produce Shepherds of exceptional intelligence combined with sound temperament and show quality. She has introduced a new Obedience routine, which might be classified as "Advanced Utility," that she standardized and demonstrated with her own dogs. She judged this class at the National Specialty of the German Shepherd Dog Club of America in 1969 when it was offered for the first time in this country as a non-regular class.

Mrs. Strickland is the mother of two children. Her daughter Susan, a graduate of the University of Delaware, assists her in training and handling, displaying great excellence at both. Her son Ronald has his doctorate in political science from Georgetown University.

Winifred's first book, *Expert Obedience Training for Dogs*, has been a best seller among Obedience books for many years. In this second book she lays down valuable guidelines for trainers, guidelines which can and should eliminate most of the regrettable methods used entirely too often in dog training.

Two statements made by the author belong, I think, in a foreword to her new book. She says, "The first requisite a person should have to become an instructor is a genuine love for dogs." This calls to mind something said two thousand years ago: "Without love you are nothing." "People have never really understood how intelligent a dog can be," is the other statement. Love and understanding for his pupil—can one be a really successful teacher without these qualities? Can he really fail if he has them? I think not. Winifred, in the field of Obedience, is living proof of the truth of what she says. She has trained her own and other people's dogs with kind, gentle, understanding firmness to be happy and well-nigh perfect workers. In this book she is telling us how to do it. It is an honor to write this foreword and a privilege to call her a close friend.

Margaret M. Megahan
AKC Licensed Obedience
and German Shepherd
Conformation Judge

OBEDIENCE
CLASS
INSTRUCTION
FOR
DOGS

I | THE IDEAL INSTRUCTOR

The first requisite a person should have to become an instructor is a genuine love for dogs. This is more important than anything else. If an instructor really loves dogs, he will not permit any handlers to be cruel to their dogs in his class nor will he introduce any training methods that promote cruelty.

Since he will have to demonstrate the correct method, or, at times, the best correction, the obedience training instructor should be a well-coordinated person with fast reflexes. If an instructor is to demonstrate an exercise, or make clear a specific point, he must be in command of the situation. Using his own dog, he should perform the exercise smoothly, first in slow motion and then in a natural manner. The student will benefit from this demonstration by watching the procedure, listening to the instructor's tone of voice, and noting the smoothness of the handling.

The competent instructor should be able to pass along his knowledge to his class in a simple and direct manner. He should be able to control the handlers and their dogs without resorting to violence, becoming impatient, or losing his temper. The use of switches, heavy throw chains, spike collars, chain leashes, rubber hoses, etc., should never be permitted. A dog should never be "strung up" (held suspended in midair by its collar) for any reason. Any instructor who practices this should be reported to the nearest humane society.

The trainer who resorts to violence to train dogs is nothing more than a sadistic bully who is satisfying his warped ego by brutally forcing dogs to obey him. His demonstrations, repulsive as they are to dog lovers, give him a large enough following among the uninformed to encourage them to try his cruel tactics. People in groups tend to accept what they hear without thinking of the consequences. It doesn't take any intelligence to train a dog with force; any unstable person can do it. Dogs are being trained in this manner every day. In some cases, such training is the fault of one callous instructor; in many cases, though, it is the result of plain ignorance, because the handlers do not understand that there is a better, more humane, way of training. There are some instructors who want to put a dog through a four-month course in six weeks; these will not take the time to be kind to their dogs.

The intelligent instructor must set a good example of patience, tolerance, and perseverance. Having infinite patience, particularly, is essential, for it takes considerably more patience to train people to train their dogs than it takes to train the dogs themselves. From one week to the next, there must be constant repetition because novice handlers have a way of forgetting the many minor details that they must learn in order to train their dogs. There will be many people who are all thumbs; they will need personal assistance. It is best to assist these handlers individually while bringing the problem to the attention of the whole class. A problem thus brought to light is likely to be remembered.

The instructor must always stress homework, insisting that the handlers practice an hour a day. The class as a whole must be inspired by the instructor to strive for perfection and smoothness of handling. He should be able to advise them how to get both.

It helps for an instructor to have a sense of humor, as there is always something amusing going on in an obedience class. A kind word, a jest, a smile, or an infectious laugh can comfort the novice handler who is discouraged to find that obedience training is work. A word of encouragement at the right moment is the difference between a dropout and a determined beginner.

The ideal instructor is a person who has foresight. To teach a handler to train his dog, he must be able to visualize the dog at different stages of his training. The instructions he gives in the Novice class will simply be the first in a series of integrated lessons. If the instructor keeps the advanced work in mind, each new lesson will be a step forward, and the dog should learn and progress from week to week without any break or interruption to mar his advance.

The instructor should be aware of the problems that arise from improper training and recognize the subsequent mistakes that occur as a direct result of using the wrong technique. By teaching the handler the correct way to control his dog, the instructor will save valuable time for the important lessons.

The ideal instructor is a person who has had actual show experience, for he will understand the problems his students will face in actual competition. Handling a dog in an obedience trial, where he is subjected to all kinds of distractions, noises, and strange odors, is completely different from class training or backyard training. The instructor who has surmounted these obstacles and problems himself is best equipped to advise his students of the pitfalls ahead. The teacher who has earned a great number of obedience degrees with a great number of dogs is most likely to have the answers to the different training problems. This is particularly true of the instructor who has been a consistent winner in obedience trials. It is, of course, a great asset if the instructor has personally had the experience of teaching and showing a great number of dogs. Different breeds react to a situation in different ways; the ideal instructor will anticipate this and advise the handler just what he can expect. There is no better teacher than experience, provided that one is able to learn and to profit by it.

There are people who have trained dogs who do not make good instructors because they persist in using old methods, old techniques, and useless routines that waste time and create errors. They are so set in their ways that they are incapable of learning anything new and are, consequently, very limited in their ability to teach others.

Then there are also instructors who train handlers in their own fashion, giving no thought to incorporating the *American Kennel Club Obedience Regulations* into the routines at the same time. It is quite possible they have never read them.

The worst instructors are those who have been at it for a few years and have lost all feeling for the dogs. Some probably started by training guard or attack dogs and feel that the answer to every training problem is force. They try to convince students that their dogs should be forced to obey, and they use one cruel tactic after another on the dogs. In order to cover up the effect this brutal treatment has on the dogs, the instructor advises the handlers to pet the dogs with a feigned "Good dog." Some dogs, thankful for the respite, wag their tails in relief. Such instructors bring out the worst in people, brainwashing them into believing it is natural and normal to train dogs by abusing them. These instructors should be boycotted, and handlers who train their dogs in this manner should be penalized in the ring. Such training is contrary to everything decent and kind.

In contrast to the aforementioned instructors, I prefer the sincere instructor who has had just a little experience but who loves dogs and respects their feelings. He realizes that a well-trained, well-mannered dog leads a happier life than a poorly trained dog because he is better adjusted in every way and sets a good example to all others. By turning out better-informed handlers and well-mannered dogs, he is doing his community a valuable service. This is the type of instructor who is willing to teach the training method that is up to date and considerate of the dogs and that promotes accurate, happy workers.

The ideal instructor is a warm person who trains with his heart. He tries to see matters from the dog's side as well as from that of the handler. He understands that an intelligent trainer uses his head to solve problems and presents a training method that brings out the best in the dogs and their handlers. He believes that the right method, with the proper use of praise, is the best way to an expertly trained dog. And although swift corrections are a part of all training, brutality is forbidden.

In this country many hundreds of people who lack the necessary experience are holding obedience classes for dogs. In order to help rectify this situation, I am going to pass along some of the knowledge I have gained through actual experience over the years, knowledge that I hope will help instructors realize that obedience training should be a series of integrated steps, and not a conglomeration of weird, unrelated ideas.

2 | HOW TO START OBEDIENCE TRAINING CLASSES

The first step in starting obedience classes is to find a suitable place. There are several possibilities to explore. If you live in an area where the weather is warm and dry, you may be able to hold the classes outdoors. The ideal location would be outdoors, in a fenced-in field where the grass is kept short. A grassy field is the best terrain for training because the grass cushions every step that the handlers and their dogs take. The turf doesn't hold the heat the way a paved surface does; this makes it more comfortable for the dog when he is working. Also, since a dog will be more apt to want to sniff grass than pavement, this fault will crop up immediately, enabling the handler to correct it in the early stages of his training.

It is also an advantage for the handlers to be able to drive their cars onto the field and park adjacent to the training area. Most of the dogs that break away from their handlers run to their own cars and are easily caught. It is a great convenience to have the car nearby if the handler has more than one dog to handle. It also works well for the handlers who bring along their children and want them to stay in the car. Many people like to watch the training classes from their cars or bring a snack and watch a couple of training classes while they relax on the sidelines.

Some public parks or schools will let responsible parties use their facilities for this purpose. It will be up to the instructor or club to see that these privileges are not abused. Many shopping centers will permit the use of a portion of their parking lots for the same purpose. This brings more people to the shopping center, and some enterprising public relations managers will even offer prizes to dogs graduating at the top of the class. We have held club shows with all the prizes donated by the merchants in the shopping center. For the merchants it is just another way to bring into the area a large group of people that would not otherwise shop there.

If you find that you have to use a parking lot for your classes, have the handlers park their cars bumper to bumper to form a large rectangle. This way the handlers and their dogs are protected from the traffic. It is hard to concentrate on training a dog and to dodge traffic at the same time.

The outdoor classes are far superior to those held indoors because of the larger working space and the great convenience this space affords. It is more pleasant working outdoors in the fresh air for both the dogs and their handlers, there is better footing for jumping, and the instructor can give his class excellent routines without worrying about cramped quarters.

It is difficult to find an indoor area that is large enough to accommodate a class of twenty or more handlers with their dogs. A school gym is just about perfect. The size is generally right, the floor is clean, the acoustics are good, and the bleachers on the sides are handy for spectators. Schools also offer the advantage of having large parking areas nearby.

Other indoor areas might be found at fire halls, skating rinks, armories, indoor parking lots, bus terminals, bowling alleys, private clubs, or recreation halls. It takes a certain amount of inquiry, but generally someone will come up with an idea, having realized that it is an advantage to have well-mannered dogs in the neighborhood.

The next step is to advertise your classes in the local newspapers. If you are not well known, you should advertise your method of training. Once you have proved your capability, the word will get around that there is a competent dog trainer in the area and more people will start asking about training for their dogs.

Be sure to give your phone number as most people like to make inquiries before they enroll in a class. If the caller wishes to register, take the handler's name, address, telephone number, breed of dog to be trained, its age, and call name. If the classes are to be held indoors, you may wish to advise the owners that their dogs must be housebroken. The owners should be required to have their dogs inoculated against distemper, hepatitis, and rabies. If it is an older dog, it would be wise to tell the handler to get his dog a distemper booster inoculation.

By having the handlers register for the class over the telephone, you will be able to control the size of the class. The series of lessons should run for a specified number of weeks. If you make it a ten-week series, the handler should be doing fairly well by the end of that time. A handler who takes the training seriously and practices correctly at home could try his dog in obedience matches after a ten-week series of lessons. However, most of the handlers will need another, more advanced, series of lessons before they are ready for competition.

Equipment: Five-foot leash, grab leash, nylon choke collar, dumbbell, three white work gloves, scent-discrimination articles, tracking harness, tracking leash, two tracking flags, five tracking poles, bench chain, and a chain choke collar.

It is a good idea to carry a small supply of equipment for the convenience of the handlers. Have a selection of top-quality leather or web leashes about five feet in length, as this is the easiest length for the beginner to use. The leather leashes should be soft and pliable and not over half an inch wide; wide leashes are too cumbersome to use. Have a supply of chain choke collars and nylon chokers on hand in all the various sizes. It is also an excellent idea to carry a supply of my book *Expert Obedience Training for Dogs* for those handlers who are sincerely interested in learning all they can about dog training. The handlers who read the book at home and take the class lessons are those who will do the best job of training their dogs. It will make the work just that much easier for the instructors.

If advanced classes are offered, I would suggest that you also carry tracking leashes, grab leashes, dumbbells, white work gloves, and utility articles. Indoor classes will need at least two rolls of rubber matting, forty feet long and three feet wide, for the advanced classes.

The instructor or club should provide two sets of jumps for the classes. These will consist of high jumps, bar jumps, and broad jumps. Heretofore, the handling and storing of jumps has always been a major headache for individuals and clubs. They were very heavy and cumbersome and needed a large storage area. Now it is possible to buy strong, lightweight portable jumps that fit together and store as easily as a bag of golf clubs. Many clubs buy extra sets and rent them out to their club members when they need them.

Another piece of equipment every instructor should have is a public address system. He will need it for classes so that everyone will hear him without his shouting, and he will need it for club meetings, dog shows, demonstrations, etc. There is a new electronic P.A. system that is ideal because it is featherweight (three pounds) and can be carried on the belt or shoulder. It is completely portable with rechargeable batteries and no cords or wires. It can be fine tuned for use in a small room, large gym, or outdoor football field. Both the jumps and the P.A. system can be obtained from Ross Carson & Company, RD2, Newark, Del. 19711.

If the instructor plans to hold a graduation night at the end of each series of lessons, he will need a supply of diplomas to present to the students who pass. These can be obtained from dog food companies or printed to order with the obedience club's name on them.

Portable jumps—ready to use and assembled; ready to carry.

Instructor using E-Z Com.

3 | OBEDIENCE TRAINING CLASSES FOR PUPPIES

It has always been my contention that dogs should be trained at a very early age, before they have had the chance to acquire any bad habits. I trained my first German Shepherd dog to do all kinds of tricks and useful little errands before she was six months old. She was taught to be obedient long before I had heard of obedience trials. I loved her dearly and felt she deserved to be trained so that she would be well mannered and accepted everywhere. Every dog that I have owned since that time has been trained at an early age. Topper of Wynthea was ready for Utility competition when he was eleven months old.

The first words a puppy learns in my home are "Puppy, No, Stay, Lie down, Good," and the puppy's name. Whole litters learn the word "Stay," before they are six weeks old. It is not that we are trying to prove anything; it is just so much easier to take care of puppies when they know a few of the basic commands. Generally, by the time they are ten weeks old, they are housebroken.

In my classes I have accepted dogs that were five months old on a trial basis. If the handler has the patience to train the puppy correctly, he is permitted to stay in the class. If he doesn't have the patience, or understanding, he is asked to let someone else in his family train the dog or to resume the training in another month.

While I thoroughly believe in training my puppies at an early age, I have never advocated early formal training for others because of the temperament of the average person. I felt that most people wouldn't have the patience and understanding to cope with the antics of a small puppy. However, last year I decided to try having a large group of people train their four-month-old puppies in my classes. They were very successful; every single handler was able to teach his puppy as much, in a specified time, as were the handlers who were training older dogs. The difference between the two groups was that the puppy group had more fun and found the work a lot easier. The methods of training were somewhat similar except that the corrections for the puppies were very mild. The puppies responded more readily to the tone of voice the handler used and were much more sensitive to corrections.

I suggest that the instructor advertise training classes for puppies who are between the ages of four and six months. A puppy four months of age is willing to accept anything you want to teach him. He will try to please just for the sake of pleasing and will be very happy if he succeeds. If he receives an adequate amount of praise and petting, he will learn his lessons quicker than an older dog. At this age the puppy has an open mind; if he can be trained to do all the right things, he will not get any bad habits. Because the puppy has not learned any bad habits, he will understand the lesson that much sooner. There is never the defiance one sometimes gets from an older dog, and any opposition the puppy gives is short-lived.

The method of training puppies is very important. The training time should be half that of an older dog. Classes should last about half an hour, and the practice sessions at home should be about twenty minutes. The training should be concentrated so that the puppy gets as much as possible from a short lesson. This is possible if the routines are very simple and direct. The puppy will understand the lesson, retain it, and progress steadily from one lesson to the next.

Whatever the temperament of the puppy, class training will be good for him, provided that the experience is always a pleasant one. Even though minor corrections will have to be given throughout the lesson, the puppy should have fun while he is learning.

The puppy class should run for a series of ten lessons, one half-hour lesson per week. The first lesson should be spent teaching the puppies to heel and sit and to stay and come. The instructor should demonstrate with a puppy the first steps in teaching a puppy to heel. At first, the puppy will try to forge ahead or go off to the side; to correct this, the instructor should jerk the puppy back to his side with just enough force to bring him back. It doesn't take much of a jerk to teach a puppy to heel. The

Holding the leash in the right hand, near his left side, the handler should guide the puppy into a straight sit.

instructor should explain that the puppy's neck is very tender and that a small jerk should suffice. The instructor should reach down and pet the puppy when he is by his side and tap the front of his leg frequently to show the puppy where he should be. He should make it fun for the puppy by laughing and reaching down and petting him. On corners he should jerk the puppy if he isn't with him as he calls the puppy's name and coaxes him to stay at heel by using a persuasive tone of voice. A puppy is always very interested in voices or odd noises, and the handler should use both to keep his puppy alert. The instructor should show his class how he uses his voice continually to keep the puppy's attention on him.

When the handler stops, he should switch hands on the leash and reach down to the puppy with his left hand to guide him into a straight sit. The puppy, at this age, can be taught to sit automatically if he gets a push or a quick tap. A combination of both should be used during the heeling routine. All the puppies that I have trained have learned to sit automatically in the first fifteen-minute lesson. When the puppy starts sitting automatically, the handler should always have his left hand down near his puppy when he stops so that he can guide him into a straight sit or pet him, or both. A big fuss should be made over the puppy who sits automatically. If the puppy gets up and climbs on the handler when he is praised, he can be excused. He should be petted and praised and then made to sit again *quickly*. This is one of the differences between training an older dog and a puppy. The puppy should be allowed to express himself and then the lesson should continue immediately.

The puppy should be petted with the left hand while the leash is held in the right.

The exception to this brief-expression rule would be a dog belonging to one of the breeds which jump up and down on their hind legs like a Yo-Yo. In this case the puppy should be jerked down as he is jumping up with the admonition "No jumping." If the handler is quick about it, he can correct his puppy in the early stages before this becomes a major problem. Handlers with small dogs make the mistake of carrying them everywhere instead of letting them walk; when they begin to teach their dogs to heel, the dogs stand on their hind legs and claw and scratch at their handlers' clothes or legs, asking to be picked up. If the handlers will stop this practice and make the puppies walk everywhere, they will soon stop jumping.

The puppy will try all sorts of tricks, depending upon his breed and his temperament. Most anything a puppy does is cute, but the handler should be firm and make the puppy mind the first time he commands him to do something. Even though the handler is guiding the puppy, or petting him, the puppy must do what he is told. When the handler makes turns, the puppy should receive a quick, small jerk, as the handler reminds the puppy to "Heel." By talking to the puppy, showing him how to stay close, repeating the puppy's name and the word "Heel" frequently, the handler can soon teach the puppy to keep up with him.

It is so easy to correct a puppy at this tender age that the handlers must be warned not to be rough with their puppies. Even the large dogs are easy to control when they are puppies. It will in no way hurt a puppy's spirit or change his personality if his training begins at the age of four months, provided that this method is used and the handlers follow instructions.

One very important point that should be stressed is that the handler should always let his puppy know that he is loved. The handler must provide the puppy with a sense of security so that he will develop complete confidence in the handler and be unafraid. The puppy that trusts his handler to be kind and understanding is the puppy who will be eager to learn and willing to work. This is the opportunity the handler will have to teach his puppy to respect him and trust him. And once he earns his puppy's trust, he must strive to keep their relationship harmonious.

The puppies should be taught to ignore each other so that they will become independent. The puppy that is permitted to sniff and play with his neighbor in class will spend his time thinking about the other puppies and trying to disrupt the class. The instructor should keep the class working every minute, except during the demonstrations and explanations, so that the puppies will be kept occupied. If they are kept busy, they won't get into mischief.

An independent puppy will become a well-adjusted dog. The puppy who would rather stay with his littermates than associate with human beings, who cries without cause, or who wants to run and hide because he is shy will become neurotic if he is not corrected when he is young. These puppies should attend classes when they are four months old. If the handlers will spend a little time each day training their puppies, they will turn out to be well-mannered, well-adjusted dogs.

There are still people who are advising others to wait until their dogs are a year old before training them. This poor advice has ruined a great number of good dogs. People who wait a year to train their dogs are in for a lot of grief. The dogs by this time are wild and unruly, and the bad habits they have acquired will be hard to break. It is possible to train a dog at any age, but the longer a person waits to train his dog, the more strict he must be and the harder it will be on the dog and the handler.

Occasionally one hears from a dog owner the plaintive cry "I wouldn't train my puppy so young. I want him to enjoy being a puppy." This naïve remark comes from a well-intentioned person who doesn't know what he is talking about. Contrast the little untrained monster who cannot be left alone in the house because he chews anything in sight and ends up either getting a licking or being locked in a room alone, usually in the basement or garage, with the trained youngster who is learning to be well mannered and is taken everywhere with the family because he is such a good puppy. Which puppy is enjoying life—the wild, uncontrolled puppy who gets in everybody's hair or the puppy who is getting acquainted with the world? Because the latter is being trained, he is enjoying every minute of being a puppy and his privileges are endless. The joy he spreads is contagious, and everyone greets him with a smile and wants to pet him. He grows up to be a beloved member of his family with his place in life secure. The untrained dog, however, very often becomes a burden and an unwanted responsibility and is passed along from one family to another until his luck runs out.

When training puppies, the handlers should be much more demonstrative and uninhibited than with older dogs. During the early stages of the training, handlers should bend over frequently to show the puppies where they should be and to pet them when they are close. The handler must be willing to forget himself and concentrate all his thoughts and attention on the puppy. Besides teaching the puppy to be obedient, the handler must keep the puppy happy and encourage him to work. Since not everyone has the temperament to teach a puppy, it will be up to the instructor to weed out any rough or inconsiderate handlers.

The instructor should explain the correct procedure used to teach a puppy the Recall exercise. With his puppy sitting in front of him the handler should hold the leash taut in his left hand behind the puppy's head. He should give his puppy the stay signal by gently placing his other hand in front of his puppy's nose as he gives him the command "Stay." The puppy will probably try to get up and follow his handler when he steps back, but the taut leash will keep him in place. If the puppy stands up, the handler must make him sit. This should be repeated whenever the puppy tries to move, and the handler should repeat the words, "No, stay," each time he puts him back. When the puppy stays for a second or two, the handler should try to step back and let the leash go slack.

At first the puppy might be quite stubborn. If he persists in getting up, the handler must hold the leash taut, give the command, "No, stay," push the palm of his right hand against the puppy's nose firmly but *not* roughly, and then hold his hand a few inches in front of the puppy's nose. If the puppy tries to jump up, the handler should place his hand on the puppy's chest and quickly push him into a sit; all the while he should be talking softly. When the puppy has decided to stay, he may turn his head

Holding the leash taut behind the puppy's head give the Stay signal with the right hand.

Each handler continues to hold the Stay signal where the puppy can see it.

to the side and appear to be looking at something. This is just a ruse and the handler should not repeat the stay command so long as the puppy remains in place. As soon as it is practical, the handler should step back to the end of the leash and, if necessary, continue to hold the stay signal out to his side where the puppy can see it. In the beginning the handler will have to repeat the verbal command "Stay" and show the puppy the stay signal many, many times.

After the puppy has stayed in place a few seconds, the handler should call his puppy by saying his name and the word "Come." If the puppy doesn't respond immediately, the handler should give his leash a little jerk. When the puppy starts toward him, the handler should praise him exuberantly, quickly guide him into a straight sit, and pet him. Puppies will learn to sit when they come in to the handler in a very short time; in fact, they will probably sit automatically during the first lesson. To accomplish this the handler must remember to praise his puppy as he is coming in; when the puppy is close, he should hold him gently under the chin or by the skin around his neck and with the other hand gently guide him into a straight sit. The puppy should be praised and petted immediately. The puppy that is started this way will enjoy learning the recall and will respond quickly.

The puppy that jumps up when he reaches his handler should be made to sit quickly with the command "No, sit," and then praised when he is sitting. The next few times the puppy comes in to the handler, he should be told to sit when he is fairly close. The handler should be ready to bend

The handler should guide the puppy into a straight sit in front as he praises him for coming.

The handler should hold the puppy gently under the chin with one hand while he pets him with the other.

over quickly to pet the puppy as he guides him into a straight sit. The handler must learn to make the corrections very quickly and smoothly so that the puppy is doing the right thing only a second after doing something wrong. His praise should come swiftly even though the handler has gently forced him to do it correctly. Since the puppy is never permitted to do anything wrong, he will remember the times when he was praised and will associate the praise with the correct things he did.

The first lesson should end with a Long Sit-Stay exercise. The puppies should be made to stay on a Long Sit for thirty seconds and then for one minute. The handlers should practice this exercise for several minutes, during which time they should leave their puppies, and return to them two or three times. The instructor should show the handlers how to return to their puppies so that they can practice this correctly at home. The handlers should approach their puppies and caution them to "Stay," as they walk around them and step into heel position. The handler should hold his leash in his left hand and extend his arm so that it is on the dog's right side.

The instructor should have the handlers make their puppies lie down while he reviews the first lesson. He should again caution the handlers not to be rough in training their puppies, encouraging them, instead, to bring out the best that is in each puppy by using a combination of praise, intelligent reasoning, psychology, love, and understanding.

This training method will appeal to the overwhelming number of dog owners who love their dogs and who realize that a dog who has been

To complete the Long Sit, each handler should hold his leash in his left hand and extend his arm so that it is on the dog's right side while he walks behind the dog into heel position.

trained with intelligence and understanding will always win over the dog who has been subjected to cruelty to force him to work.

In following weeks the instructor should add new exercises, but the practice sessions should be shorter than those for the older dogs and the corrections should never be harsh.

The Finish exercise is taught the same way one would train an older dog, but the handler should not use much force to jerk the puppy back by his side. A small jerk will be all that is necessary, but the handlers must learn to do it very quickly so that the puppy is sitting and being praised before he has a chance to think about it. After two or three times the handler should guide the puppy back with the leash and help him to sit straight. In just a few lessons the puppy will respond to the signal to finish. Eventually, he will also respond to the verbal command to finish, so the handler should test the puppy occasionally to see whether he has learned either the signal or the verbal command.

The Long Down exercise should be included in the second lesson. Teaching a puppy to drop on both signal and verbal command is much simpler than teaching a full-grown dog. Standing in front of his puppy with the leash in his left hand, the handler should raise his right hand quickly to where the puppy can see it, give the verbal command "Down," and pull the puppy down with his leash. As soon as the puppy is down, he should quickly pet and praise him saying, "Down, good, down, good." The puppy will soon be lying down when he sees the hand signal or hears

Standing in front of his puppy with the leash in his left hand, the handler should raise his right hand quickly to where the puppy can see it, give the verbal command "Down" and pull the puppy down with his leash.

As soon as the puppy is down, the handler should quickly pet and praise him saying, "Down, Good. Down, Good." If necessary, apply a little pressure to the puppy's withers to hold him down while stroking him.

the verbal command. When the puppy is down, he should be told to "Stay," and the handler should leave him, walk to the end of the leash, and turn to face him.

All verbal commands should be given in a calm tone of voice. The only time a handler should raise his voice is when he is praising his puppy exuberantly.

Each week the instructor should end the lesson with a Long Sit and a Long Down exercise. The handlers should teach their puppies to sit and stay for two minutes and to stay on a Long Down for four minutes. With practice the puppies will soon learn to stay the required length of time.

The Stand-for-Examination exercise should be introduced the fifth week of class. By this time the puppies will understand the stay signal and will be sitting automatically. It will be easy to teach a puppy to stand if the handler will walk forward with his puppy and give him the stay signal when he notices the puppy lining up his front feet. The handler can get his puppy to do this by holding him on a short, taut leash with his left hand. While holding the puppy like this, he should quickly give the stay signal and step forward to the end of the leash. If the puppy starts to move, he should be shown the stay signal and be verbally cautioned to "Stay."

After a few seconds the handler should return around his puppy and into heel position as he continues to caution him to "Stay." When the puppies understand this part of the exercise, the handler should drop his leash after he leaves him and after a few seconds he should return and examine the puppy by running his hand over his head, back, and hindquarters. Puppies like this attention and will move unless they are cautioned to stay. This is not a difficult exercise and the puppies will learn it through repetition.

To keep a small puppy standing, a handler might find it helpful to place his left foot under his puppy's tummy. He should also hold his puppy on a taut leash with his left hand as he gives him the stay signal with his right hand. Many times it will be necessary to hold the signal so that the puppy will realize he is to remain standing.

The handler should never jerk on the leash as this will make his puppy sit. The taut leash will restrain him and help him to learn what is required. By using the leash correctly, the handler will soon be able to control his puppy and teach him to stand with his front feet in line with each other. When this has been accomplished, he will find it comparatively easy to stand his puppy in this manner on a loose leash. If the puppy attempts to take another step, the handler should either say "No, stay" and place the leg back in line with the other, or have the puppy take one more step so that he would again have his front feet in line. He

Practicing the Long Down exercise with the leashes on the ground.

should make it clear to his puppy that the stay signal means he is not supposed to take another step.

If the puppy should sit at any time when he is being trained to stand, the handler should lift him up on his four feet so that he is standing squarely as he tells him to "Stand." During the time that the puppy is learning this exercise, he should also be taught to get up and stand on the verbal command "Stand." This will take considerable repetition, but the puppy will learn the command if the handler will make him stand each time he is commanded to do so.

This exercise is really not very difficult; it just takes practice. When a puppy has learned this exercise, he will be ready for the Novice Stand for Examination, but equally important is the fact that he will have learned another part of the Utility Signal exercise and the Working class Control exercise.

To teach the Figure Eight exercise, the instructor should have two handlers with their puppies in heel position act as posts while the others in the class do figure eights around them. This is a very good exercise for puppies to practice because it teaches them to ignore the other puppies while they are working. The handlers should take turns being posts each week so that everyone will have this experience. The handlers should be cautioned not to let their puppies sniff or disturb the other puppies. The instructor should advise the handlers when their puppies are lagging, forging ahead, or bumping into them. On this exercise the puppies should be taught to heel with precision and to keep their shoulders in line with their handlers' knees. The handlers should make a game of this exercise and encourage their puppies to keep up with them.

As the weeks go by, the handlers should be training their puppies to heel on very slack leads. Each handler should gradually gain control of his puppy using only his voice and his hands. At this point, the handler should remove the leash and practice working without it. If he has trained his puppy properly, the removal of the leash will have no effect on the puppy's work. The puppy will enjoy working and will be happy to stay by his handler's side.

There is no reason why a handler shouldn't expect his puppy to work with as much precision as an older dog will. It is up to the handler to insist upon perfection. A puppy can learn to sit straight if he is reminded often enough. The puppy should not be punished for sitting crooked, but he should be shown and guided into a straight sit with the admonition "Sit straight." After several weeks the puppy will sit straight upon hearing the verbal command.

The handlers should practice recalls on leash until the puppies are coming in and sitting straight in front of them consistently. Next they should practice recalls with the puppies dragging their leashes. The handlers should start practicing longer recalls as the puppies respond. A puppy will not trip over his leash if his handler will be considerate and leave it by his side or down his back.

A puppy should not be allowed to go past his handler when he is supposed to be doing a recall. If the puppy attempts this, the handler should say, "No, come," and either give the puppy a small jerk to the front or clap his hands to entice his puppy to come to him. The puppy should always be taught that "Come" means for him to take a position directly in front of his handler and nowhere else. If this point is made clear from the beginning, the puppy will form a good habit of sitting in front of his handler.

If anyone in the class has his puppy trained so well that he is ready to work off leash, the instructor should permit him to do so. This should inspire the other handlers to get busy and catch up with him. Training a puppy, or a dog, takes many hours of work, and any handler who is willing to work at it seriously should be encouraged to keep it up.

Every puppy should be taught to retrieve while he is young. This is the time when it is easy and the puppy thinks it is great fun.

There should be a ten-minute break for the puppies between the Novice class and the retrieving lesson. There are two ways of teaching a puppy to retrieve, and both are simple. If the puppy likes to chase things, the handler should play with the dumbbell himself by tossing it up in the air and catching it, making sure that his puppy is watching him. After a couple of minutes the handler should throw the dumbbell fifteen feet or so as he makes exaggerated gestures and a loud swishing noise. All this excitement should encourage the puppy to run out and get it. If he does, the handler should call him back and take it from him. After petting and praising his puppy, he should try this a few more times, making a big game of it. He should, however, be sure that the puppy picks up the dumbbell by the middle piece. If he doesn't, the handler should give the puppy the dumbbell in such a way that he must grasp the middle piece. Playing with the puppy ten minutes a day will soon make him very efficient at retrieving. He must be encouraged to retrieve the dumbbell quickly and should not be permitted to mouth or chew it.

Some puppies will not be interested in playing this game and must be taught to retrieve in simple steps. The first step is to teach the puppy to grasp the dumbbell and hold it. The handler should have his puppy on leash, and as he holds it in his left hand to restrain the puppy from moving, he should hold the dumbbell by the end and place it in front of the puppy's nose with his right hand. As he commands his puppy to "Get the dumbbell," he presses the dumbbell against the puppy's lips and, with his left hand, slips the puppy's mouth open by placing his two fingers in behind the puppy's canine teeth. He then orders his puppy to "Hold it," while he strokes him on the nose and under the chin. After a second he removes the dumbbell and praises his puppy in a very pleased tone of voice.

I have found that after a few attempts the puppy will open his mouth and take the dumbbell. Since puppies seem more eager to hold onto the dumbbell than do older dogs, it is an easy step to run backward once the puppy has taken the dumbbell and call him. As the puppy runs to the handler with the dumbbell, he should be praised and guided into a straight sit while the handler says "Hold it" and, after a second, "Out" and takes the dumbbell.

The handler should work on this exercise for a week. The next step is to throw the dumbbell six feet away and run up to it with the puppy, encouraging him to "Get the dumbbell." The handler should hold up one end of the dumbbell or wiggle it back and forth to arouse the puppy's interest and entice him to pick it up. If this is done gradually, the puppy will be quite willing to get it. If he should get stubborn about picking it up, the handler should hold his head down near the dumbbell and make him take it by holding one end of the dumbbell off the ground and wiggling it. By making it easy when he gets stubborn, he will soon be willing to pick it up every time. The handler should make the puppy get it every time he is told, even though he may have to give him a little help. This should not be practiced very long; nothing is gained by forcing a puppy to work when he is tired. I have found that ten minutes is long enough. A puppy can be taught to retrieve willingly in three weeks or less, so there is no need to make the lessons tedious.

Puppies can be taught to enjoy working and will respond with lots of spirit and precision so long as the handler makes the lesson interesting and every new experience a pleasant one. This does not mean that a puppy should not receive corrections: he will need them every day, but they should never be harsh. The puppy should be made to understand that he is being corrected for something he did wrong rather than being punished. If the handler will keep this in mind, he will find that he can train his puppy quickly by simply showing and guiding the puppy through each new step. A tug on the leash when it is needed is one small correction that is effective. A disapproving tone of voice is another very effective correction. A kind word spoken sincerely, a laugh, a smile of approval, or a hand clap given at precisely the right moment will encourage the puppy to be obedient.

If the instructor finds that there are too few puppies to start a separate class, he can include them in his regular class. However, if this is done, he should explain that there will be a difference in the way each is trained. He should keep his eye on the puppy handlers so that they don't become too rough, and he should limit the length of time they practice the different routines. The puppy should also have some rest periods during the normal one-hour obedience lesson. The different breeds should not be segregated. If the instructor will enforce the "No Barking, No Sniffing, No Snapping" rule, there will be no problems.

4 | THE NOVICE EXERCISES

A sound ten-week series of lessons
for beginners, the pet owner who
wants his dog to be obedient at home,
and the obedience enthusiast who wants
to start his dog correctly.

The First Lesson

Arrangements should have been made over the phone to have the handlers arrive about fifteen minutes early for the first lesson. This extra time will enable the instructor to check the registrations that were taken over the telephone, take the registrations of the people who have come unannounced, collect the class fees, equip the dogs with collars and leashes, and check the choke collars already on the dogs.

Each dog should be fitted with the right-sized collar. This means that when the choke collar is pulled snug around the dog's neck, there will be 3½ inches of collar left over. The large breeds, and any active dogs, should wear chain choke collars with smooth links that permit the collar to be jerked easily without catching on an individual link. The quiet dogs, many of the toy breeds, and all the puppies under five months should wear the heavy nylon cord choke collars. Chain leashes should not be permitted in obedience classes as they are worthless. They are too heavy on the dog's neck, they telegraph every correction the handler tries to make, they make too much noise, and they are hard on the handler's hands, often causing blisters.

The leash I prefer is made of nylon and cotton webbing and is about

This chain choke collar is too large; it falls on the dog's chest.

five feet in length. It is soft and strong, light on the dog's neck, easy on the handler's hands, one-half-inch wide, available in all colors, and able to be rolled up and put in one's pocket. My second choice would be a well-oiled leather leash that is soft and pliable.

The instructor should acquaint each handler with the advantages of having my book *Expert Obedience Training for Dogs* to follow along with at home. In the first series of lessons it is impractical to cover any more than the fundamental steps. A handler will have a greater understanding of obedience training if he can read all about it. Some handlers forget many of the class instructions from one lesson to the next; for them, the book explains and illustrates each step so that the handler can practice correctly at home. This book will give the dog owner a wealth of infor-

A dog should not wear a collar as high on his neck, or as tight as this chain choke collar. The correct position for a choke collar is the nylon choke collar pictured. It fits so perfectly only the rings and a couple of inches of nylon are visible.

mation that will be useful to him apart from, and in conjunction with, the class lessons.

It is a good idea to have a blown-up picture, about twenty-by-twenty inches, of a choke collar being slipped over a dog's head. A handler will remember a picture of the correct way to put on a choke collar but will forget the verbal instructions from week to week. Have this picture on display at class so that the handlers can check their dogs' collars each week before the class starts.

It should be explained to the owners of each dog that the person who is going to train the dog in class should do the training at home. It is not good for the dog for the owners to take turns training him. When a dog is trained consistently by one person all the way through the series of lessons, it will obey any adult member of the family providing that member handles the dog correctly. Problems arise through no fault of the dog but because of the ignorance of his owner.

The heavy chain choke collar on top is worthless because the links are too large and uneven. The smooth links on the bottom collar permit it to be jerked smoothly and easily.

One instructor can teach a class of twenty to thirty handlers and their dogs, if the training procedure outlined in this book is followed. If there are more than thirty handlers with their dogs, the instructor should have an assistant. A certain amount of personal attention should be given the handlers in every training class. There will always be handlers who are not coordinated or who cannot follow instructions, and they will have to be personally shown and guided along the way. .

The instructor should give the commands and instructions to the class while the assistant stands by ready to move in where he is needed. When the instructor sees a handler making a mistake, he should immediately explain the problem and the solution to the whole class. If it is necessary, he should use a dog for demonstration purposes. It is better to use his own dog than to take the handler's dog. Even with a trained dog, it is usually easy for an experienced trainer to show the class where a handler

Pass the chain through one of the rings to form a collar.

made a mistake. However, there will be times when it will be necessary for the instructor to take the handler's dog. These instances will be covered as we come to them.

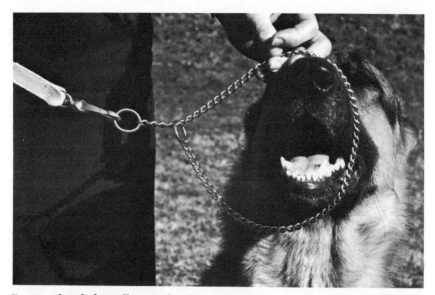

Putting the choke collar on the dog correctly. Notice the spring clip that is used.

An instructor should never take a handler's dog and abuse it, or take it to satisfy his own vanity. His job is to teach, not to terrify. The ideal instructor should be considerate of the dog and the handler. Many people are sensitive about training a dog in public for the first time; many people loathe being singled out and used as an example, and everyone expects to be treated courteously in class. People who love their dogs do not want to have them mistreated or abused. If a dog needs correction, the handler should take care of it himself. It is the instructor's place to advise him how it should be done. It should be remembered that the handlers have joined the class to learn how to handle their dogs themselves.

When an instructor, or his assistant, uses his own dog for demonstration purposes, the particular step in question must be made very clear to everyone. The best possible demonstration will have the instructor explaining the step very carefully while his assistant demonstrates it with a dog. The instructor must explain how it should be done, how it should not be done, and why this method works. The instructor and his assistant must be in complete harmony and work hand in glove at all times.

The instructor should have all the handlers and their dogs form a large circle around him. The handlers should be standing about a yard apart, and each dog should be sitting at his handler's left side. The instructor should explain and demonstrate the correct way to hold the leash. It is preferable in the beginning to hold the leash in both hands because the handler should be capable of using either hand whenever it is necessary. The leash is held short enough for the handler to keep his dog under control, long enough so that his dog can be jerked when he is away from him, and slack enough so that the dog doesn't feel any pressure on his neck.

The instructor should explain to the class that when he gives the order "Forward," each handler should say his dog's name and "Heel," and start walking on the word *Heel*. The handlers will have to be continually reminded to give the dog's name first to get his attention. Each dog should walk by his handler's left side, and when the handler stops, the dog should sit near his left leg. The instructor should explain that since the dogs will try to pull their handlers, it is up to the handlers to jerk their dogs back repeatedly, commanding them with each jerk to heel. He should also mention that when he calls "Halt," the handlers should stop and tell their dogs to sit.

The instructor should point in the direction he wants the handlers to walk, advising them to move briskly in order to keep their dogs' attention focused on them. Every few minutes he should instruct the handlers to not allow their dogs to pull them, but to jerk their dogs back. He will have to keep telling the handlers to move faster, for beginners have a tendency to slow down unless the instructor peps them up.

It is about this time that it will become apparent which dogs need to be corrected for barking. Since the instructor's advice cannot be followed if he cannot be heard, everyone will be pleased to have these dogs corrected. Usually, just one or two dogs are the culprits. The instructor should explain to the handler that if he will quickly bring his hand up under the dog's jaw as he is barking, and give him a good clop, the shock will make the dog keep quiet. The handler must make the correction himself. If he is timid about it at first, the instructions may be repeated more firmly. The handler will be embarrassed by his dog's actions and try to follow the instructions. In the rare case where a handler can't bring himself to correct his dog forcefully enough to keep him quiet, the instructor could say something like this: "I will not tolerate any barking in my class. It is impossible for anyone to hear me give instructions with that noise going on. It is the handler's responsibility to correct his dog, not mine." It is a good bet the instructor will not have to mention it again. It should always be made very clear in the beginning that any such noise will not be permitted. Although he may be tempted, the instructor should always avoid giving such corrections himself; it is his job to teach the handler how to do it. If the handler can be taught to correct his dog in class, you can be sure he will not hesitate to correct it elsewhere.

The ideal instructor should control his class right from the beginning. He should make the handlers aware of the fact that he is there to instruct them and they are there to learn.

Occasionally an instructor will get a dog in his class that has a high-pitched shriek instead of a bark. The dog can keep this shrill screaming up continually, as he doesn't need to open his mouth very wide to do so. The dog with such a tendency will be of one of the smaller breeds, such as a Miniature Schnauzer, and he will be a high-strung, nervous animal. This type of dog will also be pulling on the end of the leash as hard as he can, snapping at any dog that comes within his range. If he tries to bite another dog, he should get a sharp tap on the bridge of his nose.

There is one way to control such a dog. The dog should be jerked back sharply with the collar high behind his ears every time he lunges for another dog, screams, or tries to pull his handler on the leash. He will soon get the message and behave himself. Such dogs make life miserable for themselves and everyone near them. They should be dealt with firmly every time they act up. If they are not corrected, they will become even more difficult to manage. Dogs that are extremely bad mannered need these corrections. The instructor should explain to the owner and the class that if the dog had been corrected when he was a puppy, such measures would not be necessary.

One small dog I had in one of my classes was so obnoxious that he embarrassed his owners to the extent that they decided not to train him. I prevailed upon them to keep trying; they worked very hard with him. On graduation night this dog did so well that he graduated at the top of his class. The disciplinary training he got produced results.

A class may also include a dog that has been boss at home; he has, consequently, become very arrogant. When this dog finds he is expected to walk on leash, he becomes rebellious. He generally will plant his feet and refuse to move while his handler stands coaxing, pleading, and pulling on the leash. The dog may lie down and roll over on his back pawing at the leash or stand on his hind legs and wrap his front paws around the leash. Boxers, Dobermans, and a few other breeds will sometimes try these tactics. The solution is to have the handler keep jerking his dog sharply if he sits, stands, or refuses to walk and to drag him along the ground if he lies down. The dog will be amazed at this and find the correction so unpleasant that he will decide it is prudent for him to obey his handler. Once a dog finds his tantrums won't work, he will decide to obey. It is most amusing to see the dog's expression when he realizes his handler won't put up with such nonsense.

A dog that is overly aggressive, sharp, or vicious does not belong in an obedience class. There is no justification for exposing innocent people and friendly dogs to the imminent danger of a bad-tempered dog. Such a dog's presence in the class could be likened to a person carrying around a lighted firecracker. I will help anyone train his dog privately, but I refuse to permit a dog with an untrustworthy temperament to enter my classes. A handler with such a dog should take him to a professional trainer who will show him how to control his dog. In practically every case the untrustworthy dog has become so because his owner didn't train him when he was young, or didn't train him correctly. Since his dog is probably the product of the owner's own neglect, it is his responsibility to learn to control him before he brings him out in public. There are times when a dog has inherited a bad temperament; in this case, the handler should either take him back to the breeder, train him when he is a young puppy, or put him to sleep.

One occasionally finds a dog in class that walks on his hind legs, wrapping his forelegs around the leash or clinging to the handler's leg. Boxers, Dobermans, and a few other breeds like to do this. The correction is to jerk the dog off balance as often as necessary to keep him on his four feet. The small dogs are apt to do this most often unless the handler is fast with his correction; their owners encourage this habit by carrying them instead of letting them walk by themselves. If the handler will carry the leash in his left hand and be ready to jerk his dog as soon as it starts to jump, this bad habit can quickly be brought under control.

The instructor should explain to the class that their dogs will not be permitted to socialize at any time while attending obedience classes. He should explain to them that since their dogs are being taught to be well mannered, they must be under control at all times. Sniffing another dog is forbidden; this should be corrected with a jerk of the leash and the verbal command "No." Snapping at another dog, or the handler, must be corrected immediately with a sharp tap on the dog's nose and the admonition, "No biting." Remind the class that their dogs cannot learn anything if they have their attention focused on another dog. The dog must not be sniffing or staring at someone else; his attention must be on his handler.

The instructor might also state that the dogs should be housebroken. He should advise handlers not to feed their dogs for six hours prior to class and mention that it is up to the owner to clean up any mess the dog makes. He should caution everyone to exercise his dog before bringing him to class. A dog that makes a mistake of this kind while he is being trained should be verbally scolded. It is up to the handler to teach his dog clean habits; owners of small dogs are more prone to overlook their dogs' dirty personal habits, perhaps because the "mistakes" are small in size. I have given countless training lessons to handlers of small dogs who would permit their dogs to relieve themselves while they were working. The handler that allows his dog to get away with such social errors will find his dog disqualifying himself in an obedience ring some day.

In the beginning it is difficult for some handlers to understand how the choke collar works, and it is even more difficult for the uncoordinated handler to learn to jerk his dog. It is up to the instructor and his assistant to watch the handlers carefully, and if they see someone pulling his dog on a tight leash, they should explain this mistake to the class. The instructor should explain to the handlers that they must jerk their dogs back sharply, then immediately let the leashes go slack so that the dogs will not feel any pressure on their necks from tight leashes. This simple maneuver must be explained repeatedly week after week, for the handlers will forget it quicker than anything else. It is so normal for a beginner to hold his dog's leash close to his collar and let his dog drag him around that it becomes a difficult habit for him to break. Once the instructor gets this point across, the handler can start teaching his dog to heel. It is just as arduous trying to break the bad habits of the handler as it is the dog. A handler may even grasp his dog's collar in a futile attempt to control his dog. Telling him to have his dog's leash so loose that the clip is hanging down straight will help. Most handlers can understand this, and the instructor can ask the other handlers who are ignoring this suggestion to look at their leashes and notice whether they are holding them correctly. Gradually they will realize that the jerk the dog receives when he is away from his handler is much more effective than the one given when he is held close. He should keep reminding them that their dogs should be jerked back every time they try to forge ahead and that each jerk should be accompanied by the command "Heel." From time to time he should remind the class that the dog's shoulder should always be in line with the handler's left leg.

After the class has been heeling their dogs in a circle for about five minutes, the instructor should explain the about turn to them. The instructor should demonstrate with or without a dog, but he should explain that the handlers should either pivot or take small steps as they about turn to the right and reverse their direction. He should mention that their dogs may continue in the same direction in which they were going unless the handler jerks the dog as he is turning. He should remind them to tell their dogs to "Heel" each time they jerk their dogs.

After the class has had their dogs heeling, sitting, and making about turns for ten minutes or so, it is time to show them how to control their dogs' sits. This demonstration can be made by the assistant as the instructor explains in detail how it is done. Then the instructor should have the class heel their dogs in a circle while he and his assistant stand on oppo-

THE NOVICE EXERCISES | 37

site sides of the circle to assist the handlers. They should test each handler in the class to see whether he is controlling his dog correctly when he halts. Each handler must learn to do this correctly even if the instructor has to have that person halt three or four times. Generally, half the class will be doing it correctly after the demonstration.

The instructor should explain this maneuver every time it is necessary during the first series of lessons. When the instructor calls "Halt," each handler should grasp his dog's leash in his right hand, hold it close to his left side, tap his dog's croup with his left hand as he says "Sit," and immediately pet his dog with his left hand. The dog should be praised when he sits. The instructor should explain that each handler should control his dog's sit in this manner until his dog is sitting automatically and consistently every time he stops. The handlers should be cautioned not to jerk their dogs to make them sit. This is wrong because it causes a dog to back up a step or two to avoid the jerk. A handler with a dog of a small breed could get away with this as the dog is so light that the handler can control him with the leash, placing him just where he wants him, like a puppet on a string. However, it is far better for the handlers of small dogs to bend down and tap their dogs to teach them to sit.

During the remainder of the heeling period in the first lesson, the instructor and his assistant should be watching the handlers carefully and be ready to correct each person who does not use his leash correctly while heeling or stopping.

Hereafter when the handlers stop and have their dogs sit, the instructor should point out each handler who is letting his dog sit crooked. He should explain to the handlers that their dogs must learn to sit straight every single time from the very first sit. It is just as easy for a dog to form the habit of sitting straight as it is crooked. If the instructor will call attention to the dog who is sitting crooked, the handler will try harder to control the sit. The handlers do not like to have attention directed to them when they are doing something wrong, so they will try to follow instructions. Toward the end of the heeling period when the instructor has called "Halt," he should ask everyone to look around at the dogs. If they are all sitting straight, the class should be commended, but if there is one dog sitting crooked, let everyone notice it and then ask the handler to correct his dog.

After about twenty-five minutes of heeling, the instructor should stop the class, get everyone's attention, and review the heeling instructions that he has already given them. He should ask the group if anyone has any questions about the work. The instructor should remember that these handlers are going home to train their dogs; if they understand what he has told them, they will practice correctly and their dogs will learn their lessons.

Now the instructor should have the handlers form two lines opposite each other about thirty feet apart. He should explain that he wants every dog sitting straight at heel position. When a dog is in heel position, he is sitting by his handler's left side with his shoulder in line with his handler's left leg. The dog should be sitting perfectly straight with his toes in line with his handler's toes if it is a medium- to large-sized dog and slightly behind his handler's toes if it is one of the small breeds.

Next the instructor should explain that the class is going to do recalls. This means that the dog is going to learn to stay, and he is going to learn to come the first time he is called. It should further be explained that the dog's name should not be given before the stay command; when a dog hears his name, he anticipates action and is ready to move out of position. In the early stages of a dog's training, the handler should give his dog the stay signal and the verbal command *stay*. In obedience competition the dog's name may be used once immediately before any verbal command and/or signal when the regulations permit a verbal command and/or signal. However, in this particular case, it is neither practical nor wise to do so.

The instructor should demonstrate the stay signal by holding the palm of his right hand toward his class with his fingers pointing down, his hand held lower than his waist. This demonstration and explanation should be given several times for the people who didn't hear, didn't understand, or didn't pay attention. They should be cautioned to leave their dogs when the instructor tells them to leave, to call their dogs on his command, and to use only their dogs' name and the word "Come" when calling. Each dog should come and sit directly in front of his handler.

At this point each handler should give his dog the verbal command *stay* and the stay hand signal, walk out to the end of the leash, and turn and face his dog. After a few seconds the instructor should tell them to call their dogs. The first few times the handlers try a recall with their dogs, there will be no order or discipline. The first time a dog is told to stay, he probably won't obey and the handler will have to keep putting him back. In a class of twenty-five, you might get five dogs who will stay the first time the handlers tell them to do so. When the handlers have tried this exercise two or three times and are becoming a little frustrated, the instructor should give a demonstration with one of the class dogs.

The instructor should have the class form two lines facing each other, approximately thirty feet apart, while he demonstrates the way to teach a stubborn dog to stay. Holding the leash taut with his left hand behind his dog's head the instructor should give the dog the verbal command "Stay," in a firm, moderate tone of voice, and calmly place his right hand in front of the dog's nose for a stay signal. If the dog tries to move, his collar will be jerked back a little or he will be held in position, as the instructor cautions him, "No, stay," and holds the stay signal in front of his nose. If the dog stands up, the instructor should tap the dog's croup with his right hand as he says, "Sit," and again gives the dog the stay signal and verbal command "Stay," and continues to hold the leash taut in his left hand. As soon as possible, the instructor should release the dog's collar and leash and try to move back to the end of the leash. If the dog tries to move, the correction should be repeated. When the dog has stayed in position for a few seconds, the instructor should call him in, make him sit straight, and praise him.

The instructor should advise the handlers not to shout at their dogs when they are teaching them to stay. He should explain that there is nothing to be gained by shouting at a dog. A dog's hearing is very acute, about sixteen times better than ours, and the handler who trains his dog by yelling at him loses the respect of his dog and anyone else within hearing distance. The dog who is trained to respond to soft-spoken commands will always be more alert, reliable, and obedient. Handlers using excessively loud voices in obedience competition will be penalized.

The instructor should keep his class in order by having the handlers line up with their dogs after every second recall. Since after doing two recalls, the two lines will be working close to each other, each line should regroup and about turn so that they are facing away from each other. The instructor can control and observe a large number of handlers if they are working this closely together. If the two lines of handlers do two recalls with their dogs before they about turn, there will be a semblance of order even during the first class lesson.

After the handlers have done about four recalls, it is time for the instructor to show them how to control their dogs when they come in to the handlers. The instructor could use his own dog for this demonstration. When he calls his dog, he should start praising him in a pleased tone of voice as soon as he responds; when he is close to him, he should grasp his dog's ruff very gently with his left hand while tapping his dog's croup with his right hand to make him sit. He should give the verbal command "Sit," as he taps him, but should immediately praise and pat his dog when he sits. He should also explain that the handlers should be very gentle with their dogs when they come in to them and should hold them either very gently by the ruff, by the loose skin on their necks, or under the chin. The dog should not be petted until he is sitting. The instructor and his assistant should walk up and down the lines of handlers and help those who are having difficulty. Many of the handlers will be pointing a finger at their dogs to make them sit or stay, while others will be raising their hands too high and inadvertently giving their dogs a down signal. A few people will be letting their dogs sit everywhere but in front of them. Such errors must be brought to the attention of the entire class.

After working on recalls for about fifteen minutes, it is time to review the steps that teach a dog the recall. This time, after the handlers have tried it and have had varied degrees of success, the instructor's advice will be more easily digested and understood.

The instructor should line his class up once more and ask the handlers to have their dogs sitting at heel position. He should announce that this will be the last exercise for the first lesson. This time he will explain that he wants the handlers to teach their dogs the Long Sit exercise. He should explain that they will not call their dogs but will teach them to remain sitting, without moving, for two minutes, after which time they will return to them. Upon the command "Leave your dogs," the handlers will order their dogs to "Stay" in a quiet tone of voice and give them the stay signal. Most of the handlers will find they have to put their dogs back several times, so the first sit-stay should be for thirty seconds. At the conclusion of this time, the handlers should be ordered back to their dogs.

It is now time for the final demonstration for this first lesson. The instructor should command his dog to stay as he gives him the stay signal, then walk to the end of the leash, and turn to face him. After a few seconds he should hold the leash in his left hand and return to his dog by holding the leash on the dog's right side as he walks around the dog's left side, around in back of him, and into heel position. This should be repeated a couple of times so that everyone will understand the proper way to return to his dog. Next, have the handlers try it. The instructor and his assistant should watch closely to be sure everyone does it correctly. If any of the handlers do it wrong, they should be personally shown the right way to return to their dogs.

In closing the first class the instructor should advise the handlers to practice outdoors an hour each day. They should be instructed to practice the heeling, the controlled sit, the about turn, the stay, the recall, and the two-minute-long sit-stay. The handlers should be advised to read the first few chapters in my book, including the one on Novice exercises.

At the end of each training lesson the instructor should again encourage the handlers to bring any training problems they might have to his attention.

THE NOVICE EXERCISES | 41

The Second Lesson

If the class is not too large, additional handlers may join the second week, provided that they are willing to practice consistently each day to catch up with the others. Before the class starts, the instructor should take their registrations, explain how to fit a choke collar and demonstrate how to put it on correctly, and instruct them in the way to keep their dogs quiet during the class.

The instructor should have the handlers and their dogs form a large circle around him as he reviews the heeling routine they are to follow and practice. He should demonstrate with his dog the correct way to jerk back a dog who is pulling, the way to make an about turn, jerking the dog at the right moment so that he will learn to turn quickly with the handler, and the correct way to hold the leash while heeling and stopping so that the handler has control of the dog all the time.

People who meet me for the first time are always amazed to find that I am only five feet three inches tall and weigh just a few pounds more than my dogs. They expect to find some huge, strong, athletic type of person many times my size who depends on her physical strength to train dogs. I have trained all breeds of dogs, particularly large ones, and have developed very fast reflexes that enable me to make lightning-fast corrections. I use brain rather than brawn and depend upon my skill in manipulating the leash to teach a dog precision and accuracy.

A handler can acquire this proficiency if he will be mindful of the small things that are important in building a solid foundation in a training program. One of the first things he should practice is the proper way to hold the leash. This will vary slightly with the type of dog that is being trained. The beginner rarely holds his leash correctly, making training more difficult because of his awkwardness. The illustrations in this chapter show the right and the wrong ways to hold the leash.

If the leash is held correctly, even a small person can control a large dog. The dog's collar should be high behind his ears, and the handler should use a web or a leather leash. The instructor should watch the handlers and show them how to hold their leashes so that they will be most effective. Women will need this assistance more than men, as they have less strength in their arms. The handler should hold the leash in both hands, as illustrated, keeping the hands close together so that the strength of both hands and arms will be combined in one sharp jerk to be given when the dog starts lunging or pulling ahead. During that brief moment when he jerks his dog, he should lean back with his body and plant his feet firmly on the ground.

If a small person holds a medium- or large-sized dog on a tight leash, or on one that is too loose, the dog will start pulling and will drag the handler along behind him. To prevent this, the leash should be looped over a finger of each hand and grasped firmly in both hands so that the handler has a strong grip on it. In this manner he will be ready for anything. The leash cannot slip through his fingers, the strong, firm grip will enable him to give his dog a quick, effective jerk when it is necessary, and his right hand will always be ready to hold the rest of the leash when he needs to use his left hand. The end of the leash should never be dangling, the clip on the leash should be hanging down from the dog's collar, and the portion of the leash from the clip to the left hand should be slack, so that the dog feels absolutely no pressure at all on his neck. This is a very important point.

The instructor should repeat the instructions he gave the class during the first lesson and demonstrate the specific points he wishes to make clear. The class will need to be reminded constantly to jerk their dogs back and not to let the dogs pull them on tight leashes. An occasional handler will have to be told to make the about turn to the right, not the left, and some who may wander around in a large circle will have to be reminded either to pivot or to take small steps on this turn. Most of the handlers will have to be told not to stop or wait for their dogs on turns. At times a handler will have to be reminded to hold his leash in his right hand close to his left side when he stops so that his left hand will be free either to tap his dog or to praise it, or both. The instructor should point out to the handlers that all the work is done with the handler's left hand; this includes holding the leash, tapping the dog to make him sit, and petting him. The right hand merely assists the left by holding the leash at times and occasionally giving a signal.

By using his hands this way, the beginner will become ambidextrous and be, consequently, much better prepared to control his dog. My method of training lays the groundwork for smooth, expert handling in the first few lessons, and each subsequent lesson builds upon a strong, sound foundation. The time to teach accuracy, speed, and precision is at the beginning of the dog's training. My method ensures this, but it is up to the instructor to watch the handlers carefully to be sure that they follow the ground rules. He should instruct the handlers not to hit their dogs with their leashes, grab their dogs by the fur, or lift them by their tails. They should be instructed to praise and pet their dogs every time they do something right.

The most common error the handler will make will be to permit his dog either to forge ahead of him or to go too wide to the left. The instructor and his assistant should point out the individual handlers who are making

At the beginning, hold the leash in both hands for medium or large dogs. The leash should be tight enough for you to control the dog, but loose enough so that there is no pressure on his neck.

If you have a small dog, hold the leash in your left hand, as illustrated, and control the dog with a wrist motion.

these mistakes and advise them of what they are doing wrong. The instructor will find that many handlers have dogs that are too exuberant, too rough, or too strong for them. These dogs are generally owned by people who have waited too long to start training them; consequently, their dogs are spoiled and they now must use a more forceful approach in order to get them under control. The surest, simplest way that is not cruel to the dog is to slip the dog's choke collar (it must be a chain choke collar) up behind the dog's ears and under his chin and then to jerk the dog back. If the handler keeps the dog's collar in this position and holds the leash slack enough so that there is no pressure on the dog's neck, he will be able to jerk the dog back quickly if the dog tries to forge ahead, lunge for another dog, or jump out to the side. To be most effective the handler should jerk his dog when he is out away from him. The jerk given the dog when he is close to the handler is not effective and is more of a pull than anything else.

When the handler halts, he will have to adjust the collar, for it will slip down frequently. The choke collar should be used in this position only when the handler has a strong dog, when the dog is being obnoxious, or when the dog is being extremely stubborn about pulling. Many handlers who bring older dogs into class have tried training them before or have kept them tied in their yards; as a result of this their dogs have developed very tough necks and don't feel the jerk of the collar when it is in the normal position. The instructor should caution the handler to be gentle when placing his dog's collar high on his neck and not to pull his dog with the collar in this position. The dog must be taught that he will be jerked with a high collar if he is unruly, but will never be handled in this manner if he behaves. The correctly handled dog learns this very fast, but the majority of the handlers are very slow to practice it.

This high collar should never be used on the average dog, the sensitive dog, or a puppy, for they will respond very quickly with the collar in the normal position. The instructor should watch over the welfare of his class dogs as if they were his own. No one should ever be permitted to abuse his dog.

Not many dogs are brought up in a perfect environment. Not every family knows how to raise a puppy and fewer still know how to train one. The instructor of a dog training school will find that he has a wide variety of canine recruits lined up for instruction. Many of these will be neurotic, spoiled, aggressive, shy, or backward. Many will be sound, normal, healthy dogs. It will be his job to conduct his class in such a way that all these different canine personalities will profit by it. Although the weekly class instructions will generally be directed to the group as a whole, there will be times when individual instruction will be necessary to combat specific problems. The expert instructor knows from experience and instinct exactly what approach he should apply to each individual's problems. I will cover a wide range of problems as we go along.

During the second lesson the instructor should add left turns and right turns to the heeling routine. After the class has practiced heeling in a circle, controlled sits, and about turns for about fifteen minutes, the instructor should have the whole class form a compact group in front of him. The class should not form lines but simply stand in a group with the handlers a few feet apart. The instructor should caution the handlers not to let their dogs sniff their neighbor's dog. They should understand that a dog who is sniffing another dog is not paying attention to his handler and that a dog who isn't paying attention is not learning anything.

The handlers should also be told to give their dogs a sharp tap on the nose if they should try to bite another dog. It should be explained that dogs can be taught to get along peacefully with other dogs if they are corrected while they are in the act of being aggressive. It doesn't take many taps for a dog to learn to mind his own business. If the handler doesn't enforce this, his negligence should be brought to the attention of the whole class and he should be told quite frankly that if he doesn't correct his dog, he will be asked to leave the class. Dog fights in classes are the result of careless or negligent handlers and unwary instructors. The instructor should always be aware of any danger present and should keep ahead of the situation by warning the handlers what to expect and how to control their dogs properly.

The instructor should demonstrate a left turn and a right turn, stressing the point that both turns are sharp turns like a right angle. He should demonstrate how a dog should be jerked on the right turn to keep it heeling with its shoulder by the handler's left leg. Then he should demonstrate a left-angle turn and caution the handlers to bump into their dogs if the dogs get in their way. On all turns the handlers should be reminded to tell their dogs to heel as they make the turn.

The instructor should demonstrate and explain how he lifts his knee into the neck or shoulder of a medium- or large-sized dog as he makes a left turn so that the dog will learn to hesitate for a brief second when he makes the turn. The instructor should show the handlers of small dogs how he brushes his foot along the ground when making a turn to the left. In the beginning the handler will brush aside his dog as he makes the turn, but later he will simply take small steps. A small dog is apt to dart away from his handler's feet, so the handler should be prepared to jerk his dog back. Beginners often step on their small dogs in the early stages of training. To avoid this, the instructor should advise handlers not to toe out when they are walking. Many a small dog has been stepped on by a clumsy handler who then wondered why his dog didn't want to work near him. Small dogs will learn very quickly if they are not abused either knowingly or accidentally. When they trust their handlers, they will stick very close to them and heel with precision. Small dogs that weave in and out when heeling need to be jerked in every time they start to weave out to the left. The handler should hold the leash low in the left hand close to and in front of his left leg.

At different intervals the class should be given the commands "Forward, about turn, left turn, right turn, and halt." After carrying out a few commands, the class should be asked to regroup, as they will be scattered over a wide area. The handlers will not maintain the same pace, so the instructor will have to remind them to heel their dogs at a fast walk, which is the normal pace. Since there are quite a few individuals who do not know their left from their right, some handlers will be turning in the wrong direction the first few weeks, but gradually the handlers will get used to heeling in a group and will start correcting their dogs instead of worrying about themselves.

Once the class starts practicing the heeling exercises in a group, the instructor will notice that the handlers are more lax with their dogs. They must be reminded constantly not to let their dogs sniff their neighbor's dog, not to let them go wide, not to let them pull on a tight leash, not to let them sniff the floor or the ground, and not to let them lag behind.

Many dogs that are timid, lazy, or sensitive will lag behind the handler. This is more difficult to correct than the dog that forges. Older dogs that have been previously trained with a harsh method are wary of getting too close to the handler who abused them. To train these dogs to stay close to the handler's knee will take considerable time and patience. The handler must first gain the confidence of his dog. He can do this by talking to him, by tapping his leg in front to show the dog where he wants him, and by petting him when he is in the right position.

It should be explained to the class that a dog that is heeling with his shoulder at his handler's knee is precision heeling and that the few dogs that will do this are those who have the good fortune to own handlers who care. It will be a credit to any instructor if he can teach four handlers out of twenty to get their dogs to heel with precision. Trainers who have never been able to teach a dog to heel with precision themselves lack the

The advanced way to hold the leash. Keep the left hand against the waist out of the dog's way.

knowledge to teach others. Even though heeling can be called an elementary exercise, it is extremely important and is an exercise that will be used in every advanced class. Anyone who wants a top working dog must have a dog that can heel with precision. The time to train for this is in the very beginning.

This second week the instructor should again explain and demonstrate what to do when the handler stops: he should hold the leash in his right hand near his left side, tap the dog's croup quickly with his left hand, and then immediately pat and praise his dog. If the instructor can get the handlers to do this automatically every time they stop, the dogs will all be sitting perfectly at heel position. The most common error is for the handler to push his dog's hindquarters down instead of giving him a quick, sharp tap. The instructor should demonstrate what he means, for a dog that is tapped correctly will learn to sit automatically the first or second lesson. Even the most stubborn dog will be sitting automatically by the third week if the handler trains him this way. The handler that teaches his

Incorrect: Poor handling. Note unnatural position of left arm.

Incorrect: Poor handling. Note unnatural position of leash in right hand.

dog to sit by pushing down with the palm of his hand will end up with a slow-sitting dog that will lose points every time he sits in an obedience trial.

The dog that swings his rear end out to the left as he is sitting should be corrected by being tapped on his left hind leg. This tap, correctly placed, will bring the dog in close to the handler and make him sit straight. The dog should be petted immediately. Thereafter, before the dog gets a chance to sit crooked, he should receive such a tap and he will stop veering off to the left. These mistakes are easy to correct if the handler is alert and fast. This method is very simple and accurate and will teach a dog to sit automatically and straight every time. Yet some handlers will spend weeks pushing their dogs into a sitting position, others

Incorrect: Poor handling, leash held too tight.

will waste time tapping their dogs in a half-hearted manner, and still others will make the mistake of jerking their dogs to make them sit. The instructor will have to repeat his instructions week after week after week.

The instructor should stop any handler who is jerking his dog to make him sit. He should then demonstrate the correct way. It has long been established that the aforementioned method is far superior to any other. Jerking a dog to make him sit forces him back a little; as a result, the dog is soon stepping back to avoid the unpleasant jerk. When dogs that have had some previous training are observed, the ones which were taught to sit by using the jerking method are obvious. These dogs sit a step or two behind the handler and rarely sit straight. It is difficult to correct dogs that have been trained this way because they have already learned to distrust their handlers. This is an early example of the havoc wrought by thoughtless training.

To correct such problem dogs, the handler must try to gain the dog's confidence by handling him correctly and firmly. When he stops, he should simply hold the leash taut in his right hand, near his left leg, and tap the dog quickly on his croup by bringing his left palm forward toward his dog. This tap should never be a sideways tap or a glancing blow. If the dog sits behind him before the handler can get his hand down, he should coax the dog to sit over again by wiggling his fingers just ahead of the spot where the dog's head should be for a perfect sit. The dog should always be made to sit straight and then petted. The original error can be corrected but it will take time, patience, and work.

There are many, many similar training errors being committed by pseudoinstructors, and the handlers who are unaware of the pitfalls of training their dogs under the direction of these opportunists wonder why their dogs become confused, stubborn, and insensitive. I will endeavor to uncover these training traumas and offer a solution to the misguided

Precision heeling with the dog's shoulder in line with the handler's left leg.

handler and his dog. The expert instructor should be aware of the wrong methods of training dogs so that he can assist the unfortunate dogs that have been subjected to them.

The instructor should review the heeling method briefly and then ask the handlers if they have any questions.

The handlers should then be asked to form two rows thirty feet apart, one facing the other. The next fifteen or twenty minutes should be spent teaching recalls.

It will again be necessary to explain and demonstrate the correct procedure for teaching the recalls. After the demonstration the handlers should try a few recalls with their dogs. The instructor should insist that they form straight lines after every second recall so that they get into the habit of working as a class. This second week most of the dogs will have been taught to stay, so that some order will be possible. The handlers should be asked to wait for the instructor's commands before leaving or calling their dogs. The instructor should insist that the handlers have their dogs sitting perfectly straight at heel position before they leave them.

The handlers should give their dogs the stay command and signal, go to the end of the leash, and face their dogs. Upon command from the instructor, the handlers should call their dogs; the dogs should come and sit in front of them. When the instructor again commands the handlers to leave their dogs, the handlers can give their dogs the hand signals and verbal commands right from where they are—standing in front of their dogs. If possible, the instructor should have the class do two or more recalls before regrouping the lines. The space available will determine how many recalls the handlers can give their dogs before they must turn around and try them in the opposite direction.

At this point the instructor will probably notice that many of the handlers are pulling their dogs in to them on a very tight lead when they call them. He should explain that it is wrong for a handler to pull his dog in to him as though he were pulling in a fish. This method, used by many instructors, is another example of thoughtless training. In training a dog to be obedient, the primary consideration should always be to teach the dog to respond to commands willingly, instinctively, and quickly. If the instructor will keep this in mind from the very first lesson, he will be able to disregard all the hackneyed, obsolete methods of training that many instructors still use.

Teaching a dog to come by pulling it in on a tight leash is like teaching a dog to heel by holding the leash taut. In either case the handler is refusing the dog any freedom of thought or action. He is showing the dog that he does not trust him, he is making a simple routine extremely uncomfortable for the dog, and he is inviting the dog to rebel the first

The Recall exercise is performed the same whether it is on leash or off. The handler should keep his hands together in front of him.

The dog should come to his handler's outstretched hands.

chance he gets. He is not teaching the dog anything constructive; he is forcing him to comply. Continued use of this method will result in either a cowed dog or a rebellious one.

If the handler calls his dog and the dog does not move, he should call it using the dog's name and the word "Come." As he gives the word "Come," he should jerk the dog's leash; this will get the dog moving fast toward his handler. As soon as the handler jerks the leash, he should let it go slack and concentrate on praising his dog and coaxing him to come to his outstretched hands. He should be using a persuasive tone of voice that is moderately pitched and pleasantly exciting. He should bring his hands in close to his body as his dog gets nearer so that the dog will get the

The handler should quickly tap his dog to make him sit, then immediately pet and praise him.

habit of coming in close. When the dog is fairly close, he should gently place his left hand under the dog's chin or gently grasp a fold of skin on his neck, while he taps the dog firmly on the croup with the other hand to make him sit, and then he should immediately pet him. All this time the handler should be talking excitedly, persuasively, and pleasantly to his dog.

The instructor could at this time demonstrate the different tones of voice a handler should use in training his dog. To demonstrate the correct tone to be used in calling a dog, or praising it, I use a stranger's dog. My voice is so persuasive that the handler's dog and many others that are watching the demonstration with their handlers start toward me with wagging tails, happy smiles, and bright, eager expressions. An expert trainer can control a dog completely with his voice, and never needs to shout. It should be explained often that the handler must communicate with his dog by talking to it like a friend. If the handler is skillful about using his voice, he will establish a rapport between himself and his dog and they will become a team. It should be mentioned that a dog should not be given food when he is being trained. If the handler will make the training fun for his dog by using his voice cleverly, and by petting and praising him when he deserves it, the dog will need no other reward.

The instructor will often notice that a handler grasps his dog's collar when the dog comes to him. When he does this, the dog struggles to get away from the tight collar that is choking him, the handler gets exasperated and rough with his dog, and if the dog sits at all, he sits crooked. After several recalls like this, the dog has no desire to respond when he is called. Psychologically this method is all wrong. When a dog responds to his handler's call, he must feel confident that he will be treated kindly and

The Long Sit for two minutes the third week of class.

The Long Sit with one row of handlers.

praised for obeying. It just doesn't make sense to call a dog and then abuse him.

Nor is it sensible or wise to command a dog to stay, pull his leash so he is forced to move, and then punish him for not staying. Many trainers use this senseless method to teach a dog to stay.

If a training program is built on trust, all waste motion is avoided and the dog's instincts are utilized; if the trainer is always ready to guide, to praise, to help, to understand, and to sympathize, the progress will be rapid. The method that appeals to me is the one with the simple, direct approach. The dogs that we train are simple, direct creatures. If one is honest and forthright in training them, they will return a lifetime of pleasure and devotion.

The instructor should remind the handlers not to keep calling their dogs. The dogs must learn to respond to the first call; if they don't, they should be jerked on the second call. Dogs understand this method very quickly. They either do what they are told or they are corrected. It is as simple as that.

After the recalls have been practiced for some time, the instructor should have the handlers form two straight lines with the dogs sitting straight in heel position. The class should practice Long Sits for a few minutes. The handlers should be told to give the stay command in a soft, but firm, tone of voice and to give the hand signal by placing the hand in front of the dog's nose. The handler who throws his hand in front of his dog's nose when giving the hand signal makes the dog duck. Again, the instructor should warn the handlers not to repeat the stay command. He should instruct the handlers to stand opposite their dogs with their arms folded in front of them. If a dog needs to be corrected, the handler should be told to go back to his dog to do so. He should not try to correct his dog

The Long Down for three minutes.

at a distance by yelling commands at him or by repeatedly giving him signals. When the instructor orders his class to return to their dogs, he should watch to see that they all return in the prescribed manner, as many handlers will have neglected this when they were practicing at home. The handlers that joined the class this week will have to be shown how to do it correctly.

The instructor should conclude the second lesson by teaching the class the Long Down exercise. He should have his two lines of handlers straight, and ask the handlers to watch while he demonstrates the down with his dog. He should have his dog sitting straight in front of him, close to him but not close enough to touch him. As he gives the dog the down signal with his right hand, he should pull the dog down with a shortened leash held in his left hand. The down signal is given by raising the right hand quickly, fingers pointing up and held at such an angle that the dog could conceivably be tapped on the nose. As soon as the dog drops, the instructor must praise and pet his dog murmuring, "Down, good, down, good." If the dog tries to rise, the instructor should press down on the dog's shoulder blades as he is stroking him. By having a little pressure applied to his withers intermittently as he is being stroked on the back with the handler's right hand, the dog will understand that *down* must mean for him to keep his elbows on the ground. The verbal command "Down" must be repeated several times at this point.

The instructor should explain that this exercise should always be started with the dog in a sitting position. If the dog is particularly stubborn, the handler should give the down signal and then pull the dog's feet out from under him gently. He will have to hold his dog down quickly by pressing his thumb and fingers behind the dog's shoulder blades before he tries to struggle to his feet. The praise and petting should be given at once.

The handlers should then be asked to step in front of their dogs; next they should command and signal their dogs to go down. As soon as a dog is down, the handler should tell it to stay, leave it, go to the end of the leash, turn, and stand facing it. After a couple of minutes, the instructor will order the handlers to return to their dogs, adding that they should return the same way they did for the Long Sit exercise. At this time the instructor should mention that the dogs are supposed to remain down until the handlers order them to sit. He should mention also that when he calls, "Exercise finished," the handlers should reach down and pet their dogs; after that they may order them to sit. He should advise the handlers to include the Long Sit and the Long Down exercises in their practice sessions at home at least once a day.

The second lesson is concluded after the instructor has advised the class to practice for about an hour each day all the work they covered during the lesson.

The Third Lesson

If there is a space problem where the classes are held, the first ten minutes of heeling practice should be in a circle for the first three or four weeks. If space is not a consideration, the class should start group heeling the second week. Each week the heeling period should last for about twenty-five minutes. The instructor should be watching the handlers carefully to be sure they give their dogs the right corrections. As long as the handlers continue to make handling or training errors, the instructor will have to repeat the instructions. It is only by this constant repetition that the handlers will learn how to control their dogs.

The third week the handlers will learn how to control their dogs when changing from one pace to another. The instructor should ask the handlers to stand where they can see him demonstrate with his dog. He should explain and demonstrate the speed at which the handler should walk during the slow pace, as compared to the normal pace. The slow pace is really very slow, while the normal pace should always be a fast walk. Dogs work much better and are more alert if the handler moves briskly. The instructor should mention this every time he notices one of the handlers moving slowly when he should be walking at a normal pace. Beginners erroneously believe that if they move slowly, they will have better control of their dogs. Nothing could be further from the truth.

Hold the leash taut in your left hand about a foot from your dog's collar.

When you say, "Joll, heel," jerk him back past your left side as you step back with your left foot.

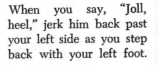

He should turn in toward you, and, as he does, bring your left foot back in line with your right. The leash should be slack at this point.

Tap your dog to make him sit.

He sits.

Immediately pet
and praise your dog.

When a handler works a dog slowly, the dog becomes bored, is distracted by anything and everything, has time to get into mischief, and loses interest in the whole procedure. The handler that moves quickly will have a fast-moving dog that will keep his eye on him. The dog that watches his handler will learn more readily and perform more accurately.

The instructor should also explain that during the fast pace, the handler is to run, but should not run so fast that he leaves his dog behind him. He could explain that the dog should be reminded to heel each time the handler changes his pace; however, if the dog lags, the handler should encourage it to stay up with him by tapping his left leg in front, by speaking to the dog pleasantly and persuasively, and by petting the dog when it is close. Occasionally it helps to jerk the dog, but this should not be done very often. If the dog forges ahead or gets playful when the handler changes pace, the handler should say, "No, heel," and jerk the dog back. When the dog is back in heel position, the handler should praise and/or pet it. The handlers should be advised to practice turns and changes of pace constantly when they are practicing at home. By combining these maneuvers and practicing them consistently, the handler will gradually teach his dog to heel on leash.

The instructor should include numerous about turns, left turns, right turns, and the three different speeds—slow, normal, and fast—during the course of each lesson for the rest of the series. Since the heeling routine is of prime importance to beginners, about half the lesson should consist of heeling practice.

The third week the class will learn how to incorporate the Finish with the Recall exercise. The instructor should have the class do several recalls. It will be necessary to repeat all the instructions for the Recall exercise. After about ten minutes, the instructor should have the class take positions where they can watch a demonstration. The instructor or his assistant should demonstrate while the exercise is explained. The instructor should explain that the dog should sit perfectly straight in front of him, close to him but not touching him, and he should advise them that small dogs should not sit between the feet of their handlers. He should hold the leash about twelve inches from the neck of a medium- or large-sized dog and about two feet from the neck of a small dog. The leash should be held in the left hand with the palm facing down. Then, when the handler says, "Hussan, heel," (preceding the command with the dog's name), he should step back with his left foot, jerking the dog back with enough force to land him behind the handler. At this point the handler should bring his left foot up beside his right as his dog turns in towards him, steps up, and sits at heel position. As the dog steps into heel position, the handler should switch hands on the leash and tap the dog on the croup with his left hand to make him sit. He should pet the dog immediately while he praises him enthusiastically.

This demonstration should be repeated five or six times while the instructor explains the pitfalls to the class, so that they will be aware of the mistakes they should avoid. They should be warned that if the handler moves his right foot, he will be defeating the purpose of stepping back with his left. The dog follows the handler's left leg as he steps back, and after he turns, he follows it back again to heel position. If the handler were to step back with his left foot and then his right, the dog would be standing behind the handler at an angle; subsequently, his sit would be crooked. Many handlers, when they first try this exercise, get confused and take all sorts of different steps, which in turn confuse the dog. The handler should be told not to move out of position at all.

The handlers should be cautioned to turn their dogs in toward them after they have jerked them back. A dog is able to keep his eyes on his handler if he is turning toward him. This makes the exercise easier for the dog.

The instructor will find that most of the handlers will pull their dogs back with tight leashes. This common error causes the dog to execute the finish very slowly. Since the object should be to teach the dog to move briskly whenever he is doing something, the handler must get in the habit of teaching his dog to move quickly right from the beginning. Pulling a dog back on a tight leash to teach him the Finish exercise is very uncomfortable for the dog. A handler who practices this will soon find the dog becoming stubborn and resentful of the treatment he is receiving. Without realizing he is to blame, the inexperienced handler will feel the dog is getting worse instead of better. If the handler would try to analyze the situation, he might understand how unpleasant and unkind he is being to his dog.

The formula applied here is one that dogs understand. Use the direct approach, make the lesson short and simple, make the correction quick and to the point, and be sincere and generous with praise and petting.

The handler must remember to control the dog's sit when the dog steps into heel position. He should use the same method he used when teaching the dog to sit during the Heeling exercise; that is, he should switch hands on the leash, tap the dog on the croup to make him sit, and then pet him immediately. In the Finish exercise, a dog will often sit with his rear end out to the left; the handler should watch for this and be ready to tap his dog on his left hindquarter before he actually sits. If he is quick about this, his dog will soon learn to sit straight at heel position.

The handler is holding the leash the wrong way. This weak grip on the leash causes the handler to pull the dog back instead of jerking. The handler is standing too far away from her dog.

Wrong: The handler should be holding her leash near her left leg. Note incorrect position of dog.

All errors in dog behavior can be traced to the handler. If the handler doesn't train his dog exactly right, the dog will begin to make various kinds of mistakes. If this method is followed accurately, it will produce excellent results. If the instructor permits the handlers to insert their own variations, the results will be far from satisfactory. As long as the handlers are under the trainer's supervision, he should insist upon perfection. Later, when the handlers are trying their dogs in obedience trials, they will be very thankful they received such excellent basic training. Good training habits learned in the beginning soon become the only way to train. Many people who have attended my basic classes and have moved away, start training classes themselves because they find they know more about training than the other people in their area.

The instructor should have the handlers form two lines facing each other about thirty feet apart; he should then ask them to step in front of their dogs. Next he should ask them to keep practicing the Finish exercise until he or his assistant can get to them. He should then watch each handler do three or four finishes to be sure that he understands the exercise and is practicing it correctly.

The instructor will find all kinds of mistakes being made; it is this personal supervision that will be most helpful to the handlers. Pulling the dog back instead of jerking him back is the most common mistake. Permitting the dog to turn out instead of in toward the handler is also common. In some cases, the handler might be stepping back with both feet, or not at all, or stepping forward a few steps after the dog turns or turning sideways instead of staying in one place or pulling the dog around without moving anywhere.

Many handlers forget to make the dog sit, many allow the dog to sit crooked, and others forget how to hold the leash in order to control the sit. There will be many, many errors, but the instructor can straighten them all out in ten minutes if he will just give everyone a little personal attention. This is extremely important because the handlers must be able to practice this exercise correctly at home.

Every once in a while a handler will join the class who has a dog that has been partially trained; this dog may have been taught to finish by going past the handler's right side, behind him, and so into heel position. However, since the dog sits straighter, looks smarter, and works quicker with the left-hand finish, I always suggest changing over. Also, knowledge of the left-sided finish is suggested for today's Utility class, so it is wise to teach the dog in the beginning. After the *handler* has accepted the suggestion, the dog will learn very quickly. It takes the dog only three or four days to learn the new method, and he will rarely go back to the old way.

When a handler uses her own variation of the Finish exercise anything can happen . . .

. . . and often does!

Getting the handler to accept something new, however, is much more difficult. Too many people cling to methods that are pathetically outdated and make their dogs suffer for it.

The handler with a small dog should hold the leash in his left hand. All in one motion he should jerk his dog back and make it turn. It is extremely easy to teach a small dog to finish, yet often a handler will make it difficult by pulling his dog back hesitantly. When the dog gets halfway past the handler, he will start jumping all over him, begging to be picked up. At this point the handler humors the dog, who immediately takes command of the situation. Instead, the handler with a small dog should take a small step back when he is teaching his dog the finish. Small dogs can learn the finish in one lesson when they are trained in this way.

A handler who has a large dog may find it difficult to get his dog past his left side. This will be particularly true if the handler tries to pull his dog back; the dog will resent this and either plant his feet or start pulling in the opposite direction. In order for a small person to teach this exercise swiftly, he should slip the dog's choke collar up behind his ears and up under his throat and hold it loose enough so that there is no pressure on the dog's neck, but taut enough so that it won't slip down. When he gives his dog the verbal command "Heel," he should give his dog a sharp jerk and hold the leash with both hands. The jerk should be big enough to propel the dog past the handler's left side, at which time he should be turned in toward the handler and told to sit when he steps into heel position. Advise the handlers, however, not to continue placing the collar up on the dog's neck after he understands the exercise. This method is only to help the handler control a dog that weighs almost as much as he does. If the dog knows that the handler can make him move whenever he wants to, he will be more cooperative.

When the instructor is satisfied that everyone in the class understands the finish, it is time to combine the recall with the new Finish exercise. The instructor should have his class do two recalls and then ask them to stand where they are and do the Finish exercise. This routine of two recalls and then a finish should be practiced several times. If a dog is given a finish every time he does a recall, he will soon decide to skip the sit in front and go straight to heel. Rather than let the dog start anticipating the finish, it is wise, in the early stages of his training, to do at least two recalls before doing a finish.

The class should then be asked to line up in straight rows to practice a Long Sit exercise. This time the instructor could advise the handlers to lay their leashes on the ground in front of their dogs and step on the ends of them. With arms folded they should stand facing their dogs. The instructor should insist that the handlers be firm with their dogs and make them stay when they are told. He should also caution them to give a quiet stay command, again explaining that it is never necessary to shout at their dogs. The handler who shouts at his dog is trying to intimidate the dog into obeying. If he will just use a quiet tone of voice it will have more effect on the dog. The handler should give the dog one verbal command and one signal; if the dog moves, the handler should immediately correct him. At first the handler should correct his dog with the command, "No, stay," and put him back exactly where he was. If the dog is quite stubborn or rambunctious, and keeps getting up and moving out of position, the handler should intercept the dog, give him a sharp tap on his nose, saying, "No, shame, bad dog, I told you to stay," and put him back. The dog will not break many times if he is corrected like this. The handler and his dog should learn early in the training that obedience means an immediate response to the handler's command, not commands.

The dog that whines or barks should be stopped with the verbal command "Ssssst, stop that." If that doesn't work, the handler should tap the dog under the chin sharply. The barkers and whiners that have been completely spoiled require a harsher method. The handler should, after all else has failed, lift his dog on his back toes for a second with the leash while he gives it a sharp tap under the chin and the command "Stop that." The correction should be repeated whenever necessary. One more suggestion to cure a whiner: put the dog on a ten-foot lead and lay the leash on the ground behind him. Every time the dog whines a helper should give the leash a good jerk as the handler gives the command "Stop that." The handler, however, should place the dog back in position since the dog's attention should always be on him and not the helper. One rarely sees these spoiled creatures in a class, but if the case arises, the instructor must understand how to handle them.

If a dog should lie down when the handler has left it on a Long Sit, the handler should return to his dog without talking to it, lift it into a sitting position with the leash, and give it the stay signal and the command "Sit, stay." Make the correction short and simple, and the dog will retain it.

The instructor should let the handlers know that he expects their dogs to be sitting and staying for at least two minutes by the third lesson. If there are some dogs that do not stay, the instructor should announce to the class that they should practice the stays at least two or three times a day at home.

The instructor should also advise handlers not to let their dogs sniff, and if they do, to correct them immediately. To do this, the verbal command "No sniffing," should be given along with the correction so that the dog will eventually learn to stop sniffing when he hears the verbal command. If a dog is sniffing while he is heeling, the handler should jerk his head up sharply; this should be done every time the dog sniffs. Generally it will be necessary to place the dog's collar high on his neck so he will take heed of the correction. If a dog is sniffing the floor when he is on a Long Sit, the handler should go to his dog and jerk his head up, saying, "No sniffing." If a dog insists on sniffing the dog next to him, the handler should tap him on the nose, saying, "No sniffing." Dogs will learn not to sniff each other when they are working, provided that the handlers are quick to correct them and are never lax about it. People with hounds or sporting breeds can break their dogs of this annoying habit by keeping after them. They learn not to sniff when they are working in obedience trials or when they are practicing the exercises; this, however, does not stop them from sniffing when they are hunting.

After two minutes the handlers should be told to return to their dogs. The instructor should again mention that the dogs are not supposed to move out of position when the handlers return. After a few seconds, he will call, "Exercise finished," and the handlers should then pet their dogs. It isn't necessary for the handlers to pick up their leashes as they return to their dogs, as they are working toward the goal of taking them off leash entirely. Not picking up the leash is another subtle way of showing a dog that his handler trusts him.

The handlers should be asked to line up once more with their dogs sitting straight in heel position. When this has been accomplished, the instructor should ask them to stand in front of their dogs, drop them, and leave them as soon as they are down. By doing this, the instructor can quickly determine which handlers are having difficulty putting their dogs down.

During the third lesson, there will be three or four handlers who can't make their dogs go down. If a dog still won't drop after the handler has been practicing with him at home by pulling down on the leash or slipping the dog's front legs out from under him, the instructor should show the handler the quick way to do it. A clumsy handler will unwittingly be rough with his dog by pulling, jerking, and overhandling him unnecessarily. The quick down method must be taught this handler's dog before he rebels.

It is better for the trainer to teach the dog to go down than to let the dog be abused. The short method is to give the dog the down signal, and if he doesn't obey, simply to lower the hand on the dog's nose with a sharp tap. The type of tap one gives the dog depends on the size of the dog. A toy poodle can be tapped with one finger and the tap will be effective. A Saint Bernard would need a four-fingered tap. The object is to make the dog drop quickly and then immediately pet and praise the dog as the handler murmurs, "Down, good, down, good." By handling the dog in this manner, the dog will realize he is not being punished but is being taught an exercise. A dog can be taught the down in one lesson and will retain it for his entire lifetime. However, there are some people who do this so poorly that the instructor should do it for them. When they go to tap the dog, they either tap too lightly or miss him completely. After they have swung at the dog and missed a few times, the dog gets very proficient at ducking; some even get fresh and will take a snap at the handler's hand after he has missed several times. Dogs are quick to take advantage of an awkward handler.

Many times an explanation will be all that is necessary, and the handler can try this short method at home. This would be the best solution for extremely nervous dogs, particularly small ones. If they are in a quiet place, without distractions, they will learn quickly. In class it is difficult for the handler to get through to them because they are so overwrought, but once they know what to do, they will obey in class.

Once the dog is down, the handler should stand at the end of his leash, which has been placed on the ground, and face his dog with his arms crossed. After a few minutes the class should be asked to return the same way they did for the Long Sit exercise. The instructor should advise them not to let their dogs get up, but to pet them while they are lying down, then after a few seconds order them to sit.

If a dog gets up at any time, the handler should return to him and make his dog go down again. When a dog is on the Long Down, he may lie over on his hip in a comfortable position. He should not be forced to lie down in a straight line, as this would be very uncomfortable for him. However, he should not be permitted to lie flat on his side, as this is too relaxed a position. The dog should always be alert when he is executing a command.

The instructor should close the class by advising the handlers to practice all the exercises for an hour each day outdoors. Most dogs become very obedient indoors when they realize they can't get away from their handlers. The training is more difficult outdoors where there are many more distractions.

The Fourth and Fifth Lessons

The fourth and fifth lessons are primarily spent practicing what was done in the third. The instructor should repeat any instructions that will help the handlers teach their dogs to heel properly.

Most of the people who join my beginners' training classes are interested only in learning how to make their dogs behave. They know nothing about obedience trials, obedience titles, or obedience exercises and have no interest in showing their dogs. They want to train their dogs to behave in the shortest time possible with the least amount of effort. The routines used in the beginners' classes are designed for both types of handlers: the dog owner who is only interested in having a well-behaved pet and the obedience enthusiast looking for expert instruction. In either case the dog must be trained to be obedient; this means he must respond to his handler's first command, be alert and attentive at all times, and be trained to work with precision and accuracy.

It is just as easy to do something right as it is to do something half-heartedly. The pet owner must be shown that his dog can be trained to be well mannered if he will practice with him correctly. If his dog is not making progress in class, the handler is either not following instructions carefully or is not training his dog at home. Hundreds of pet owners who have joined my classes just to teach their dogs to be well mannered were so encouraged when they found that their dogs responded to the training that they went on and showed them in obedience trials.

An instructor should never stop trying to teach his handlers to work with skill and precision. Each handler is very fortunate if he can train his dog under an expert instructor who will constantly correct and advise him. Even the most inept handler will learn something worthwhile. I have heard many instructors say that they don't bother to teach their beginners any precision because the dogs are just pets. This is the wrong attitude to take and can only lead to sloppy work and poorly trained dogs. By setting a good example with his own dog, the instructor should try to get his class to visualize what a delightful world it would be if every dog were well mannered and expertly trained. I trained my first dog because I wanted her to be obedient; at that time I had no interest in or knowledge of dog shows. Although she was of show quality (when I finally did show her she won a major in her first show), I considered her a pet. An instructor should consider every handler a prospective obedience enthusiast, and if his instruction is expert enough, he will gain some recruits for this sport.

My classes have always had many different breeds of dogs in them, and this is exactly the way I like it. Any dog, regardless of his size, gains much more experience by working in this type of class than he would in a class that was limited to his size or his particular breed. Of course a handler could show his dog in just specialty shows, providing that he had a popular breed and that enough of these shows included obedience classes. Nevertheless, he might have a long wait between shows or have to travel quite a distance to find shows in which to compete. On the other hand, if he were to show his dog at any all-breed shows that included obedience classes or at any obedience trials, he would be able to compete somewhere almost every weekend. In this case, many different breeds of dogs and many different sizes of dogs would all be competing with his dog in the same class. The dog that has had the experience of training with other breeds in classes is the one that will be steady in a show. The class work will also give the handler added confidence.

Some instructors limit their classes to one breed or take only small dogs because they are afraid an all-breed training class would upset the small dogs. An instructor who has control of his class will be doing the small dogs a favor by including them in his group, for they will benefit by the experience more than any other dogs. I have had many small dogs enter my classes as pampered, nervous, neurotic pups and graduate as confident, self-assured, well-mannered dogs. An obedience class should help all the dogs in it; in order to do just this, I include special heeling routines in my classes from the fourth week on.

In a class of thirty or more dogs, half will usually be large dogs while the other half will consist of small or medium-sized dogs. After the class has been heeling in a compact group for about ten minutes, I have them stop and position themselves about five feet apart. I ask the handlers of the large dogs to stand with their dogs in heel position, and stay where they are while the rest of the class heel their dogs between them, walk beyond them a short distance, then about turn, and walk past them again. Next I ask the handlers of the smaller dogs to stand while the large dogs and their handlers practice walking and turning near them, the object being for the handlers to control their dogs when they are heeling past other dogs or when they are being approached and passed by other dogs. The small dogs get used to passing close to the large ones without having a tantrum, and the large dogs learn to behave themselves as the small dogs walk by them.

Each group should have several turns at walking by the dogs and handlers in the other group. The instructor should caution the handlers to correct their dogs if they try to bite or sniff another dog. The handlers should teach their dogs to ignore the dogs they are passing and should praise them when they do so. If this routine is included in the heeling practice each week, all the dogs will soon become accustomed to ignoring each other. This routine is particularly beneficial for the handlers for it gives them the opportunity to test and correct their dogs. A dog who has a tendency to be antagonistic, nosy, shy, or boisterous can be quickly disciplined at this time, and the handler can give his full attention to his dog so that the correction will be effective. During the regular heeling routine, many handlers are so busy trying to remember what they are supposed to do that their corrections are ineffective. This situation gives them a chance to get better control over their dogs.

Handlers with small dogs practice heeling them past large dogs.

It is now time for the instructor to add some variations to the Recall exercise. After two or three straight recalls in which the dogs travel the length of the leashes, or about six feet, the instructor should announce that they are going to try something new. He should explain that each handler should give his dog both the verbal command "Stay," and the signal and go back to the end of the leash. Upon command from the instructor, the handler should call his dog; if his dog doesn't move, he should jerk it toward him. Once the dog is moving toward him, he should run backwards a few steps, praising and beckoning to him. The handler should then stop and let the dog come to his outstretched hands and sit straight in front of him. This procedure teaches the dog to come in quickly. A dog should respond instantly and move quickly when called; this is the first step toward that goal. The leash should be slack except for the moment it is jerked.

Besides teaching the dog to come the first time it is called and to trot in briskly to the handler, this exercise will also teach the dog to sit straight in front of the handler. A sit will often be the factor that decides who will win first place at a dog show. The dog who has learned to sit straight in the early stages of his training will be the dog who sits straight most consistently. The instructor should insist that every handler make his dog sit straight in front of him every time he is called, even if he has to adjust the dog's sit or make him sit over again. The handler should get in the habit of saying, "Sit straight" to his dog when he finds it necessary. It doesn't matter where the dog is sitting, whether it is at heel position, in front of the handler, or at a distance on the Long Sit, if the handler is consistent in telling his dog to "Sit straight," his dog will eventually do so on command. This will save a great deal of time later when the dog is learning the advanced work.

All breeds of dogs are guilty of the sloppy sit in which the dog will sit over on one hip with his hind leg folded underneath him. To correct this sit, the handler should reach under the dog and pull his foot out far enough so that the dog is sitting erect. Gradually, the dog will begin to correct himself when he sees the handler reaching down to adjust his leg, or he will respond to the verbal command "Sit straight."

Another sit that should be corrected while the dog is still working on leash in the early stages of his training is the sit in front after a recall. The aforementioned recall procedure should be practiced for a few weeks. If after this amount of time, the dog is still going off to the left or the right instead of going to the handler's hands when he approaches him, he should receive a short quick jerk with the leash when he is off to the side and again be reminded to "Come." The handler should attract his dog's attention by talking to him, clapping his hands, or tapping his leg in front.

Straight sit.

Wrong: Sloppy sit.

Right: Straight sit.

Wrong: Great Dane is not sitting up straight.

Dogs go off to the side because the handler lets them. The correction or bid for attention should be given as the dog starts to veer to one side, not when he has gone past the handler. The instructor should remind the handlers to give their corrections fast. When the dog sits in front of the handler, he should be petted gently. The instructor should show the handlers how to pet their dogs. Most people do this the right way instinctively, but there is always one handler who pounds his dog as roughly as he pleases. He thinks that because he has a big dog, he has to be rough with it. This is ridiculous. The big dog should be trained to be gentle through gentle handling and a soft tone of voice. It is considerably more impressive to see a large dog respond to a soft tone of voice and be well

Insist that your dog sit perfectly straight in front of you each time he comes to you. Your hands must be placed down at your sides whenever the dog returns to you.

mannered than to see a big, rough dog acting like a wild animal. The instructor should insist that such a handler either be kind to his dog or leave the class. One rarely has a handler, though, who will not listen to reason.

The training method used should be the direct approach. A dog will learn and retain the lesson if he understands what he is supposed to do and has complete confidence in his handler. The simple routine of teaching a dog to stay and to come is very natural, and any dog can learn this in one lesson. The important point here is to be firm when making the dog stay, and firm but very pleasant when teaching him to come on a loose leash.

There are many other methods used to achieve the same goal, but these take longer and use subterfuge in training, which I believe is unnecessary and a complete waste of time. The dog eventually learns to come to his handler despite this method because he is an infinitely patient creature and hasn't the means to voice his objections. However, it is unjustified to use subterfuge to teach a dog to come when a direct approach will give such excellent results.

Take, for instance, the Come Fore routine used by some instructors. The dog is heeling by the handler's side when suddenly he is jerked toward the handler who begins to run backwards. This is a completely unnatural way of teaching a dog to come and sit in front of the handler. The dog, who should be concentrating on his heeling and perfecting his heeling technique, must worry about being jerked unnecessarily. The handler is pulling his dog in to him on a tight leash as he is stepping back, a maneuver that encourages the dog to dislike the leash and distrust his handler. Most of the dogs that heel poorly have been exposed to poor training techniques such as this one.

Another thoughtless routine that I disagree with is teaching the dog to drop while he is heeling by his handler's side. Some instructors have their handlers step in front of their dogs suddenly, while they are heeling, and jerk them down. This is their method of teaching a dog to go down. Again the dog's heeling routine is interrupted unpleasantly and unnecessarily, and after a few such incidents the dog becomes very wary and suspicious of any movement the handler makes. I am often told by handlers who attend my clinics that their dogs would rather work off leash than on, and upon pursuing the matter I find that they have tricked their dogs with senseless routines while they were teaching them to heel on leash. Again I must stress that if one is to expertly train his dog, a genuine feeling of mutual trust must be established between the dog and his handler.

The dogs should all be staying for the prescribed length of time during the Long Sit and the Long Down exercises. The dogs should be able to remain sitting for three minutes during the Long Sit exercise, and they should be able to stay down for five minutes during the Long Down exercise. If there is a dog that is not staying for this length of time, the instructor should make it clear to the handler that his dog is not being properly trained at home. It is a good idea to find out why the dog is not getting the practice at home when it is so obvious he needs it.

The Sixth Lesson

If any of the handlers were going to drop out, they would have done so by the sixth lesson. It is customary to lose a few handlers after the first few lessons. There are many legitimate reasons for this, and the instructor should expect it. Some bitches come in season and must be confined at home for three weeks. In my classes I let the owners make up these three lost lessons in my next series of lessons. In the interim, I suggest that the owners attend the classes and continue the training at home. The fact that a bitch is in season will not prevent her from learning her lessons at home.

Since there could be hundreds of reasons that a handler may drop out of class, it is wise for the instructor to keep in touch with his students so that he can offer his encouragement and assistance if it is needed. It is at this point that many of the handlers will begin to fall by the wayside if the instructor is not on his toes. Many people reach a certain level of achievement in the early training and would never make any further progress if they weren't encouraged each week to try harder. Many times the dog becomes bored because the attitude of the handler is that of indifference. Some people are so pleased that their dogs are behaving themselves at home that they feel they don't need to practice any longer. Many people will state that their dogs do the work perfectly at home, even though they do nothing commendable in class. Dogs generally do better at home where there are no distractions and where the handlers fail to notice their mistakes.

In order for the instructor to get the most out of his class, he must always be there with a word of encouragement, a helping hand when the going seems rough, or a word of warning for the careless or insensitive handler. The sessions should be practically all work, but a few humorous moments will make the lesson more enjoyable. If the instructor keeps everyone working and occupied, the hour lesson will pass very quickly.

The instructor should demonstrate with his dog the progressive heeling stages. He should demonstrate (1) the leash being held in both hands in the beginning for the medium- to large-sized dogs (the handler of a small dog should always hold the leash in his left hand); (2) the correct way to hold the leash to control the dog's sit when the handler stops; (3) the leash being held in the left hand when the dog is heeling with more precision; (4) the automatic sit with the leash still switched to the right hand so that the dog can be petted; (5) the completely loose leash with emphasis now placed on voice control; and finally, (6) the leash being held in the left hand with the arm folded in front of the handler's waist with the right arm swinging down by the handler's right side. Some hard-working handlers may have already reached this final stage; it is reasonable to expect a handler who has trained another dog by my method to make rapid progress with his second dog.

Some handlers, though, will still be heeling their dogs with tight leashes

A typical Novice class for beginners.

and many will be pulling their dogs around on the about turns and right turns. The instructor should stop the class every time he sees a handler doing this, and explain the error and the correction to him in a voice loud enough for everyone to hear. Some people never become good handlers because they can't bring themselves to correct their dogs with any degree of firmness. The dog senses the owner's feeling of helplessness and takes advantage of him. Some people find it almost impossible to train their dogs in a class but do admirably when given private lessons. Then, once they learn the fundamentals, they can rejoin a group. However, with each succeeding lesson the instructor should note a definite improvement in the way each dog is handled and in each dog's deportment. With this method of training, at least 90 percent of the handlers will be making progress. The percentage might improve from class to class depending upon the handlers.

The majority of the dogs will be sitting automatically when the handlers stop during the heeling routine. When the class has reached this stage, it is time to teach them the Stand-for-Examination exercise. The first part should be demonstrated to the class by the instructor as it is explained. The instructor should show the class how he orders his dog to heel and then takes a few steps forward; when he notices that his dog's front feet are in line with each other, he gives his dog the stay signal and

"Stay." Can. Ch. and O.T. Ch. Joll vom summerland, UD.

A class practicing the Stand-for-Examination exercise.

As you walk forward slowly, quickly hold the leash taut and give your dog the Stay signal and the verbal command "Stay."

At first, when you return to your dog, hold your dog's right hind leg so that he won't move or circle.

verbal command "Stand, stay." All this time he has been holding his dog's leash taut in his left hand. With large dogs a taut leash means folding it until it is about twelve inches long. He quickly moves away from his dog to the end of the leash and turns and faces him. After a few seconds he cautions his dog to stay and returns to him by walking around his left side, then behind him, and thus into heel position. At this time he holds the leash in his left hand with his arm extended. He explains that the dog should remain standing for at least five seconds when he returns to him, then he tells his dog to "Heel," and as they move forward, he praises his dog.

The instructor has already explained this return procedure to the handlers as they used this same method when they returned to their dogs after the Long Sit and the Long Down exercises.

The second time the instructor is demonstrating this part of the exercise, he should tell the handlers what to expect when they try it with their dogs. If the handler does not hold his leash taut in his left hand, the dog will keep moving; this will make it hard for the handler to control him. The taut leash will restrain the dog while the verbal command *stay* plus the stay signal will help him to understand what is expected of him. The handler must never jerk up on the leash at this time or he will force his dog to sit. To prevent a dog from moving or sitting when the handler starts to leave his dog, he should hold his dog's right hind leg at the stifle as he gives him the command and signal to stay. To prevent the dog from turning when the handler returns to his dog, he should reach over the dog's back and hold his right hind leg. If the handler senses that the dog will sit when he returns to heel position, he should be ready to caution the dog to "Stand," in addition to reaching down to hold his dog's hind leg. It is even necessary at times to hold the dog's leg when the handler is standing in heel position, for a dog will often sit at the last second when the handler is back by his side.

This exercise is slightly more difficult for the handler with a small dog because he will usually sit before the handler can get down to him. The best way to teach the small dog is to hold the leash taut, give him the stay signal, and command him to "Stand, stay." By this time the dog has probably sat, so the handler should lift the dog into a standing position and repeat the verbal command, "Stand, stay." By holding the dog in a standing position with one hand supporting its tummy and by pressing and stroking the dog's back with the other hand and by repeating, "Stand, good, stand, good," the handler will soon teach the dog the exercise. When the dog understands that he should stand on the signal, the handler can teach him the rest of the exercise.

The instructor should explain and demonstrate to the class the proper way to lift a dog into the standing position. The dog should be lifted with the handler's arm, never by his tail or his ears or his skin or his fur. If the instructor sees someone abusing his dog in this way, he should bring the incident to the attention of the class and condemn such treatment. Every time a handler has to lift his dog into a standing position, he should command his dog to "Stand."

The instructor should emphasize the point that when the handler returns to his dog, he should stand there for a count of five, not letting his dog move. After the five seconds have passed, he should tell his dog to "Heel," and as they move forward, he should praise and pet his dog.

After the instructor has demonstrated this exercise four or five times, he should have his class move forward and then say "Stand your dogs, leave them." After a few seconds he should say "Return to your dogs, stand there for a count of five, then walk forward and praise your dogs."

I have found that most classes understand this portion of the exercise after they have practiced it six or seven times. If a class is slower to learn the first part of the Stand, the following step could be delayed until the next week's lesson.

The instructor should demonstrate the next step with his dog. He again gives his dog the command to "Heel," holds his leash taut, walks forward and quickly gives his dog the verbal command to "Stay" and the stay signal, walks out to the end of the leash, and turns to face his dog. This time he places the leash on the ground in front of him, returns to his dog and examines him by running his right hand down the dog's head, back, and hindquarters, walks around the dog, goes back out to the end of the leash, picks it up, and returns to the dog in the usual manner.

The instructor should explain to the class that each handler should examine his dog quickly with one sweeping motion from the dog's head to his croup. The dog should be cautioned to stay when the handler approaches him and while he is examining him. Friendly dogs want to move and wiggle all over if they think they are going to receive some attention and need several stay commands. This exercise is not difficult, and the dogs learn it by repetition.

The instructor should have the class practice this step six or seven times. He should not spend too much time on each stand, but should get the class to work quickly. He should add the command "Examine your own dog," to the others to cover this new step. He should conclude the practice by advising the handlers to practice this exercise the coming week until their dogs stand without moving while they examine them.

The instructor and his assistant should watch the handlers, helping those who are making mistakes and commending those who are doing the exercise correctly. One common error is for the handler to leave his leash

If you have a small dog, hold the leash taut in your left hand and place your left foot under your dog's stomach to prevent him from sitting as you give him the signal and verbal command "Stay." At first bend over this far to give him the signal. Later, when he is trained, it will not be necessary to bend over to give him the signal.

near the dog and simply pick it up when he is in heel position. Instead, the leash should be left far out in front of the handler so that the dog can get used to the handler's returning to him from this distance. If this point isn't stressed to the class, the handlers will do it wrong; but if each handler understands the exercise, he will practice it correctly at home. This personal coaching the instructor gives his class is vital to their complete comprehension of the exercise.

The instructor should explain to his class that this routine is primarily an exercise used in obedience and conformation classes. However, it is an exercise every dog owner should teach his pet, for sooner or later the dog will be taken to a veterinarian for treatment, and it will be a tremendous help to everyone involved if the dog stands quietly while he is being examined.

The class should have another short heeling practice, and then the instructor should have them take positions to watch a demonstration of the Figure Eight exercise. Two people who have been placed facing each other about eight feet apart should act as posts while the assistant with his dog demonstrates. He should start the exercise from a position in the center of the two posts but one step back so that he will be squarely facing the instructor several steps away. The instructor should explain that the handler may start either to the left or to the right, but that it is easier for a dog to keep up with his handler if he starts out to the left. He should explain that the handler should keep close to the posts and should teach his dog to keep close to him without bumping either him or the posts. On the inside turn, the dog might crowd him; if so, he must push him aside with his right hand or bump him with his knee. On the outside turn, the dog will probably lag or go wide; here the handler must be alert and encourage his dog to keep up with him by saying something pleasant to him, tapping his leg, or giving him a jerk with the leash. The assistant should continue heeling his dog in the Figure Eight pattern five or six times more while the instructor is explaining the exercise to the class. The assistant should stop two or three times in different places so that the class will understand that halts are included in the exercise. If the assistant gives the necessary corrections to his dog as they are going along, it will be of special benefit to those watching. If his dog is doing the exercise perfectly, it would be well for him to take one of the handler's dogs so the class could see how an untrained dog will react when he does the Figure Eight exercise for the first time. Many times the class will learn a great deal just from watching an instructor or his assistant correct a dog at this time, providing he does so correctly.

The instructor should explain that although there will not be enough time during this lesson to try it out with the handlers, he would like everyone to practice it at home each day before the next lesson.

The class should practice longer recalls now, and the instructor should be prevailing upon everyone to insist upon prompt responses, fast recalls, and straight sits. The handlers that are making good progress with their dogs may drop their leads, while the others should hold their leads and back up swiftly when they call their dogs. The instructor should advise the handler who drops his leash to let it fall by his dog's side so that his dog won't trip over it when he moves forward.

An assistant instructor demonstrating the Figure Eight exercise to a class.

Once in a while a dog will break loose and run to someone who is watching from the sidelines instead of obeying his handler's call. The most effective way to stop a dog from doing this is for the handler to get his dog, who is on leash, and as he runs backward to his place in line, he should jerk his dog toward him several times, each time saying, "Come." The instructor should notice whether the handler follows his instructions. It is important that the handler run backward while facing his dog and that he jerks his dog sharply as he says, "Come." He should then finish by having the dog sit in front of him for a few seconds before he praises him.

If the handler will correct his dog's first impulse to be disobedient, he will not have any major problems when he takes his dog off leash. Dogs are always giving their handlers little signs and signals of things to come. An alert handler or instructor can keep two steps ahead of a dog by correcting him in the early stages. This is the intelligent way to train a dog.

The class should end the lesson with two Long Sits and two Long Downs. All the dogs should be doing this exercise correctly. If some are not, the instructor should give them some personal assistance while the other dogs are staying.

The Seventh Lesson

By now, the majority of handlers will be able to control their dogs during the heeling routine, and most of the dogs will be sitting automatically with an assist now and then by the handler.

After the class has practiced heeling for ten minutes, it is time to show the handlers the first step they should practice prior to working off leash.

Using his own dog or a handler's dog, the instructor should tuck the end of the dog's leash in his belt. (A handler without a belt could throw the end of the leash over his right shoulder.) He should explain as he is demonstrating that he wants the handlers to learn to control their dogs with their voices and their hands. Of course if a handler's dog lunges for another dog or goes out of control, he should jerk the leash, but the handler must learn how it feels to control his dog without a leash. The instructor should demonstrate how to clap hands on turns to get the dog's attention, how to pet the dog's shoulder to praise him for staying at heel, and how to control the dog with the voice at all times. The handlers must be instructed to talk to their dogs as often as it is necessary to keep their dogs' attention focused on them. A dog that is heeling perfectly should keep his right eye on his handler so that he will be prepared for any move his handler may make. The dog that looks straight ahead or off to the left can easily be fooled into making a mistake by a clever trainer. The dog that heels expertly cannot be fooled and will keep his shoulder at his handler's knee no matter how many turns he makes or how often he changes pace. The instructor should demonstrate how he controls his dog when he stops. He should heel forward a few steps and then halt. If his dog doesn't sit automatically, he should tap him instantly to make him sit. If the dog is forging ahead, he should place his right hand and arm in front of the dog's chest to restrain him while he taps the dog quickly with his left hand to make him sit. The dog should be petted immediately with the left hand.

After demonstrating for a few minutes, the instructor should have his class form a group in front of him in order to give them some heeling practice without benefit of the leash. The handlers will be quite surprised to find how little control they have over their dogs unless they can keep their dogs' attention focused on them.

The handler should hold the leash loosely while someone examines her dog.

This is an opportune time for the instructor to stop the class and explain how important it is for the handlers to practice training their dogs on a loose leash. The handler who has been consistent about keeping a loose leash on his dog will have no problem when he tries this exercise. Since the dog is not used to feeling any pressure on his neck from a tight leash, it will make no difference to him whether his handler tucks the end of his leash in his belt or removes it entirely. However, the handler who persists in holding his dog on a tight leash will find he has no control of his dog at all. He will be grabbing at the leash constantly, like a crutch, to keep his dog near him. The instructor should advise these people that they are falling behind the other handlers in the class and they will have to practice correctly if they expect to graduate from the class.

The class should practice this free heeling for about five minutes the first time and then practice heeling the regular way for about ten minutes. Some instructors permit only two or three handlers to work on the floor at one time because they cannot control any more than this. I believe in

Four handlers are practicing the Figure Eight exercise simultaneously. With eight handlers and their dogs acting as posts, everyone is getting excellent experience.

giving my classes plenty of actual work; I believe handlers can learn a great deal more by steady practice and helpful correction than they can by watching a few people work their dogs. Obedience training looks deceptively easy from the sidelines. When the watchers try the exercises themselves, they are completely ignorant. The best instruction has all the handlers participating at the same time. There is great security in numbers, handlers are less shy, everyone has a problem of some sort, and everyone profits by each other's experiences. The quickest progress is made by getting the handlers interested in themselves as a group. As a unit they will want to keep up with each other. Consequently, an instructor should limit the number of handlers he takes in his classes to the number he can work together as a group. In some cases where the instructor is inexperienced, even ten handlers will tax his knowledge.

The instructor should then announce that they are going to practice the Stand-for-Examination exercise. They should practice the first two steps of this exercise: leaving the dog standing and then returning to it. Next they should practice leaving the dog standing, examining the dog, and then returning to it. He should have the class review the work they started during the sixth lesson. If the handlers are doing well with their dogs, the instructor should advise them to have members of their family or neighbors or friends examine their dogs for them at home so that their dogs will learn to stand for strangers without moving. It may be necessary to give some extra assistance to any handlers having problems with this exercise.

The remainder of the heeling practice should be devoted to the Figure Eight exercise. The instructor should have several handlers and their dogs act as posts while the rest of the class practices figure eights around them. In a class of forty handlers, I use eight handlers and their dogs as posts. This way we have four handlers doing the figure eights simultaneously. It saves a great deal of time, and twice around the posts gives each handler valuable experience. Each week we have different handlers act as posts. Whether the handler and his dog are acting as posts or are heeling in the figure eight pattern, the experience of working so close to the other dogs is excellent. The instructor should keep a sharp eye on everyone, though, to be sure they do the exercise correctly, keep their dogs under control, and praise their dogs when they do well.

The instructor will find that many handlers will hold their dogs too tightly. They should be told to keep their leashes just loose enough to put no pressure on their dogs' necks but tight enough to be ready to jerk the dogs back sharply in case they lunge suddenly. Each handler must be reminded to keep his dog by his side and not let it sniff, go wide, lag behind, or forge ahead. Each dog will need help for one reason or another. The instructor should also make sure that each dog sits straight every time he stops. The dogs acting as posts must be corrected if they try to sniff or bite the working dogs. This is a splendid opportunity for their handlers to teach them to ignore the other dogs.

Recalls and Finishes should be practiced at this time. Then the Long Sit and the Long Down exercises should be practiced.

The instructor should advise the class that graduation exercises will be held the tenth week of the series. The assistant should distribute printed instructions that explain the individual exercises that will be part of the obedience test. Every handler and his dog will be put through the first three exercises alone and will be judged on the merit of their work individually. The Long Sit for one minute and the Long Down for three minutes will be group exercises; all the dogs in the class will do these two exercises together.

The graduation test will consist of five exercises:

1. Heeling on Leash. The handler may not give his dog any extra commands or signals during the heeling exercise. He may give his dog's name and the command "Heel" every time they start heeling. Two sits will be included in the routine and the dog will be expected to sit automatically without any help from his handler. A right turn, left turn, about turn, fast, normal, slow, and halt, in any order, will be part of the heeling pattern. When the judge says, "Exercise finished," the handler may pet his dog.

2. Stand for Examination. The Stand-for-Examination exercise will be done on leash. The handler will give his dog the verbal command and signal to stay, leave his dog, go to the end of the leash, turn, and face his dog. The judge will examine his dog. Then, upon order from the judge, the handler will return to his dog and wait for the judge to say "Exercise finished" before petting his dog.

3. Recall. The dog may work off leash or drag his leash, at the handler's option. The handler will give his dog the stay command and/or signal, leave his dog sitting, stand about twenty feet from him, turn, and face him. On order from the judge, the handler will call his dog verbally, and the dog should come in briskly and sit in front of his handler. Upon order from the judge, the handler will send his dog to heel position for a straight sit. After the judge says, "Exercise finished," the handler may pet his dog.

4. The Long Sit.

5. The Long Down. These exercises will be practiced as a group. The Long Sit will be for the duration of one minute; the Long Down will be for the duration of three minutes. The judge's commands for the Long Sit are "Sit your dogs. Leave your dogs. Return to your dogs. Exercise fin-

ished." The commands for the Long Down are given in the following order and begin when the dogs are sitting by their handlers' left sides: "Down your dogs. Leave them. Return to your dogs. Exercise finished."

The Eighth Lesson

The class should begin the eighth lesson by repeating the heeling practice, including ten minutes of free heeling. During this time if there are any handlers who are doing quite well, they could be invited to try heeling their dogs completely off leash. There may be a handler whose work shows that he is ready to try this but who is unsure of himself. To gain more confidence, this handler should unclip the dog's leash while he is petting him and hold the leash in his left hand with the ends hanging down. The dog will see the leash hanging down and behave as he does on a loose leash. The handler will become more confident when he finds his dog is behaving normally and after a few minutes will be willing to try heeling with the leash folded in his pocket. If the handler is relaxed, the dog will heel as well as he did on leash. The handlers should be encouraged to try heeling their dogs off leash in their own yards. If they try this for short periods of time during the daily practice sessions, the dogs will become trustworthy.

The instructor should have his class practice a few Stands for Examination, letting the handlers examine their own dogs. By this time the majority of handlers will have taught their dogs to stand quietly while they are being examined. The class should hold on to their leashes the next time they try the exercise while the instructor and his assistant examine the dogs. The first time this is tried, there will be only a small percentage of dogs that stay without moving. Some will be shy, nervous, or so pleased and happy that they will wiggle and walk forward a few steps, and others will wag their tails so hard they move out of place. Whatever the reason for the dog's moving, it means the handler will have to practice this exercise more diligently during the coming week. The dogs will all learn to stay after they have had a bit more experience, particularly if they have strangers examine them at home.

The handlers should be ready by now to try fifteen-foot recalls off leash. If they are doing well, the distance could be increased to twenty feet. This would be far enough for a large class, as the temptation for a dog to bolt is greater when he sees other dogs running near him. A handler can control his dog at this distance, but the average handler would run into problems at a greater distance. Since the object is to eliminate problems and not create them, the length of the recalls in this series of lessons should be limited.

During the period when the class is practicing recalls, the instructor should notice how well, or how poorly, his class is doing the Finish exercise. Despite the fact that he has been advising them how to do them for the past few weeks, there will be handlers that still do the finish poorly. The instructor should have his dog on leash and demonstrate the many phases of the Finish exercise: jerking his dog back correctly, guiding the dog into heel position with a loose leash, giving the finish signal by swishing the left hand back, and giving just the verbal command. He should then show the class that his dog will execute the finish with either the verbal command or signal, without the handlers having to step back.

After the demonstration he should have the class try the finish all these different ways. They should be instructed to practice the finish from now on without stepping back for the dog. The instructor should explain that if the dog doesn't go back far enough, the handler should quickly step back with his left foot and jerk his dog back. If the medium- or large-sized dog doesn't go back far enough, he will not have room to turn and will end up sitting crooked. When the handler has had more experience, he will be able to gauge the exact amount of room his dog needs in order to turn and sit straight, depending on the dog's size and agility. The instructor should explain this point to the handlers. This can also be made very clear by demonstrating the finish with several dogs of different sizes.

The class should be taught how to incorporate the come signal with the verbal command "Come." The instructor should demonstrate the come signal: he holds the leash in his left hand, raises his right hand out to his side and brings it in swiftly to his chest, then drops it down by his side. He should explain that if the dog doesn't respond the first time, the signal should be repeated as the verbal command is given. As soon as the dog starts to move toward the handler, he should be praised in an excited tone of voice. A dog responds to signals faster if the handler is exuberant and excited when he praises him for coming.

The remaining time should be spent practicing recalls with the verbal command and signal. The finishes should be practiced with the handler's not stepping back unless it is absolutely necessary.

The class should end with a Long Sit and a Long Down. The instructor should have the handlers stand in front of their dogs and drop them, give them the stay command and signal, and leave them. After the dogs have stayed on the Long Down for five minutes, the handlers should return to their dogs and pet them. Next the instructor should have the class line up with the dogs sitting in heel position. He should have each handler, in turn, give his dog the stay command, step out five feet in front of his dog, and face him. Then he should be asked to drop his dog quickly on signal and command. The dog should drop immediately.

If the dog doesn't drop, the handler should approach the dog and repeat the hand signal. If the dog doesn't drop this time, he should be tapped quickly on the bridge of the nose. When the dog is down, the handler should say "Good, down," and pet his dog. He should then go back to heel position, and the next handler should try to drop his dog at a distance.

This method will reveal which dogs still need help so that the instructor or his assistant can give them personal supervision while the rest of the class is practicing another Long Sit and Long Down. The class should be instructed to teach their dogs at home to drop on a verbal command or signal and to keep increasing the distance between them and their dogs until it is twenty feet.

The instructor should again remind the class to practice an hour each day to get their dogs ready for the individual tests on the tenth week. These tests will determine which dogs are ready to advance.

The Ninth Lesson

The instructor should devote this whole hour to practicing all the exercises the class has been learning for the past eight weeks, and the instructor should still insist upon perfection in everything they do.

The routines practiced during the eighth lesson should be repeated. The instructor should notice improvement in the heeling exercises since the handlers are now aware that they must depend less upon the leash and more upon their handling technique. The dogs also should be more polished when they execute the Finish exercise, as the handlers have now had the opportunity to practice the different stages of the finish on leash. If the handlers have asked strangers to go over their dogs while they stood them for the Stand-for-Examination exercise, the dogs should be much steadier. The handlers should have advanced to a point in the Recall exercise where they are doing twenty-foot recalls off leash. Of course, this never applies to everyone; there are always some handlers who, for one reason or another, will have to repeat a class. This is quite normal.

The instructor should end this lesson by having the handlers drop their dogs individually at a distance of twenty feet. Most handlers are quite proud of the fact that their dogs have learned to do it. It is also a very practical exercise—one that the handlers will use quite frequently at home.

The Tenth Lesson

There is a great deal of excitement at graduation time. The conscientious handlers who have worked hard at training their dogs for the past nine weeks are anxious to see whether they can pass an actual test. The handlers who have not practiced consistently at home are apprehensive over the way they expect their dogs to work in the tests. All are just a little nervous because their dogs are still unpredictable creatures and they feel unsure of them.

If there is time, the instructor should give the handlers a ten-minute capsule of class work: some snappy heeling with changes of pace and several turns to wake up the dogs and get the handlers to relax; two Stands for Examination with the handlers examining their own dogs; five minutes of Recalls at twenty feet; and Finishes with every second recall. As the class is working, the instructor should brief them about the test: no extra verbal or signal commands when the exercise has started; praise permitted after the judge says "Exercise finished." No corrections permitted during the test.

The assistant should give each handler a numbered armband. The instructor should judge the class since the class work for each handler for the past few weeks counts toward the decision whether the handler fails or passes. The instructor will know which dogs have made consistent progress because of their handler's efforts and deserve to go on to an advanced class.

The instructor judges each handler and his dog in numerical order. After all the dogs have been judged, he has the class line up for the Long Sit and the Long Down exercises. At the conclusion of the judging, the instructor should determine which handlers deserve to pass. The training certificates that have been partially completed can now be finished and signed by the training instructor.

Additional certificates should be given out to the handlers that have failed to pass the first series of lessons. They should be encouraged to try another series of lessons. There are some handlers who sincerely want to learn but are just so uncoordinated that it takes them two or three times longer to learn the work than it does the average person. By repeating the same class, this handler will be able to grasp the work better and gain better control of his dog. This experience not only will benefit the handler but will be of great value to his dog. The dog must have a good foundation in order to teach him to be a reliable worker.

The instructor should pass the certificates out to everyone and encourage them to continue training their dogs.

There are many ways to make graduation exercises interesting and exciting. The training certificates could be tied with ribbons like diplomas, trophies could be awarded, refreshments could be served, a movie could be shown of an advanced class, and the advanced work could be demonstrated by a skillful handler. It could be an occasion when obedience people get together to share their experiences and enjoy dog talk.

It is my opinion that the handlers who have made definite progress over the weeks and who have been conscientious about training their dogs each day should be permitted to go on to the advanced work even if their dogs failed one or two of the five test exercises. This is not proof that the dogs can't do the work. The handler is generally nervous when he takes his first test and transmits this feeling to his dog. When a dog senses that there is something unnatural about a situation, he suddenly suffers a lapse of memory. Much to the embarrassment of the handler, he acts as if he never heard of the exercise he is expected to do or he suddenly becomes very self-conscious and aware that he is being watched. Under these circumstances he will not act normally and will not do the creditable job that the instructor realizes he can do. These dogs simply lack experience.

It would be a complete waste of time and show very poor judgment on the part of the instructor if he were to make these people repeat the beginners' work. If given a chance, these handlers will be so grateful they will work with renewed interest and vigor to prove the instructor was right in believing in them. If there are any borderline cases, it is best to let them try the advanced work on the condition that if they can keep up with the class, they can remain in it.

5 | THE ADVANCED
NOVICE CLASS

A ten-week course for handlers at
every level of training who want to gain
positive control of their dogs off leash
through expert class instruction.

First, Second, and Third Lessons

The Advanced Novice class should include the handlers who graduated
from the Beginners' Novice class and anyone else who is training his
dog in the Open, Utility, or Working classes. This class offers the handler
and his dog the best possible experience; any dog who does the work
perfectly here can win in shows. This combination of Novice and experienced handlers has a very steadying effect on everybody, including the
dogs. The Novice workers can learn a great deal by working alongside a
veteran who is unruffled by anything we do in class. The advanced dogs
that come into this class for practice exert a great influence over the
beginners who tend to copy them. A Novice dog who works next to a well-
mannered dog becomes calm and easier to handle when he finds he is
being ignored by his neighbor. This work is particularly important for the
advanced dogs because of the heeling involved and the increased number
of sits that must be executed in the Open, Utility, and Working classes.

Before the instructor begins this class, he should explain to the handlers
that he is going to give them class obedience instruction that will enable
them to become top handlers. In order to accomplish this feat, he is going
to correct every little error they make so that they will be aware of them.
He should tell them that they will learn enough in the next ten weeks to

enable them to earn their Companion Dog degrees with high scores. He should let them know that he expects them to practice with their dogs an hour every day, follow instructions implicitly, correct any mistakes their dogs make immediately, and develop fast reflexes. He will want to see the handlers give soft-spoken commands, signals without any body movement regardless of the size of the dog, and sincere, exuberant praise and petting for the dog when it is deserved. The handlers should always be attentive if they expect to have alert dogs. He should mention that this will be a fast-moving class and that every handler, regardless of his breed of dog, will have an equal chance to become a top handler. The most successful training method and expert instruction available will be used; it is up to the handlers to utilize them.

The class should start out each lesson with a brisk heeling session with all the Novice dogs on leash. The handlers should always walk at a brisk pace during the heeling practice, except for those instances when the instructor orders them to go fast or slowly. The instructor should be very critical of any handling errors and point them out continually. This is the only way the handlers will learn to handle their dogs flawlessly, for most of them will be unaware of their mistakes. Some of the obvious faults the instructor should correct in the coming weeks are mentioned here. These will be repeated by different handlers from time to time, even though the mistake and the correction is brought to the attention of the entire class. A handler is more apt to remember a mistake when he is personally corrected for it.

Any handler who is still pushing his dog down to make him sit should be told to tap his dog instead, and the instructor should watch him until he starts doing it correctly. The handler has formed a bad habit, and even when he starts tapping his dog, he will leave the palm of his hand on the dog's croup. It might take several lessons to get this handler to do it right, but he will eventually learn if the instructor bears down on him. By the time the handler learns how to do it, his dog will be sitting much faster.

The handler who is making poor turns will need constant surveillance. This is a common fault and one that can be corrected with the right instruction. On about turns, the handler should take small steps or pivot quickly on the soles of his feet without raising himself. He should not hesitate on the turns nor should he turn so fast that he leaves his dog behind him. It should be a natural turn for a person who walks at a brisk pace. There should be no body motion in the turn: the handler should not throw his shoulders forward as he is coming out of the turn as this is a signal to the dog. He should not bend his head down while making the turn, as this is another body signal. The dog's shoulder should remain at the handler's knee on the turn, and he should not drop back so that his nose is at his handler's knee—this is lagging. To correct this, the handler should jerk his dog just enough to bring him up where he should be. The handler should never make a military turn or take long steps at this time, as either turn would make it difficult for the dog to keep up with him. The first turn gives the dog a signal that his handler is going to turn, while the other turn makes the dog lag.

The handler with the small dog should jerk his dog with his hand held low near his left side. He should be careful to point his toes forward when heeling with his dog as he will eventually step on his dog if he walks with his toes pointing out. When making about turns, he should take small steps and be prepared to jerk his dog if he forges ahead or goes wide after the turn. If the handler will watch his steps when making about turns with his small dog, there will be no need for the dog to go wide to avoid the handler's feet. Another common fault of small dogs is that they weave in and out as they are heeling. They must be taught to walk in a straight line; this can be accomplished by guiding the dog with the leash held as described.

The small dog should also learn to sit straight when the handler stops. In the beginning the small dog will have a tendency to sit too wide, too far ahead, too far behind, sideways, or at an angle with one foot held up. The handler should correct these sits by reaching down to straighten them as they occur; later he could lift his dog a little with the leash, making his dog get up and sit again with his legs tucked in straight. If the handler has been consistent about saying "Sit straight," every time he has corrected his dog, the verbal correction should be working now. If the small dog is lagging, the handler could try getting him up by talking to him excitedly or pleasantly and by tapping his leg near his knee. I have found that this always works for me when I am training small dogs. However, if this doesn't work with the handler, he should try jerking his dog every time he lags. If the handler does it correctly, this will always work with every small dog.

Small dogs are naturally fast workers and can be ruined by handlers who drag them around, treat them like babies, or fail to realize that they enjoy working with spirit. The spoiled pet who walks on his hind legs and clings to the leash when his handler stops should be jerked with the leash at the right time to stop this nonsense.

Another error common to a small dog is his having to step over to the handler to sit when he stops. The dog should be heeling a certain distance from the handler as they are moving along; when the handler stops, the dog should immediately sit where he is. If he has to walk over to the handler to sit, he was heeling too wide in the first place. Even one step would be an error. One must always compare the performance of a small dog to that of a large one. It would be considerably more noticeable if the Saint Bernard were to take a step or two to get close to his handler before he sat, but it would be no more an error for him than for his small friend.

A small dog can be controlled while heeling if the handler is constantly alert, jerking the dog every time he needs it and praising the dog when he is in heel position. The dog's shoulder should be at his handler's left leg on turns, as well as on the straight heeling; if there is any variance, the handler should be quick to correct his dog. If the handler notices his dog making a mistake, such as darting ahead on a turn, he should be ready to correct it the next time they turn. Dogs always repeat their mistakes until they are corrected.

The small dog should sit with his shoulder at his handler's left ankle. Some people find it hard to decide where a small dog should sit. The important point to remember is that the dog should sit in the same place every time he sits. In other words if he sits with his shoulder in line with his handler's left leg or ankle, he should sit there every time, not in front of this position at times or behind his left foot on occasion. It is up to the handler to insist upon precision every time.

Most toy dogs can be trained with a nylon collar and a lightweight leash. I prefer to use a nylon web leash with a small clip on it so that there is no weight or pressure on the dog's neck. Because a small dog can make no heeling error that cannot be corrected with the left hand, training him by holding the leash in the left hand is easy. When the handler stops, the dog can be held in position, with the leash switched to the right hand, while he is tapped quickly with the left hand to teach him to sit fast. He should then be praised in a pleased tone of voice.

Any hounds in the class, such as beagles or bassets, will have to be corrected every time they sniff. If the problem is acute, the handler should slip the dog's collar high on his neck and jerk it every time the dog lowers his head to sniff. As the handler jerks his dog's head up, he should say "No sniffing." Any dog can be broken of this habit provided that the handler is persistent with his corrections right from the beginning. It will be more difficult to correct an older dog and might take longer since the dog is more set in his ways, but he should receive the same kind of correction. Whenever a handler is faced with a problem of this type, the instructor always wonders whether the handler will be more persistent than his dog is stubborn, for if he is, the handler with the perseverance will win and the dog will give up his bad habits.

The long-coupled dogs, such as Dachshunds and Bassets, can be taught to sit straight if the handler will correct them every time they sit crooked. These dogs will sit over on their hips if permitted to do so, but will learn to sit straight as soon as they realize their handlers will not tolerate this. At first the handler should reach down and pull the crooked leg out from under the dog, later a little nudge with the handler's toe will have the same effect, and later still the verbal command "Sit straight," will be all that is needed.

When a dog sits behind his handler's left leg, the handler can correct him by pushing him over with the side of his right foot. If the dog has done this a couple of times, the handler can prevent him from doing it again by placing his right foot in line behind his left. Rather than sit on his handler's foot, the dog will sit straight.

The handler who steps over to his dog when he stops must be cautioned about this. When the handler stops, he should remain where he is without moving. If his dog sits ahead of him, out to his side, or crooked, he should either adjust the dog or ask his dog to sit again by ordering him to go to heel. The instructor should be on the alert for this handler error and correct it every time he notices it.

Then there is the handler who does not praise his dog because he says his dog will go to pieces if he does this. So they both work in complete silence except for the criticism the dog receives when he does something wrong. This, of course, is a sign that the handler doesn't know how to control his dog and he offers this as an excuse. From the beginning of this dog's training, he should have received praise every time he did something right. If the dog had tried to jump around and go wild at that time, the handler should have held him by his ruff forcefully while he petted him with the other hand gently and murmured a few soft words of praise to him. The dog would have been gentled in a short time. If the dog had eluded the handler and jumped up at his face out of control he should have received a sharp tap on his nose which would have made him stop jumping. Then the handler should have held him at heel position by the ruff, petted him, and praised him. The handler must have a firm grip on the dog's ruff or the loose skin on his neck, but he should not hurt or pinch the dog at this time. In other words the dog should be taught to accept praise so that later there will be the communication between the two that every handler–dog team needs. This communication between the handler and his dog is essential if there is to be any rapport between them, and the handler who neglects this point is missing the most wonderful relationship one experiences in training dogs.

In my classes I insist that each handler establish communication with his dog. Sometimes it is hard for a handler to learn to talk to his dog because he feels self-conscious, but there is such a significant difference between the performance of dogs who are lucky enough to have understanding handlers and that of those who have silent handlers who never consider their dogs as partners, that he gradually sees that he must train his dog with more feeling and compassion. With constant prodding from the instructor, even the most reticent handler will be able to give his dog spontaneous words of praise.

The instructor should be continually urging the handlers to react fast to any given situation and to be speedy in giving a correction, a pat on the dog's head, a word of praise, or a word of warning. When he sees a handler correcting his dog too late or praising him too slowly, he should chide him saying something like, "Oh c'mon, you can get down there faster than that," or on the second offense, "What makes you so slow? Faster, faster." I have never found handlers in the advanced classes who minded constructive criticism, for they realize I am trying to help them become top handlers.

There is no need for a handler to feel that he must slow down his pace to meet that of his small dog. Small dogs are very fast and can easily outrun their handlers, so any lagging should be corrected. By using a combination of voice persuasion, praise, petting, and sharp jerks, the dog should be made to stay up with the handler. If he is being particularly stubborn about hanging back and trying to mope along, as some are wont to do at times, the handler should walk twice as fast as he normally would and jerk the dog repeatedly until he decides to stop balking and start working. This is simply a case of showing the dog who is boss. In this instance the instructor will find that getting the handler to train his dog sensibly is a major problem. The handler will usually feel that his small dog is like a piece of fragile china, whereas in reality he is a tough, spunky little fellow who knows exactly how to get his own way. The instructor should show the handler how to jerk the dog, immediately reaching down to pet him as they are heeling along. The handler should be asked to try the same thing in front of the class so that he won't feel guilty if it is necessary for him to jerk his dog in order to teach it to heel. The instructor should use a little psychology at this time and commend the handler if he does it correctly, encourage him if he tries, or make a joke of it if he does poorly and persuade him to try harder.

Large dogs can be induced to stay up with the handler by using the same combination of corrections. The handler could also try tapping his leg in front to show his dog where he wants him or playing with his dog while heeling to keep him alert and induce him to stay up with his handler. This shouldn't be overdone, however, to the point where the dog gets out of control. The handler should always be in command of a situation like this with the instructor standing by ready to guide him if need be.

The heeling practice for the first six weeks of the Advanced Novice series of lessons should include ten minutes of heeling on leash except for those who have advanced degrees or their Companion Dog degree. The instructor should take advantage of this time to instruct the handlers how to correct their dogs each time they start heeling wide. If the dog crowds too close to the handler when he is heeling, the handler should walk with a goose step which will keep the dog away from him or tap the dog lightly on his cheek to warn him not to walk too close. Crowding, provided that the dog doesn't actually interfere with the handler, is the least offensive of the heeling errors. A dog that crowds the handler in the beginning is apt to correct himself after he has had a little experience and gained some confidence. He is generally anxious to please his handler, and in his eagerness, he stays close to him. It is, in the beginning, a good fault and easy to correct.

The dog that bumps his handler by weaving in and out has a more serious problem; this error is made by many dogs in the advanced classes. These dogs have never been taught the fine points that expertly trained dogs have already learned. The size of the dog is of no consequence, for all dogs are apt to weave while heeling unless the handler corrects his dog every time it errs.

Since lagging is the most difficult heeling problem to correct, it should be regarded as the most serious error. The dog who has been taught to keep his shoulder in line with this handler's left leg at all times is the dog who can be considered the perfect heeler. It takes knowledge, skill, and practice to teach a dog to heel properly, but this can be accomplished with any breed of dog. However, every dog cannot become a perfect heeler for many varied reasons. The main reason a dog lags is that he hasn't been taught to heel correctly. A dog is no better than the handler who is teaching him and the handler is handicapped unless he receives expert instruction. Even then the instructor is not responsible for poor training or lack of training the dog receives at home. A dog that lags can be corrected if the handler will concentrate on the problem and encourage the dog to stay up with him by using his voice persuasively, tapping his leg, jerking the leash occasionally, and praising and petting the dog at the right moment.

The dog should be taught to stay up with his handler in the beginning and should be corrected every single time he lags. This is something most handlers neglect to do because it is hard work. The instructor will find it necessary to keep reminding the handlers to talk to their dogs or correct them every time they lag. If the handlers are made aware of the problem, they will try to do something about it. For lagging alone, a dog can lose ten or more points from his score. Heeling is important, and the instructor should impress this fact upon his handlers while they are in the Advanced Novice class.

One rarely sees a dog that forges in the advanced classes, because forging is the easiest error to correct. One simply jerks the dog back when he starts forging. Heeling wide is a sign of poor heeling and can be seen in many Novice classes at shows. The handler should jerk his dog toward his side when he sees him going wide and make his dog maintain the same distance from him all the time. If the dog tries to go wide when he is off leash, the handler should use a very short grab leash on his dog so that he can reach out quickly and jerk his dog toward him if it is necessary. When a dog that has been working well off leash goes wide, the handler should put his finger through a ring of the dog's choke collar and jerk him in close.

Occasionally the instructor should walk his class up to a wall and call, "Halt." Most of the dogs will hang back instead of stopping in heel position. They will refuse to heel toward a barrier because they do not yet trust their handlers to stop in time. After the handler has practiced stopping a few times this way, his dog will be willing to stay with him. This routine should be tried indoors and out, for it is quite possible that some thoughtless judge will walk the handler up to a wall or fence and call, "Halt." This has happened to me on occasion.

The first six lessons of this series should include Figure Eight practice on leash for the Novice handlers. This exercise is rarely done correctly in shows. There one will often see a handler adapt his pace to that of his dog, hold the dog on too tight a leash, give the dog extra hand or body signals, jerk the dog with the leash, or make wide turns around the posts. The dog either lags, forges ahead, crowds his handler, bumps into his handler or the stewards, cuts a turn, sits crooked, heels too wide, or heels behind his handler's left leg.

The most common mistake handlers make at a show when they are doing the Figure Eight exercise is to make unrealistically wide turns around the stewards. By allowing his dog to take him in a wide arc around each steward, the handler is losing the practical value of the exercise. This exercise should be a test of the dog's ability to heel closely around people, as on a crowded street, without touching anyone, and to do so by maintaining a pace that keeps his shoulder in line with his handler's knee at all times. The judge who appreciates the skillful handler-and-dog team will penalize any Figure Eight performance that is less than perfect. The instructor should remind his handlers of these points and insist that they practice the exercise correctly.

The first thing a handler should learn is where to stand in relation to the Figure Eight posts. With the two stewards standing eight feet apart, the handler should position himself so that he is facing the judge opposite him and standing centered between the two stewards, but one large step back from the middle. This position is ideal for starting in either direction, and the judge can see instantly whether the dog's sit at heel position is straight or crooked. The handler should always check his dog's sit before he starts to be sure he is sitting straight.

A dog that crowds his handler on the inside turn, where the dog is close to the steward, should be tapped on the cheek with the handler's right hand and then encouraged to heel close by being petted. Sometimes the dog can be corrected by being bumped with the handler's knee as the dog is crowding. The handler can use his foot if he has a small dog.

The most difficult fault to correct is lagging. Many dogs that lag will do so most of the way around the Figure Eight, while others will lag only on the outside turn, where the handler is next to the steward. This can be corrected by making a game of the exercise. The handler can tap the front of his leg to show the dog where he wants him; he can entice the dog to stay up by using a persuasive tone of voice; he can jerk the dog occasionally; and he can and should often change pace from normal to fast to keep the dog alert. If the dog persists in heeling behind the handler's left foot, the handler should make a wider outside turn, jerking the dog up and out to the left as he reaches back with his right foot and gives the dog a good shove over to the left. This is not a kick and does not hurt the dog. Stubborn, lazy, or hard-headed dogs will try to avoid working by dropping behind the handler's left foot; although this is a difficult fault to correct, the method mentioned above always works if the handler will use it consistently. I would penalize this type of error more than any other because I know it can be corrected if the handler will work on it.

It will take many weeks, probably the whole series, to teach a dog to do the Figure Eight exercise correctly. The instructor should be there to guide and advise the handlers so that they will make progress from week to week.

The instructor should include a variety of Stand-for-Examination exercises during the advanced series of Novice lessons to encourage steadiness in the handlers' dogs. During the first three weeks the instructor should have his class practice the following routines.

The first exercise is to have the handlers heel forward as a group, stand their dogs, turn and walk away from their dogs to the end of the leashes, and turn to face them, commanding them to stand and stay. Friends who are watching from the sidelines will be asked to come out on the floor and examine the dogs. After the examination has been completed, the handlers will return upon the instructor's order, "Back to your dogs." The dogs will be praised after the instructor's command "Exercise finished." This exercise should be repeated several times.

All through the training routines, the instructor should use expressions in his classes that a judge would be apt to use in a show. If a handler is

Handlers petting strange dogs who are practicing a Sit-Stay.

familiar with the commands and terms that are used in shows, he will feel more at ease when he is in actual competition. I believe in making my class work harder than actual show work so that the latter will seem simple by comparison. I feel it is important to explain the obedience regulations as they apply to each exercise so that the handlers will be fully prepared for competition. At times, a handler might forget some of the regulations because he gets nervous, but once he has been penalized, he will be more apt to remember the rules.

The next routine is for the handlers to heel in a large circle, sit their dogs, and leave them. They should then walk forward toward the dog ahead of them. After they have walked in and around each of the dogs, they should return to their own dogs and praise them for staying. Any dogs that break should be corrected immediately. The handler should keep glancing back at his dog as he is walking the circle to be sure his dog is staying. The instructor should insist that the handler return to his dog promptly if he needs to be corrected. The next time the handlers should try the same routine, except that they should leave their dogs sitting, turn, and then walk toward the dogs behind them. As they approach each dog, they should pet him around the head. If a dog shies away, the handler of the dog should stay with him, forcing the dog to stay as the other handlers approach it. Each time the dog is petted, the handler should praise and pet him so that the dog will relax a little. Shy dogs require patient training, but the handler must also use firmness and praise. Since shy dogs will hide behind the handler, the handler must brace the dog with his foot behind him while he makes the dog stay and permits a stranger to pet him. After a few weeks, the handler will be able to leave him sitting at the end of the leash while a stranger pets him. Overcoming shyness is a slow process, but if the handler will persevere, he will get good results.

While the instructor has his class on the floor for heeling practice, he should give them additional instruction in the Finish exercise. The handlers in the advanced class should be doing a commendable job of sending their dogs to heel after a recall and should be conscientious about having them sit straight. If the instructor feels his class is ready for the next step, he should expand the exercise. At first he should give a demonstration and explanation with his own dog. With his dog sitting at heel position, he should take a quarter turn to the right as he orders his dog to heel. The dog should immediately get up and move into heel position as the instructor pivots. Then he should make a quarter turn to the left by pivoting and taking a very small step while remaining on the same spot. While executing this turn, he should order his dog to heel; the dog should get up and go to the heel position by turning at his left side. The instructor should explain that the handler should not step forward but should remain in the same spot, making the quarter turn by pivoting and taking small steps.

Learning this new finish will not pose any problem for the handlers who have taught their dogs to go to heel quickly and accurately. The others will have to start practicing more effectively. This exercise calls for precision work that can be reached only through practice. The instructor will find, though, that the handlers and their dogs will become very proficient at doing these finishes as the weeks go by in the second series of lessons.

Again, the Novice handlers are learning something that will benefit the overall performance of their dogs. This new finish will help their dogs to understand where they belong every time they are in heel position. They will more readily understand the command *Heel* and be able to zip into heel position no matter where they are sitting when the command is given. And again, this method is teaching another part of a Utility exercise.

The instructor should have his class utilize this Finish exercise when the dogs are heeling. If a dog should make a mistake and sit quite crooked while heeling, the handler should simply tell his dog to go to heel. By letting the dog correct himself in this manner, the dog will soon understand that if he sits crooked, he should get up, go to heel, and sit straight. I have always taught my dogs the real meaning of the heel position so that they could learn to correct their own sits if it was necessary. It is one of the first steps I use to teach a dog to think for himself.

The instructor should have the class practice various kinds of recalls during the series so that the dogs will become very reliable and very accurate. The first three weeks should be spent in teaching the dogs to come in swiftly, happily, and accurately. The dog that responds to his handler's call by moving slowly might be acting this way for several reasons. Perhaps the handler is making the exercise dull; in this event, he should clap his hands, praise his dog in an excited tone of voice when he starts moving, laugh a little, and be ready to help his dog sit straight. If the dog thinks he may have a little fun, he will run in to find out. If the dog runs away, the handler should go up to him and jerk him back to his place in line repeating the command "Come," every time he jerks him. If he runs away several times, the whole class should join in and say, "Shame, bad dog, shame," whenever the dog gets near them. The smart aleck who wants to show off will be quite deflated by such a cool reception and find himself much better off with his handler. At such a time, the instructor should caution the handlers not to laugh, for the dog who is looking for excitement would enjoy this too much. When a dog runs away from his handler and the handler has to go get his dog, the instructor should insist that the handler run backward to his place in line as he jerks his dog toward him with the command "Come." This will break the dog of this annoying habit.

If there is a stubborn dog in the class that has been trained by some other method and is disobedient about doing recalls at a distance, the handler should put the dog on a thirty-foot leash. Every time the dog tries to run away, the handler should jerk him back with the leash. The dog can never completely run away, for someone can always step on the leash and prevent him from doing so. When the dog finally decides to behave, the leash should be shortened until it can be removed entirely.

I do not believe in throwing heavy chains at dogs in classes, or anywhere else, in order to get them under control. There are no dogs that are so disobedient they need to be hit with a chain. There are other ways to discipline a dog that are more effective and are not cruel. When a chain is thrown in a class of dogs, someone is going to get hurt. This is the reason it is thrown in the first place. Small dogs are terrified of such brutality, sensitive dogs are frightened by it, and large dogs are ready to duck and run the second time the punishment is given. Many dogs get very upset when they see another dog being punished. The effect it creates is the same as if they were receiving the correction themselves. A highly intelligent, sensitive dog, regardless of his breed, does not like to see another dog punished in a violent way. It makes an impression on him that time will not erase. It is just such a thoughtless act as this that makes a dog neurotic.

There are misfits in the dog world just as there are in human society, and although we have correctional institutions for human beings, we don't have any comparable facilities for dogs. Some dogs are vicious because of their inherited traits, others because of their environment, and still others because their owners have encouraged them to be mean. Many large dogs become wild, rough, and intractable through the neglect of their owners. A good number of dogs are penned in their yards where they are tormented by children; after being subjected to this type of torture, they take a dislike to all children. Some dogs become mentally unsound because of a combination of unfortunate experiences.

A few of these dogs can be admitted to obedience classes, but the bulk of them need force training to straighten them out. This is a job for an experienced, professional trainer, who should train the handler and his unruly dog privately. Most of these dogs are not fit to join a class of normal dogs. Since dogs have a habit of copying each other, it is best to limit the class to untrained dogs that are not a serious menace to the other dogs. Occasionally I will find a handler who is able to control his dog after three or four private lessons and is then able to join the class. Generally, however, the owner wants a quick, cheap answer to his dog's problems, and one that will not involve too much work on his part.

A handler may experience some difficulty with his dog's going to either side of him instead of sitting straight in front of him when called. He can correct this quite easily either by holding his leg out to block his dog's path as he gives the command "Come" and motions, with his hands together, to the dog to come close in front of him or by giving the dog a sharp jerk to the front with his collar and motioning the dog into position with his hands as the dog starts to one side. In either case the dog should be praised when it sits in front. If the handler will remember to use his hands effectively to show the dog where he wants him to sit and to use the side of his foot to line his dog up in front of him, his dog will soon start trying to sit straight. The instructor should keep reminding the handlers how important it is to be gentle with their dogs when they come to them. The handler should try to keep his hands down by his sides.

The dog that comes in too fast—and there are many of these—should be stopped or slowed down with a *sit* command when the dog is a few yards away. This will slow the dog down so that he won't crash into his handler. With this type of dog, the hands should be held outstretched in front of the handler's body so that when his dog is close, the handler can say *easy* and hold his dog so that he doesn't touch him.

Dogs rarely sit straight in a class 100 percent of the time. The important point to get across to the handlers is that they should correct their dogs whenever it is necessary, no matter how often that may be. As the handlers and their dogs become more proficient, the instructor should impress upon them the importance of teaching their dogs to sit straight on the verbal command without any physical assistance. By the time this series is half over, the dogs should be sitting straight in front at least half the time. They should be sitting straight at heel position about 90 percent of the time.

To prevent a dog from forming the habit of holding his head down when he comes in, the handler should hold him gently under the chin, scratching him there with one hand while he strokes his head with the other. In this way the dog will form the habit of holding his head up and will be more likely to sit straight if he has his eyes on his handler. It is important to talk to the dog conversationally at this time to hold his attention.

The handler of a small dog should bend over to straighten his dog's sit at first, then gradually get his dog to look up at him by making a noise with his hands, talking to him, or saying his name and a word of praise. It is just as easy for a small dog to be attentive and watch his handler as it is large one.

If there is adequate space, the instructor should have his class do two or three recalls before they do a finish. It is excellent practice to have the class leave their dogs, walk away from them some forty feet, turn to face them, and then call their dogs in to them one at a time. The dog being called learns to come in very fast this way, and the other dogs learn to wait their turn. The dog is staying because he has learned to be obedient, and after watching several other dogs being called to their handlers, he will be so eager to work that he will just fly in when it is his turn.

If a dog does not come when it is called the first time, the handler should walk up to it quietly, give the dog a jerk toward him with its collar, and then run backwards to his place in line with his dog trotting toward him. This same type of correction should be given to the dog that responds very slowly. A slow dog may need three or four good jerks as the handler is running backwards. This correction may be necessary every time the dog walks in slowly, but it is very effective.

Recalls should be practiced alternately with the voice command and the signal so that the dogs will become expert at obeying both. The instructor should show his class the correct signal to use when calling a dog. He should raise his right arm out to the side, shoulder high, sweep it in to his chest, and then place his arm back down by his side. Any time a signal is called for in class, the instructor should repeat the correct signal as some handlers tend to use sloppy signals that confuse their dogs. The dog that waits for his handler's signal and ignores a signal from a stranger who is standing close by is the dog that is well trained, alert, and sharp. This is the dog that will be on his toes when he goes into competition.

The ideal instructor should stress the importance of perfection. Perfection is possible to attain if useless, nonsensical, obsolete routines are avoided. The routines mentioned here will help a dog become a willing, happy, alert worker who, without anticipating, will respond briskly to his handler's first command. The other half of the team is the handler who has been taught to respect his dog. He has learned that his dog must obey his first command or be corrected. He has learned that more can be accomplished with a dog if he appeals to the dog's finer instincts and encourages him with praise and petting than if he tries to force him into obedience. He has found out that if he wants an alert, fast-working dog, he must be equally fast and alert himself. If he wants a smooth-working dog, he must learn to be a smooth handler; he must practice all the tips this method offers to produce a smooth-working, natural team.

The instructor should have his class form a straight line with five feet between each handler, their dogs sitting straight at heel position. He should then have the class practice dropping their dogs at a distance. This should be started at a distance of five feet, and as the dogs learn to drop quickly, the distance should be increased. The instructor should explain that the dogs are to drop very fast without moving out of position. In other words, when a hand signal is given, the dog must drop like a shot without crawling forward, rolling over on its back, or lying flat on its side. If the dog doesn't drop fast, the handler should run up to him and make him do so. He should not shout at his dog or throw anything at him. The very stubborn dog should receive a tap on his nose to make him drop faster. Many times a dog will drop at a distance if the handler takes one heavy step forward and gives the drop signal a second time. This shouldn't be repeated too often, however, or the dog will get wise and begin to wait for the second signal. The handler should always be thinking ahead of his dog. The instructor should be ahead of the whole class at all times with the right answers and conclusions.

The instructor should have his class practice these drops for a short time each week until all the dogs will drop immediately on signal. This exercise and routine can then be skipped for a few weeks. Once a dog has learned to drop fast at a distance, it is no problem to drop the dog on a recall. This first step prepares the dog for the Open exercises. Again, we are way ahead with our advanced training.

If a handler wants to practice dropping his dog with a verbal command, he should be permitted to do so, but he should not be allowed to shout at his dog. A dog can be taught to drop on recall with a verbal command given in a moderate but firm tone of voice. If the handler elects to use a voice command, he should make his dog obey him immediately. He should not keep repeating the command in a progressively louder and more desperate tone of voice. The trick is to insist that the dog drop the first time the command is given in a normal tone of voice, and if the dog ignores it, he must immediately be tapped on the nose. Such a correction as this will induce the dog to be obedient even if the command is given in a soft tone of voice. The voice must be raised just enough for the dog to hear the command; this will vary a great deal. The voice the handler uses in the quiet of his backyard is much softer than the voice he uses in an armory full of barking dogs where a loudspeaker is blaring away.

The Long Sit and the Long Down exercises should be practiced every week. The whole class should practice these exercises together. The Novice people should stand opposite their dogs about forty feet away from them, and the advanced people should go out of sight of their dogs. The handlers who are watching their dogs should immediately go to their dogs and correct them if they do something wrong. The handlers who are out of sight should be called back to correct their dogs. If there is an advanced dog who has become ring-wise and lies down on the Sit or sits up on the Down, the instructor or someone else should stand by ready to correct him by jerking him into position without saying a word to him. In this case the handler has given the dog the command and the dog has been disobedient, not because he has forgotten the command but because he was obstinate, so the correction, to be effective, should be made silently and swiftly by a stranger.

The Long Sit should be practiced for at least three minutes; the Long Down should be practiced for at least five minutes. When the handlers leave their dogs, they should all leave at exactly the same time, walk about forty feet away from their dogs, and turn around to face them with arms folded in front of them. The advanced people should leave the training site in single file. When the handlers are ordered to return to their dogs, the advanced people should file back and the whole class should return to their dogs at the same time. This is similar to the show procedure: if the class will practice this way, the dogs will become very used to the routine and will be more likely to stay when they are competing in a show.

When the handlers have been practicing the Long Sits and Long Downs for a few weeks and the dogs have become quite steady about staying, it is time for the instructor to explain a few of the finer points of these exercises. Whether the exercises are being done on leash or off leash, the handlers should walk their dogs into position in line on leash. When the whole class is lined up, the handlers should remove their dogs' leashes and place them about three feet behind their dogs. The instructor should explain that if they were competing in a show, the numbered armband that the steward would give each handler would be weighted down with the dog's leash so that it wouldn't blow away. The number on the armband should be visible to the judge.

The handlers should stand at ease, and upon the order "Leave your dogs" from the instructor, the handlers should give their dogs the stay command and/or signal and leave them. When a handler has reached the point in his training at which he feels his dog will stay when he is told, I suggest that he try leaving his dog with just the verbal command "Stay." The verbal command is smoother and more professional than the hand signal and verbal command given together. The handlers are advised not to raise their voices when giving the command, but to give it in a moderate or soft tone of voice. The word *stay* should not have the intonation of a question but should be spoken firmly. Many years ago I initiated the soft tone of voice as the criterion for training dogs and the soundness of my theory is now recognized universally.

However, it is high time that judges penalized the handlers for screaming "Stay," at their dogs while doing the Long Sit and Long Down exercises. This breach of the rules is quite unnecessary and gives obedience a black eye. Nothing seems quite so offensive to the spectator as the sight and sound of fifteen handlers screaming "Stay," at their poor dogs. I have heard many conformation judges condemn obedience for this reason alone. Although the practice has always been particularly obnoxious to me, I place the blame exactly where it belongs, in the hands of the instructors who should give better instruction, the handlers who should be familiar with the rules, and the judges who should enforce the obedience regulations.

If a handler is feeling nervous in the show ring, he might feel more secure if he gives his dog both the verbal command and the signal, but if the dog has been trained with the verbal command in class, the signal should not be necessary.

If the dog is given a signal, either alone or in conjunction with the verbal command, it should be made with one hand and arm only. This practice is another example of expert training that should apply to all breeds of dogs regardless of size. We have trained hundreds of small and medium-sized dogs, and have found that there is no valid reason why the handler should have to bend over or kneel to give a stay signal to his dog.

The handler should give any breed of dog the stay signal by placing his right hand down in front of him, palm toward the dog, fingers pointing down. If he has a small or medium-sized dog, the dog should be taught to look at him when he is giving it commands or signals; it should never be necessary for the handler to crawl around on his knees in order to get his dog's attention. If he will just give his dog the stay command and signal and leave him, the dog will soon start watching him. If the dog disobeys, he should be corrected immediately. This time he should receive the stay signal only. Remember that a dog can see the signal held waist high even if he has his head on the floor. It is up to the handler to make his dog pay attention.

When the instructor has his class lined up for the Long Down exercise, he should have the handlers wait until he gives them the order to "Drop your dogs," before they do so. Everyone should drop his dog at the same time. If verbal command is used, it should be spoken firmly but softly. The down signal should be the same for all breeds of dogs. There should be no exception made for the size of the dog. The way many people down their dogs, one would think the dogs couldn't turn their heads or raise their eyes. This exercise points out the poor handlers quicker than any

Give your dog the Down signal without bending over. Teach him to watch you.

other at a show. The handlers of small dogs find that my method helps tremendously with the rest of the work, for it makes their dogs become more attentive and alert.

The Long Down exercise should be practiced for five or six minutes with the leashes placed behind the dogs and the routine the same as that for the Long Sit exercise.

The instructor should caution the handlers not to pet their dogs immediately upon their return, but to wait five or ten seconds until the call "Exercise finished." After the conclusion of the Long Down exercise, the handlers should reach down and pet their dogs for staying before asking them to sit. If a dog gets up when he sees his handler returning, the handler should put him down again and then walk around him a few times before stopping in heel position. The dog must get used to the handler's walking around him; by cautioning him to stay and, if necessary, holding him in place, the handler can soon make the dog understand what is wanted.

The instructor should ask his class to follow the same pattern every time they take their dogs outdoors to give them a lesson. Each handler should ask his dog to "Get the leash," which should be located where the dog can reach it. At first the handler should take the dog over to it and pick it up saying this phrase: "Leash, leash, get the leash." After showing it to his dog, he should then clip it to his collar and take him outdoors. The incident should be a pleasant one so that the dog will associate the leash with a happy occasion. Later, the handler should hand the leash to his dog and let him carry it to the door where it should be clipped to his collar. Eventually, the dog will learn to get the leash and carry it to the door or bring it to his handler. Throughout the instruction, the word *leash* should be repeated continually so that the dog will learn the name as well as the act. It is very practical to teach a dog the names of articles that are familiar to him.

Fourth, Fifth, and Sixth Lessons

The instructor should give his class a half hour of heeling practice, including the routines that have been described earlier and incorporating the Figure Eight exercise. Emphasis should always be placed on perfection, and the instructor should always be firm with the handlers, insisting that they do everything correctly. By being vigilant at all times, the instructor will be able to make top handlers out of his students. By establishing an esprit de corps, the handlers will take pride in each other's accomplishments as well as in the success of their own dogs.

Heeling off leash. Incorrect: This is unnatural. Hold your left arm folded in front of you, out of your dog's way, and swing your right arm down by your side in a natural manner.

From the fourth week on, most of the heeling practice should be done off leash. At first, if the handler is hesitant about taking his dog off leash, he should try his skill at controlling his dog with his voice and his hands by throwing his leash over his shoulder or tucking the end of it in his belt. He should endeavor to keep his dog close to him by talking to him, petting him on his left shoulder when he is close, making a game of about turns and right turns by reaching down and guiding him playfully, clapping his hands or saying the dog's name on a turn to keep the dog attentive, or grunting "Uh, uh" when the dog is about to do something wrong.

The handler should graduate to holding the leash folded in half with both ends dangling down where the dog can see them; the leash should be held in the left hand with the arm folded in front. This step gives many handlers the confidence they need. After this, they can either take the leash off completely or use a five- or six-inch grab leash so that they can jerk the dog quickly if it is necessary. Figure Eights should be done on leash by those handlers who are working for a Novice degree and off leash by the advanced handlers.

During heeling practice the instructor should demonstrate the heeling signal, which is given by scooping the left hand forward, and the handlers should practice this until their dogs start forward instantly when it is used. If a dog doesn't start heeling on the signal, the handler can either give the verbal command "Heel," simultaneously with the signal, or quickly grasp the dog's collar and jerk him forward. Once the dog learns the signal, the handler should use it often enough that his dog will remember it. Not only is the handler teaching his dog another signal that will be used later in the Utility Signal exercise, but he is teaching his dog a signal that will make him more attentive and responsive to commands.

From the fourth lesson on, the instructor should include a variety of routines in his class that will make the work more interesting and keep the handlers and their dogs alert. The instructor should never let the lessons become boring, and these particular routines will keep things lively.

The instructor should have his class form a large circle, or two circles one within the other if the class is large, with the handlers spaced about five feet apart. The handlers should stand their dogs and leave them as they did when they practiced leaving their dogs sitting in the circle. If there is a dog who is too shy to permit a stranger to examine him, his handler should remain with him, but at the end of the leash. The rest of the handlers will examine every dog they come to before returning to their places in the circle. This is a perfect way to correct a dog who is shy; so many strangers examine the dog that he finally submits without protest. After five or six weeks the shy dog will be able to be examined as easily as the others.

If a dog tries to bite the examiner, his handler should remain with him. When his dog growls or snaps at someone, he should give it a sharp tap on his nose, saying, "No, shame, bad dog." When the dog permits a person to examine him without resenting it, the handler must praise and pet his dog, saying, "That's it, good boy."

Handlers examining each dog in circle as they come to him.

Give the Stay signal as your dog is bringing his left foot up in line with his right. This method looks smoother than any other. It is perfect teamwork and expert handling.

The judge will examine your dog off leash at a show.

Another version of this exercise is for the handlers to form a long line, take one step forward, stand their dogs, and then leave them. The person at the far end of the line should then walk to the other end as each person moves forward and examines each dog as he comes to it. Since all the dogs will be facing the same direction, the handlers will be passing them on both sides, some handlers examining the dogs and the rest moving back to start over again, until they step into heel position next to their own dogs. The handlers must keep an eye on their own dogs, being ready to run back and correct them if they move or to caution someone else's dog to "Stay," if it attempts to move while being examined. As soon as each dog does well on leash, the exercise should be practiced off leash.

These routines teach a dog to be steady during the Novice Stand for Examination, the Graduate Novice Stand, and the Utility Group Examination. By the time the Novice dogs are ready for Utility, they will have learned many of the Utility exercises. This is one of the reasons that my method is so up to date and fast. It applies to all breeds of dogs. It is easy to teach any dog with this fast, accurate method of training, but it is very difficult to retrain a handler who has been using one of the old-fashioned methods of dog training. It will require a concentrated effort on his part to correct his bad habits.

The instructor should watch the handlers each week to be sure they correct their dogs swiftly and properly. By the time the handlers have reached this class, they should be using the smooth, professional way of standing their dogs which I originated. The handler should hold his dog's leash taut in his left hand, lower than shoulder height. As his dog moves forward, at the precise moment the dog has his weight on his right foot, the handler should give his dog the stay signal and command "Stand, stay," holding the leash taut so that the dog cannot move forward. As the handler gives the signal, the dog will bring his left foot down in line with his right, and the handler should immediately go out to the end of the leash. Now he has his dog posed with both of his front feet in line. The dog looks good, feels balanced, and is very likely to stay in that position without moving. This was achieved very smoothly, without the handler having to fuss and fiddle with his dog. Once the dog acquires the habit of doing this, the handler will be able to do it off leash. Again, he has taught his dog a Utility exercise in the Novice class. This method is smooth and natural with both handler and dog being taught to work together as a team.

The instructor should point out that the Novice Stand-for-Examination exercise will be done off leash in a show and that the handler should be about six feet from his dog. He should stress this point because in shows many Novice people walk fifteen or more feet from their dogs and have to be told to come back or, in some cases, are penalized for a handler error. The handler is supposed to be familiar with the Obedience Regulations before he competes in a show. It is conceivable that some judge will deduct points if a handler stands too far from his dog because it is a handler error.

An expert instructor will mention the mistakes people make in shows so that his class won't repeat them. The class should also be urged to read the AKC Regulations that are in the back of this book. They should study these rules which are also free in booklet form to anyone writing to the American Kennel Club, 51 Madison Avenue, New York, New York, 10010. Often a person remembers things he has read better than things he has only heard. However, if a handler is penalized in a show because he has done something stupid, he will remember it forever. With the high entry fees at shows today, the handler is really paying for his mistakes.

From the fourth lesson on, the instructor should try a variety of recall routines in this class to make the work more interesting and to keep the handlers and their dogs alert. He should have the class form a straight line with all the dogs sitting straight at heel position. Upon the command "Leave your dogs and scramble," the handlers should walk some thirty feet away and face someone else's dog—one that is at least two places away in line. He should have the handlers call their dogs one at a time; the dogs should go to their handlers and sit straight. Since the dogs will be approaching their handlers from an angle, all the Novice dogs will sit crooked until they have been taught otherwise.

Every once in a while the instructor should have the class call their dogs at the same time. The inexperienced dogs will often sit in front of a perfect stranger. This is sometimes seen in shows, and although the spectators find it amusing, the handler isn't very pleased about it. It indicates that the dog either lacks this type of training or is confused.

To teach the dogs to do the angled Recall exercise, the instructor should demonstrate short recalls with his dog. The handlers should practice these recalls every day at home until the dog actually understands what the handler wants when he says, "Come." If my dog were to come to me and sit straight when I called him from a distance of forty feet, it would be gratifying but certainly no guarantee that he knew what he was doing. However, if from the same distance he came to me from an angle off to my left or an angle off to my right or even with my back turned to him and sat perfectly straight, then I would believe he understood that "Come" could only mean to sit straight in front of me.

The instructor should have his dog sitting at a right angle from him, some six feet away. When he calls his dog, the dog should come to him and turn enough so that he sits straight. The instructor should then try the

Try angle recalls. Stand facing away from your dog. Hold your hands out to guide the dog to you as you say "Come."

same thing at a left angle and get the same results. And last he should try leaving his dog a few feet away with his back to his dog. The dog will move all the way around until he is in exactly the right place before he will sit straight.

Since it is more difficult for a dog to do this when he is close to his handler, the practice should start with the dog about six feet away. After the dog has been called, the handler should not do the finish but should, instead, tell him to stay, leave him, and then call him from another angle. The pattern should change with every recall. The correction, if the dog tries to sit crooked, should be "No, come," and the dog should be straightened with the handler's hands or the side of his foot. No words should be used in the beginning which might confuse the dog. This little routine

When he is close, guide him into a straight sit with your hands, as he looks up at your face, and encourage him with your voice as you say "Good, come."

Try the same thing without using your hands. Control him with your voice.

Keep his attention on you as you talk to him.

should be practiced every day until the dog gets the idea. He should have it down fairly well within one week.

I have taught my dogs to sit straight in front of me regardless of the angle or direction from which they started. Although this training doesn't guarantee a perfect sit every time in a show, dogs that have had it can be expected to sit straight through force of habit and, in this case, that means good practice habits.

When the dog begins to move over and line himself up for a straight sit, the handler can begin to lengthen the recalls, but should still practice them from odd angles. The handler should add straight routines to the practice session now. After trying the more difficult recalls, it is surprisingly simple to get straight sits when the handler is in line with his dog. If the instructor has a large class, doing this kind of short recall is impractical, but he should demonstrate with his dog so that the handlers can practice at home. In class, they can get similar experience by practicing the angled recalls at distances of fifteen, twenty, thirty, and forty feet.

The instructor should remind the handlers to stand up straight and keep their hands down by their sides. In accordance with the AKC regulations the hands must be placed down by the handler's sides whenever his dog is returning to him. This is the only time that it is mandatory.

Although the handler has trained his dog to sit in front of him by motioning to him with his hands, he should gradually stop this practice. Now he should call his dog after he places his hands down by his sides and only move them if it is necessary to assist his dog to sit straight. By talking to his dog and/or guiding him with one hand or the side of his foot, he will soon have his dog centering himself in front of him.

From the fourth lesson on, each dog should finish every time he does a recall. The one exception is the time the handler is working on odd-angle recalls. If the dog is beginning to anticipate the finish, the handler should then do two recalls to every finish. If the handler finds that his dog is anticipating the recall on the instructor's command, the instructor should give the handler two or three orders to finish before the handler sends his dog to heel. In such a case the number of orders to be given should be mentioned to the handler beforehand. The handler will find it wise to hesitate after the instructor gives the finish order so that he can catch his dog in the act of anticipating and correct it. This error is easily corrected this way. The same type of correction applies to dogs anticipating any command given by the instructor.

The class should practice the Long Sit and the Long Down exercises as described previously.

Dogs taught to Sit this closely in class will become very reliable in a show.

Seventh, Eighth, and Ninth Lessons

During the seventh, eighth, and ninth lessons, the instructor should give his class heeling practice, including the routines that have been explained earlier. Most of the work should be done off leash, and the handlers should be instructed to practice all the exercises off leash at home. There may be some handlers who do not practice at home often enough for them to do all the work off leash in class. The instructor should have these handlers use grab leashes on their dogs so that they can make quick corrections when necessary.

The instructor should include all the routines that will help the handlers perfect the Figure Eight, Stand-for-Examination, and Recall exercises with their dogs.

From the seventh week on, the instructor should include in the recall practice another routine that provides excellent discipline for the dogs. The class should form a straight line with their dogs sitting straight at heel position. The instructor should then ask every second person to step forward about eight feet with his dog. Then everyone should be asked to leave his dog and form a single line some thirty feet from the dogs. The dogs will be called singly; it will be a great temptation for the dogs remaining to break and go dashing to their handlers. The dogs that break should be scolded with the verbal "No, shame, bad dog, I told you to stay." A dog that persists in breaking when he has been told to stay should receive a stronger correction.

When a dog breaks, the handler should move forward toward him; the spot where they meet is the place where the dog should be corrected. If it is an older dog, he should be given a sharp tap on the bridge of his nose and the verbal scolding. If it is a young puppy, a jerk on his collar and the verbal scolding should be all that is necessary. A dog corrected in this way will not continue to anticipate the recall or disobey his handler.

When disciplining a dog with a tap, the tap should sting but should not be so heavy that it injures the dog. I have had to admonish some strong-handed people for overdoing this correction. If the tap stings the handler's hand, the dog will feel it, and that is certainly sufficient. If the tap is given correctly, it may never have to be repeated. Only one tap should be given. One often sees a handler swinging at his dog trying to hit him, but missing every time; this may encourage his dog to get fresh and take a nip at him. Nothing is gained in this case, and the handler's dog is quick to take advantage of his master's awkwardness. If the handler is inept, he should hold his dog's ruff, or the loose skin around his neck, with one hand while he taps him with the other. A dog will not become hand shy if the handler taps his dog occasionally. A dog will become hand shy, however, if the handler is so clumsy that he keeps hitting at his dog and missing, or hits his dog repeatedly. But then a dog will shy away from any correction that is not administered intelligently. A dog should never be hit with newspapers, sticks, or leashes, as nothing can be gained from this treatment. A handler who taps his dog during the course of a lesson might do so once or twice, but the balance of the time he should be petting his dog with his hands.

I will mention here another type of correction this is quite heartless and unnecessarily cruel. Some groups of people who train dogs for attack work have found that they can force their dogs into submission by using brute strength every time the dog attempts to disobey. The reason I mention it here is that this sadistic approach to training is beginning to appear in public training classes. There is no reason for using such unwarranted, forceful corrections in a class that consists of pets and show dogs. The correction I speak of is "stringing a dog up." This means that the handler lifts the dog off his feet by his collar and dangles him in midair until the dog is limp. This is a very ugly scene to witness and takes a much stronger stomach than mine.

In my opinion the only dog that could possibly deserve such extreme punishment is a dog that has attacked another animal without provocation and nearly killed it or has viciously attacked and injured a human being. I could never condone such action in any obedience class and would advise anyone who sees such cruelty to report the trainer and boycott his classes. It is only by reporting and rejecting this type of training that the people who love dogs will be able to keep obedience a healthy sport.

The following is a very good routine that can be practiced by a class consisting of Advanced Novice, Open, and Utility dogs. The instructor

A novice dog responds to his handler's call while all the open dogs remain where they were dropped on Recall.

should have the class form a straight line with the dogs sitting straight at heel position. The advanced dogs should be scattered among the Novice dogs. The handlers should be told to leave their dogs and to walk out about thirty feet from them. The advanced dogs will be called to their handlers singly and dropped when they are halfway in to them. Then the Novice dogs will be called individually all the way in to their handlers and should finish without command from the instructor. The advanced dogs will then be called in either individually or all at the same time. The class could also practice using signals to call their dogs. Routines such as these make the dogs very steady and reliable.

The class should finish these lessons by practicing the Long Sit and the Long Down exercises. If there is room, the instructor should have some handlers practicing the Open or Utility exercises behind these dogs who are practicing stays. Spectators should be encouraged to make all the noise they want and to clap their hands from time to time. The dogs should learn to work with all kinds of distractions around them. If there are no distractions at class, the handlers should make a few, such as running past the dogs when they are staying, calling to them, or giving them signals from the sidelines.

When a handler and his dog are ready to graduate from this class, they should be ready to go into a show and compete for their Companion Dog degree. If the end of the series comes at a time of year when there are no shows in the area, the handler should continue to practice in this class while he works on his Open degree. In this way he will keep his dog sharp while teaching him something new. Every instructor will have to set his own price rates according to the area in which the classes are held.

However, I believe handlers should be able to practice in this particular class free of charge if they are also working on an advanced degree.

The instructor should remind every handler to read the *American Kennel Club Obedience Regulations*. They should be advised to read the material that pertains to the Novice work and be encouraged to ask questions about it. During the course of the series, the instructor should advise them about the regulations from time to time as specific incidents arise that are pertinent to the subject. By the time the test rolls around, the handlers should understand the exercises and know exactly what is expected of them. Throughout this series of lessons, all the work the handlers learn conforms with the *American Kennel Club Obedience Regulations* so that even if a handler forgets the regulations, he will still be practicing them correctly.

The Tenth Lesson

The test that is given in this class should be exactly the same as the handlers would get if they were to compete in a Novice class. The penalties should also be the same, so that the handler will have an idea how well or how poorly he did. It is best to be honest and realistic about the test so that the handler can practice any exercises his dog did poorly. If the handler gave body signals unintentionally or gave double commands, it would be most helpful for him to find this out before he competes in a show.

It is a good idea to conduct the test as it would be judged at a show, with the assistant or an experienced judge presiding, rather than the instructor. The experienced handlers should help by giving out armbands and acting as stewards in the ring. If the experienced handlers wear armbands that read WE ANSWER QUESTIONS, the Novice people will not feel shy about approaching them. No matter how much training a beginner has had, he can always think of a question he would like answered at his first test.

The exercises and the maximum scores in the Novice classes are as follows:

1. Heel on Leash	40 points
2. Stand for Examination	30 points
3. Heel Free	40 points
4. Recall	30 points
5. Long Sit	30 points
6. Long Down	30 points
Maximum Total Score	200 points

When the judge has finished judging the class and has announced the winners and the scores, he should give out sample judging sheets so that each handler can study his test scores. The information on the sheets will tell the handler where he and his dog failed. These sheets are available to clubs, judges, instructors, etc., and many of the leading dog-food manufacturers are pleased to distribute them free of charge. These judging sheets can be used at Club Fun Matches or Club Obedience Tests, but it is against the rules for a judge to pass them out at AKC-Sanctioned Matches or point shows.

The competition for the Novice test will be a little more exciting if a trophy or two is awarded to the winners. The instructor could give out prizes that would encourage the handler to keep his dog in top condition. An obedience dog will work better if he is in excellent health and is groomed every day. An obedience dog who competes in shows should always look his best; he does not have to meet the breed standard, but he should be a shining example of good care and grooming. The prizes could include brushes, combs, shampoos, cedar dog beds, leashes, nylon collars, food or water dishes, a thermos for a dog's water supply, dog bags, or many other similar items.

6 | CLUB PRACTICE MATCHES

Club practice matches are great fun and everyone involved enjoys them. It takes the combined efforts of a small group of people to keep the match running smoothly and efficiently.

A new training club could start in a small way by having practice matches every month. These matches are very easy to arrange and set up. If at all possible, they should be held at a different location, preferably a member's backyard, each month. This gives the dogs the experience of working in strange locations, which is a must if the dogs are to gain poise and self-confidence.

Two of the men could be in charge of setting up the rings. The club should own the rope and stakes, and these should be used for each show. The measurements for the ring should be those stipulated in the obedience regulations for an outdoor Utility ring—forty feet long by fifty feet wide; this ring could be used for all the classes. The dogs should get used to working in a ring that is the official size.

The object of these practice sessions is to give the dogs a chance to work in strange surroundings and to give the handlers the opportunity to handle their dogs individually in front of an audience. Dogs and handlers who do very well in class are surprised at how poorly they make out in the first few practice sessions.

Until a dog becomes acquainted with the world, he is likely to be caught staring at the new sights instead of following his handler around the ring. The handler, on the other hand, gets nervous when he finds himself the center of attention and forgets all the good advice the instructor has been giving him over the past months. When he gets his score sheet, he is amazed that he made so many handler errors.

The handlers should be given numbered armbands, which can be obtained free from dog-food companies or distributors, and they should learn to wear them while they are working their dogs in the ring. Later they should place them with their leashes behind their dogs during the Long Sit and the Long Down exercises. All these small steps will make the transition from practice matches to sanction matches to point shows that much easier for the handlers and their dogs.

If the club has someone qualified to judge, or some friend who has completed the Utility degree, or even a member who has competed in shows, his services would be most helpful to the handlers who are practicing with their dogs. If not, the instructor should judge the handlers and point out the errors made, the reason for deducting points, and the handler errors. If this is done, the audience can follow along and keep a mental score. The instructor should understand the obedience regulations from cover to cover before he attempts this, as passing along misinformation is worse than giving no information at all. Just reading one small passage from the obedience regulations is not enough. The instructor should understand them thoroughly and instruct his handlers to read them several times; then, when the handler has queries about them, the problems can be discussed intelligently.

Once a year my club puts on the most sophisticated fun match I have ever seen. We call it a practice match, and the handlers have the option of either correcting their dogs in the ring and taking the penalty or letting the dog get away with errors and trying for an unusually nice trophy. Many handlers feel it is worthwhile forfeiting the trophy to be able to correct their dogs in the ring. Since handlers are not permitted to practice or to correct their dogs during sanction matches or point shows under the present obedience regulations, a fun match is the only place where a dog can receive the discipline he sometimes needs. We do stipulate that the dog must be corrected quietly without disturbing anyone else and that the correction can consist of only a verbal correction or a small jerk on the dog's collar. A dog that requires more drastic corrections than these is actually in need of more practice. We do not permit handlers to abuse their dogs in any way. A handler may return once, if necessary, during the Long Sit or Long Down exercises to correct his dog, but must give the correction in a quiet tone of voice. The handler is scored as if the dog failed.

A ring ready for the Working class.

Regulation rings with a five-foot aisle between them.

We use an outdoor field that is completely fenced in. The rings are located near a group of trees that give welcome shade to the dogs and their handlers. We have four regulation-size rings—one for each class. (We were the first obedience club in the country to include the Working class at a match.) The rings are set up side by side with a five-foot aisle between each ring; the aisles are closed to traffic. Next, the whole ring area is enclosed in a second set of ropes with a five-foot aisle all the way around it; this keeps children back where they belong. It also keeps spectators and their dogs back from the working area—some untidy people drop food alongside the rings where the dogs are working and some people unwittingly let their dogs crawl under the ropes and distract the dogs working in the ring. The grass in the rings and the surrounding area is cut short and is green and velvety like that of a golf course. At the entrance to each ring, we have a sign that gives the ring number, the class, and the name of the judge.

The two club members who put up the rings at our show every year have figured out an ingenious way to make the rings without cutting the rope. The rope is stored on a large spool and is unwound as the men are setting up the rings. When they come to an entrance, they simply bury the rope in the ground by lifting the sod on one side with a spade and running the rope down one pole and up another. In this manner the rope that forms the rings is one continuous length that is wound up on the spool at the end of the show. It makes the rings look very neat and professional, and it is easier to take down at the end of the day. We have our own steel posts that are painted to match the rope.

A number of attractive trash containers are placed around the grounds to encourage everyone to keep our showgrounds clean; so far we have never had to pick up litter at the end of the day. Clean outdoor rest rooms are placed a short distance from the show site so that the handlers won't need a guide to find them.

We have an excellent public address system that is run by one man who takes care of the four rings all day long. He reminds each handler when it is his time to be at ringside, calls the dogs together for the Long Sits, Long Downs, and Group Examinations, and calls all the class winners to ringside. He also announces the winners of each class and their scores. At most shows the spectators never hear the scores unless they are in the front row at ringside. He explains the requirements for the nonregular classes before they start. If there are other obedience shows coming up, he mentions the show, the place, and the date.

Free parking is available near the working area. Good home-prepared food is offered at reasonable prices. We give our judges a specially prepared lunch that is attractive and appetizing.

We try to use ingenuity in selecting the trophies for our show. They are always prizes a person will use or treasure, and they always suggest a certain theme. We have had trophies from the Far East, woodenware from New England, pottery from well-known artists, equipment or toys for the dogs, articles one would use at a dog show—such as picnic baskets, folding chairs, thermos bottles—and trays of all shapes, sizes, and materials. There is no end to the variety of trophies a club can offer at a show. Selecting them just takes imagination.

We generally publish a catalog that describes the classes and gives pertinent information, such as the judges' names and addresses, background of the club, trophy donors, etc.

A practice ring, complete with a full set of regulation jumps, is set up apart from the working rings and out of hearing distance. The majority of the handlers take advantage of this opportunity to warm up their dogs before competing. The jumps that we use in our working rings are also regulation jumps, freshly painted and easy to adjust to the correct heights. Furnishing the judge with regulation hurdles that will conform to the measurements needed for every dog competing in the class is the least an obedience club can do when holding a trial.

The overall impression one gets from seeing this Fun Practice Match for the first time is that of a lawn party at a country club. Everything is very neat, quiet, and attractive, and one is not conscious of the mechanics of it because it is being run so smoothly and efficiently.

We try to get a different person each time to be the show chairman so that each club member will eventually have this valuable experience. By participating in the club events, the members have a greater appreciation for the work that is carried on behind the scenes at matches of all kinds.

We try to make every feature of our annual fun match as close to perfect as possible.

HOW TO HOLD AN
7 | AKC-SANCTIONED
OBEDIENCE MATCH

A club AKC-Sanctioned Obedience Match will be beneficial to everyone concerned. Sanctioned Obedience Matches shall be governed by such regulations as may be adopted by the board of directors of the American Kennel Club. Scores awarded at such matches will not be entered in the records of the American Kennel Club nor count towards an obedience title.

The first step is for the club secretary to write to the American Kennel Club, 51 Madison Avenue, New York, N.Y. 10010 for a free copy of the *Regulations for Sanctioned Matches*. With these regulations as a guide, the club members should not find it very difficult to put on a match.

The club should name a show chairman who will supervise the show. The show chairman will name the people he would like to serve as subchairmen; each of these subchairmen will name several members he would like to have serve on his committee.

The trophy chairman and his helpers will solicit trophies and cash donations from business firms and friends. He will order the ribbons for all the classes and any special ribbons desired, such as Highest Scoring Dog in Trial, Highest Scoring Dog in Open B and Utility, etc. The trophies are the responsibility of this chairman; he should display them on a table at the show and see that they are taken to the judge when he is ready for them.

The food chairman and his group will arrange to get food donations and sell food at the show. He will also have special luncheons prepared for the judges who are officiating at the show. This committee will decide what food will be sold, how much will be charged, and how the food will be displayed. The club members should be asked to bring some kind of food to the show that could be sold by the food committee. Some of our members cook hams and turkeys to be used to make sandwiches while others make tarts, brownies, cookies, cupcakes, pies, and regular cakes. Girls wearing attractive aprons in the club's colors could walk around the showgrounds carrying colorful baskets filled with sandwiches to sell to the spectators.

The gate chairman and his assistants are in charge of collecting admission fees and entry fees. As the entry fees are collected, armbands and entry forms should be distributed to the exhibitors. The chairman should be ready to hand over the receipts of the show to the show chairman an hour after the entries close, unless the club plans to go on collecting admissions at the gate.

The entry chairman and his committee will take the entries the day of the show. This is one of the key jobs the day of the show, and the efficiency of the committee can guarantee a successful show. Everyone on this committee should know exactly what he is going to do the day of the show so that long lines of people will not be waiting to register.

The handler who has paid his entry fee and received his entry form and armband should report to the entry table. Here the information on the entry form will be recorded and passed along to the judge of his class.

The grounds chairman has a very important job. He needs men to serve on his committee who are reliable, resourceful, energetic, and congenial. This committee will be in charge of all the equipment—jumps, rope, posts, chairs, tables, and signs. They will set up the rings, see that the grass is short if the match is outdoors, park cars, handle the public address system, provide signs for the other committees, place directional arrows at numerous crossroads to direct people to the showgrounds, provide tables and chairs for each ring, place the jumps in the right rings, erect the show signs, and order the portable toilets. This committee will also be in charge of closing down the show.

The publicity chairman will mail out flyers to all those who might be interested in attending the show; notify newspapers, radio stations, and TV stations; and distribute posters to stores which will display them. Members who are attending other shows should pass out flyers while they are there. The chairman of this committee should try to get some favorable publicity in the local newspapers before and after the show.

The show chairman will have the busiest job of all. At the first show committee meeting, many important things should be decided: where the show will be held, the date of the show, the opening and closing times for entries, the time the judging will start, the classes to be offered, the judges who will be invited to officiate, and the fees that will be charged. The show chairman will have to contact the judges and get their consent to judge, look the show site over to be sure it is suitable before obtaining permission to use it, be certain the date meets with everyone's approval, give all the information to the American Kennel Club on their special forms, and handle all the correspondence that will follow. He should also arrange to have the show covered by insurance.

It will be necessary to call meetings from time to time to check the progress of each of the committees and to see that things are going smoothly, efficiently, and peacefully. A good chairman is the club's greatest asset; he can make or break a show. I have seen one chairman make a clear profit of five hundred dollars on a match by working hard with every committee, and I have seen another person take it over the next time with the same group of people and lose money on the show.

The show chairman must plan to have at least two hundred dollars in small bills and change at the show. This should be divided between the food chairman and the gate chairman, who in turn will give him receipts for the specific sums they receive. After the show, the entry chairman should compile a list of the entrants in alphabetical order so that the club will have a list of the people who supported their show. This is the beginning of an active mailing list, and as the years go by, it will be an important item to maintain.

The American Kennel Club is always willing to help a sincere, hardworking group of people to accomplish its goals. The club that has elected a slate of officers, drawn up a set of bylaws similar to the sample supplied them by the AKC, proved that they are capable of holding sanctioned matches, and worked successfully as a congenial group should have no trouble becoming a recognized obedience club.

THE IDEAL
OBEDIENCE TRIAL

The location of the obedience trial is important. If outdoors, the ground should be level and the grass should be thick and cut short. Trees should be nearby to provide shade for the handlers and their dogs. If possible, the rings should be set up under the trees so that it is more comfortable for everyone concerned. If there are no trees, ample tenting should be provided for the exhibitors and their dogs.

The rings should be formed with double ropes: the first to form the ring and the second to form a five-foot aisle around the first. The club that uses fencing to form the ring should add a rope ring around that.

If indoors, there should be ample space for the double rings and the spectators. If the floors are slippery, they should be entirely covered with wide rubber matting. Two strips of four-foot-wide rubber matting should be provided for the jumps in the Open class. The Utility-ring floor should be entirely covered.

The rings should be regulation size. Many specialty clubs have the mistaken notion that judges want a huge ring; if the ring is too large, the judge will simply have to change the ring size when he sees it.

The club giving the show should let the exhibitors arrive and leave according to their individual schedules. The way some all-breed clubs force the exhibitors to arrive by a certain time and stay until a certain hour is both archaic and senseless. By forcing the exhibitors to stay, they hope to make more money from the spectators, but this creates massive traffic jams and numerous other problems as a result of such greediness.

The club should inform each exhibitor of the number of entries in his class, his dog's number, and the first and last numbers so that he can determine the approximate time that he will be judged. Clean rest rooms should be provided nearby with water, soap, towels, etc. If these are not provided, the exhibitors should complain to the show chairman. Free parking should be provided near the working area. Chairs should be furnished around the rings. Good food at reasonable prices is a welcome feature.

Good stewards should be in every ring. They do not have to be experienced, so long as they are willing, alert, and courteous. The steward should not usher a handler into the ring until the judge signifies that he is ready. A handler should not be expected to wait in the ring when the judge is not ready for him. A boring, prolonged wait will sometimes take the edge, or fire, from a dog's performance. The stewards should give out the armbands at the beginning of the class. In the advanced classes, the steward should make a notation in the catalog of the height that each dog jumps. When a handler has completed the exercises and is leaving the ring, the stewards should be adjusting the jumps for the next dog. This is a great timesaver for the judge; although the judge will measure the height of all dogs who jump less than three feet, he will rarely have to change the jumps—there are very few handlers who do not know what height their dogs are at the withers.

When the handler and his dog are in the ring and the dog is sitting at heel position watching, the steward should put the handler's articles on the ground, placing eight of them six inches apart with his hands. The two unscented articles should be placed untouched by the steward or the judge on the judge's table or chair. When the exercise is over, the steward should place the two used scented articles in a plastic bag, provided by the club. If the show doesn't furnish the handler with a bag for his used articles, the steward should at least keep them separate for him. The handler might want to use the rest of his articles the next day, and this will save him the trouble of washing them. If one steward will pick up the articles while the other places the handler's gloves down for the judge, the judging can be expedited. The judge will designate or mark the spot where he wants the gloves to be placed. It is also a nice gesture if one steward will have the handler's articles ready for him after he finishes all the exercises and is ready to leave the ring. Efficient stewards should always be ready to act as posts for the Figure Eight exercise, take the handler's leash when he is ready to work off leash, give the handler the dumbbell when he needs it, take it from him when it has been used and place it on the table, and inform him where the judge would like him to stand for the next exercise. The stewards should stand at the ring entrance unless they are working. Too many stewards stand near the judge's table and interfere with the dog's work.

The club should offer trophies that have been chosen with a little ingenuity. Anyone can make a phone call and order statuettes of different sizes. The trophy chairman should be chosen who has good taste and imagination. Even the silver plates and bowls are overdone. Why not some handcarved figures of the different breeds of dogs, monogrammed glasses or glassware, woodenware of all kinds, beautiful ceramics, exquisite china dogs, traveling bags of all shapes, sizes, and materials, picture frames of all kinds, etc. There is an endless variety of trophies waiting to be chosen by the trophy chairman who dares to be different.

The club should give the exhibitors clear directions to enable them to find the show site. Sufficient dog-show signs should be displayed at intersections and turns to direct the exhibitors to the showgrounds.

9 | *THE OPEN CLASS*

A ten-week course that includes a
Retrieving Method that never fails, the
Drop on Recall, Jumping instructions,
Handling Tips, and new routines to make
every dog steady and reliable.

The First Lesson

The heeling routines have already been covered in the Advanced Novice
classes, so they will not be discussed here. The instructor should begin the
Open class by teaching the Drop-on-Recall exercise. The instructor should
demonstrate the drop with his dog and explain that the down signal is
given by raising the right hand and arm quickly; the signal should not be
held more than three seconds. A handler may use either hand to give the
signal, but he will find it is most effective to drop his dog with the right
hand. By using the right hand consistently, the handler can avoid confusing the dog. The instructor should also explain that once the signal is
given, the dog should drop immediately and should never take extra steps
or crawl forward. When the dog is called in from the down position, he
should respond quickly and willingly. The sit should be straight and the
finish should be made with precision.

The instructor should have the class line up about six feet apart in a
row. He should remind them to keep their hands down by their sides.
At first the handlers should practice dropping their dogs one at a time.
The first handler in line should leave his dog, walk about thirty feet from

him, and turn and face him. The first time he drops his dog, he should do so when the dog is about ten feet from him. If the handlers have already been through the Advanced Novice class and have practiced the drop at a distance, the dog will understand the exercise. It is fairly simple to teach the dog to drop on recall once he has learned the other exercise. However, if the dog does not drop for the handler when he gives the signal correctly, he should run up to the dog and say, "Down," repeating the down signal. He should then take the dog back in line and try it over again. This time the dog should respond to the signal. Each handler in succession should try the drop, until everyone has had a turn. Then the whole routine should be practiced again. If any particular dog doesn't drop, he should immediately try it again. The instructors should get the handlers to move fast so that valuable class time won't be wasted waiting for them.

In succeeding weeks the dogs should learn to drop at different points, until they become proficient at dropping anywhere. With sufficient practice a dog should be able to drop immediately whenever the handler gives him the down signal. The handler should know his dog so well that he should be able to drop him at any given point.

The dog's name may not precede the hand signal but may precede the verbal command. The handler has the option of dropping his dog with either the down signal or the voice command in a show, but he cannot use both at the same time. He should practice both ways at first, and when his dog will respond to either method, he should then decide which he prefers to use and concentrate on using that alone. I always suggest that the handler use the hand signal as its use will train the dog to keep his eye on his handler and will teach him to be attentive. The signal is part of the Utility Signal exercise, and by using it in the Open work, the dog is preparing for the Utility class. In my opinion, any routine that serves a dual purpose is vastly superior to any other.

When a dog is learning to drop on recall, he should be praised when he drops quickly. The praise should be given spontaneously, and the handler should teach his dog to accept the praise without getting excited. If the dog should get up when he is praised, he should be dropped again, told to stay, and praised again quietly. The dog that is excitable might have to be restrained a few times at first, but he will eventually learn to accept the praise by just wagging his tail. It is much better to teach the dog to control himself and accept praise under any circumstances than it is to ignore the dog because you are afraid that if you pet him, he will go to pieces. A handler could hardly be considered a good trainer if he has no more control over his dog than this.

While the dog is practicing to drop on recall about ten feet from his handler, he should be trained to drop very quickly. If he learns to drop

The handler gives her dog the Down signal by raising her right hand and arm quickly.

She immediately returns her hand down by her side.

quickly at this distance, it is unlikely that a problem will arise when he is dropped farther away from his handler. If any dog doesn't drop quickly, the handler should again raise his right hand and arm, say "Down," and step forward threateningly with his right foot. If the dog is exceedingly fresh or stubborn and refuses to drop, the handler should run up to the dog, repeat the down signal, and tap the dog on the nose. The next few times the dog drops, the handler should walk up to his dog and pet and praise him; as he leaves him, he should caution his dog to stay.

The handler who uses the verbal command "Down" to drop his dog should not shout or scream at him. This would be penalized in a show. The command should be given firmly but just loud enough for the dog to hear it. Although it is permissible to use the dog's name prior to the verbal command, I feel it takes too much time. A fast dog would be close to the handler before the *Down* portion of the command was given. The word "Down" alone is sufficient.

Once the dog has dropped, the handler must concentrate on getting his dog to come in to him quickly. He can accomplish this by calling the dog in an excited tone of voice, praising him, jumping up in the air, clapping his hands, and looking generally pleased. The dog will respond to this kind of treatment and learn to move briskly.

The retrieve should be started the first night so that all the dogs in the class will be ready for competition by the end of the ten-week series of lessons. The instructor should have dumbbells on hand for the handlers to purchase. It is difficult to get dumbbells that are the right weight, size, and proportions, and those that I have seen in most pet supply stores are inferior in every respect. However, most of the pet supply stands at dog shows carry the right kind. The dumbbell should be made of wood, and the ends should be painted a flat white so that the dog can see it easily. The type of dumbbell I prefer using for German Shepherds has a middle piece that is three and three quarters to four inches long and three quarters of an inch in diameter. The ends are two and one-half inches square and one and one-half inches wide. I use the same proportions cut down for a small dog or increased for the large breeds. Any dumbbell so proportioned is comfortable for the dog to work with.

The ideal time to teach the retrieve is when the puppy is about five months of age. This applies to the puppy who wants to come to his handler willingly and instinctively. If the puppy has been coming when he was called because he expects to be petted and praised, he will continue to do so when he is retrieving the dumbbell. It is natural for a puppy to run up to an object that has been thrown and pick it up. It is also natural for him to bring it in to his handler if the handler calls him and praises him as he is coming in. If there are any young puppies in the Open class, the instructor should be very patient and gentle with them and try the method explained in the chapter on puppies.

The following is the method I have used to teach the retrieve to my dogs, and other people's dogs, over the past umpteen years. I also use the same approach and method in my classes and have had 100 percent success. I have yet to meet a dog that couldn't be taught to retrieve if this method is used.

The instructor should use one of the class dogs that does not know how to retrieve for the demonstration. If the instructor and the dog's handler will do it correctly, the dog will be retrieving happily and willingly in three weeks.

The first step is to teach the dog to take the dumbbell when the instructor hands it to him and to hold it until he takes it away from him. If this is done correctly in the beginning, any other problems that arise will be minor.

The dog should be on a five-foot web or leather leash. The instructor

A correctly proportioned
dumbbell.

should try handing the dumbbell to the dog a few times with the command, "Get it." The first two or three times he tries this, he should open the dog's mouth gently and put the dumbbell in it. If the dog doesn't get the idea right away, the instructor should sit the dog in a corner, stand by his side facing him, and place his right foot directly in front of him to block his path. The whole class should be standing in a semicircle watching the demonstration. The instructor should hold one end of the dumbbell in his right hand, keeping his fingers off the middle section, and place it about one inch in front of the dog's nose. The dog's choke collar should be as far up on his neck as it will go; that is, it should be directly behind his ears and under his chin. The instructor should place his left hand on the collar and draw all the excess collar through the ring. To draw the collar tighter, he will apply pressure with his left thumb, pressing on the ring as he pulls out more of the collar with his fingers. This forces the dog to open his mouth.

Some dogs will rear up on their hind legs when pressure is applied to their collars, some will submit passively, some will grab the dumbbell quickly, some will grit their teeth and turn their heads from side to side to avoid the dumbbell, and the occasional mean-tempered dog will try to bite. These reactions will be encountered only during the first lesson.

The dog will turn his head to avoid the dumbbell so the instructor should keep moving the dumbbell so that it is always in front of the dog's nose. The instant he opens his mouth, it should be there for him to take. As the instructor places the dumbbell in front of the dog's nose, he should say, "Hussan, get it," in a firm but quiet tone of voice. He should use the dog's name each time he gives the command. When the dog opens his mouth and takes the dumbbell, the instructor should let go of the collar immediately, caution him quietly to "Hold it," and quickly stroke his nose gently with one hand as he strokes him under the chin with the other. The gentle stroking will pacify him, keep the dumbbell in his mouth, and prevent him from mouthing or chewing it. The dog should be praised in a happy tone of voice. The instructor should be generous and sincere with

The collar is tightened smoothly.

"Get it." "Hold it."

his praise. The instructor should then have the handlers try it with their dogs, standing by ready to help anyone who needs assistance.

After the handler has tried this method a couple of times, he should test his dog to see whether he will take the dumbbell without having pressure applied to his collar. The handler should put the collar up high, but he should coax his dog to take the dumbbell two or three times, using a persuasive tone of voice. If his dog doesn't respond, he should again apply pressure to the collar. From now on, he should give his dog a chance to obey before applying pressure. The dog will soon realize that it is more fun to take and hold the dumbbell than to be stubborn. The majority of dogs will learn to do this the first lesson. The handler should not teach his dog to retrieve for more than ten minutes at a time at first.

The instructor should make it very clear that the handler must be very gentle with his dog. He should tell him to be sure that the dog takes the dumbbell from him; the handler should never place it in the dog's mouth. The dog must of his own accord, even though pressure is applied, reach out and take it. The handler must be careful that he takes the dumbbell without banging the dog's teeth or gums. He should apply pressure very smoothly, stroke his dog's nose and chin gently, and talk soothingly and reassuringly to him.

It is not unusual for a dog to start reaching out for the dumbbell, hold it for a few seconds and give it up on the command "Out" during the first lesson. The dogs that learn this step during the first lesson will be retrieving the dumbbell willingly within three weeks.

The instructor should personally help each handler get his dog started on this exercise so that each one will practice correctly at home. He should also warn them not to try any additional steps with their dogs without his supervision. The handler who tries to push his dog too fast will end up having to start all over again. Many people have difficulty with their dogs because the dogs start out too fast and don't actually learn how to take the dumbbell, hold it, or pick it up off the ground. It isn't enough for the dog to learn how to run out and get it at a distance. The dog should understand each step thoroughly before he goes on to the next one. If this exercise is taught correctly, the dog will have no problem retrieving other articles in more advanced classes.

After the handlers have practiced this exercise in class long enough to understand the first step, the jumps should be set up and all the dogs should practice jumping. The class should be divided into two groups; while one group is working on the high jump, the other can be working on the broad jump. The class might be divided according to size—one group for medium or large dogs and the other for small dogs. In either case the groups can form lines and take turns jumping their dogs over the hurdles. Everyone enjoys this work, including the dogs.

For the small dogs, the high jump should be set up with one eight-inch board and two broad-jump hurdles that have been turned over onto their sides. The large dogs should start the high jump with two eight-inch boards and three broad-jump hurdles, the first and third on their sides and the second one flat in its normal position.

The instructor should demonstrate how to teach a dog to jump. He should explain that the dog will understand he is to jump if the handler takes the jump with him the first few times. When the dog understands that he is to jump the hurdle, the handler may then run up to the jump with his dog and quickly run around the side of the jump as he guides his dog over the jump with the leash. When all the dogs are jumping these hurdles with ease, the hurdles can then be raised or extended.

The handlers should be cautioned to keep their dogs on leash the first few days they practice so that their dogs will get the correct rhythm. As each handler approaches the jump with his dog, he should say "Hup," to his dog at the precise moment that it is most advantageous for the dog to clear the jump. The dog, if started correctly, will rely on his handler to say "Hup" at the right moment, and later when the dog is jumping by himself at a distance, the handler will be able to control the dog. Very few dogs are natural jumpers; this is the way to perfect their timing.

Every handler in the class should be instructed to get himself a set of jumps, including the bar jump, so that he can practice at home during the week.

The Second Lesson

During the second lesson, the class should again practice the Recall and Drop-on-Recall exercises. It is a poor system to practice a Drop on every Recall, because it will slow the dog down and he will start to anticipate the drop. The dog should be dropped every third or fourth recall, unless he does the drop poorly; if this is the case, he should repeat the drop until he does it right. Occasionally, the handlers should switch places and practice angled recalls. If the whole class will practice recalls like this for ten weeks, the dogs will become very good at it.

After practicing the Recall and Drop-on-Recall exercises, the instructor should then work with the handlers who are teaching their dogs to retrieve dumbbells. If there is a handler who has not succeeded in teaching his dog to take and hold the dumbbell, it is probably because he is either manhandling his dog; shouting at him; jerking his collar; shoving the dumbbell in his mouth; banging his teeth or gums with it; keeping the collar tight after the dog has taken the dumbbell; placing the dumbbell in the dog's mouth, grabbing his jaws, and clamping them together over the dumbbell; or hitting his dog with the dumbbell in a fit of temper. Any one

Lift the dog with the leash as you run toward the jump and take a detour around it at the last second.

At first, turn two of the hurdles on the high side; then lift your dog over the Broad Jump with the leash as you run with him.

or combination of these things will frighten the dog and cause him to be stubborn or disobedient. It follows that the dog will take a sudden dislike to the dumbbell. This handler will have to start over again and be kind and patient with his dog.

As soon as the dogs start taking the dumbbells, they should practice away from the corner. The handlers should proceed in stages now. First each handler should encourage his dog to reach out a foot or so to take the dumbbell; then when the dog does this consistently, the handler should gradually lower the dumbbell to the ground and have him get it there. Next, the handler should let the dog walk forward and take the dumbbell; as he does so, the handler should swing around quickly and run backwards, urging his dog to come to him. When his dog comes in front of him, he should caution his dog to "Hold it," place one hand gently under his chin, and tell him to sit. By placing his hand under his dog's chin, he will prevent him from dropping the dumbbell.

Some dogs and handlers progress faster than others. Rather than hold back the handlers who are ready for the next step, the instructor should explain it to them so that they can practice at home. The next step is for the handler to throw his dumbbell a few feet and command his dog to "Get the dumbbell." The handler should run along with him, repeating the verbal command so that the dog will remember the words.

During the many months I spent working and experimenting with the Working class exercises, I discovered that my dogs did not actually know the names of the articles they were using. This made it very difficult for them to retrieve the articles by name alone, as required in the Vocabulary exercise. They thought they could run out and pick up the first object they came to, and they were surprised to find I wasn't pleased with that idea. I have found that when teaching a dog to retrieve, it is just as easy to teach him the name of the article at the same time. By using this new method, the dog learns two important things: to retrieve—an exercise he will use in some advanced classes—and the name of the object he is retrieving—added knowledge he can apply in the Working class, or in everyday life. In scent discrimination or search work, when I give the command "Get mine," my dog realizes he must search for an article with my scent on it. I strongly urge all instructors to use this new method, as it is another stepping stone to advanced training. The handler should give the command softly but firmly, and the dog should start out on the last word of the command. I feel the dog's name should be omitted for the sake of brevity.

If the handler has a dog that absolutely refuses to pick up the dumbbell, he should lift one end of the dumbbell with his fingers or wiggle one end to arouse the dog's interest. Within a week the dog should be fooled

"Get it," as you walk forward slowly and hand the dumbbell to your dog at his level.

Throw the dumbbell six feet away, run up to it with your dog and encourage him to retrieve it as you say "Good, get it."

When the dog takes the dumbbell, quickly run backwards as you say "Come, hold it."

"Come."

"Hup."

into picking it up by himself as the handler pretends to lift one end. Actually he is just covering one end with his hand. There may be a dog who is downright stubborn about it; if the handler will force his dog's head down and apply pressure to the collar as he did in the beginning, his dog will pick up the dumbbell. He might have to do this once or twice before his dog realizes that he must obey his handler. It is better for the handler to apply pressure to the collar than to stand there nagging his dog

Lift your dog over the Broad Jump with the leash as you jump with him.

when it is obvious the dog has no intention of picking it up. Outside of plain cruelty, there is nothing that ruins a dog's spirit more completely than an owner who continually nags.

The class should spend the remainder of the second lesson practicing the high and the broad jumps. The jumps should be made a little more difficult this time by increasing the height of the high jump and lengthening the broad jumps.

The Third Lesson

The third lesson should start off with a variety of recalls and drop on recalls.

The handlers who are ready for the last retrieving step should be asked to line up. Every time a handler starts his retrieve practice, he should hand his dog the dumbbell with the command "Get it"; when his dog takes the dumbbell, he should order him to "Hold it." After a couple of seconds he should take the dumbbell from his dog with the command "Out."

The handler should now take his dog off leash and send him out after the dumbbell by himself. At first he will have to run out a few steps with him, but gradually he should stop this and let the dog go out by himself. There will be a dog who will refuse to go out unless the handler takes the first step or two with him. The handler should correct this by quickly

Have your dog sit eight feet in front of the jump. Hold the leash as illustrated as you stand near the first hurdle. Give your dog the command "Hup," and when he moves forward, run alongside the jump. If necessary, lift him over the first few times.

taking his dog's collar and scooting him out toward the dumbbell as he orders him to "Get the dumbbell." This will give the dog the idea that he has to go out alone. It is imperative that the handler time his praise correctly. A dog that hesitates over the dumbbell will very often pick it up if he is encouraged at the right moment. When I am conducting a class, I always praise the handler's dog myself, so that I can get the ideal response from him and the handler can note my timing and tone of voice.

The dog that is taught to retrieve this way is prepared to retrieve anything for his handler. This method makes teaching the dog to retrieve the scent discrimination articles and the glove considerably easier. He is also prepared to carry articles for his handler since he understands the words, *get it,* and *hold it.*

If a dog keeps mouthing or chewing the dumbbell, place a strip of aluminum around the middle piece of the practice dumbbell. This will break the habit.

The class should continue working on the high jump and the broad jump, but now the bar jump should be added to this routine. The dogs should start practicing going over the bar jump with the bar set very low. As each dog becomes proficient, the bar should be raised to the height the dog would be required to jump in a show. Puppies are the exception; they should jump one third or one half the required height, depending upon the age of the puppy, his breed, and his physical condition.

The instructor should know what height each dog is required to jump in a show so that he can pass this information along to the handlers. In the Open and Utility classes, every dog that jumps less than thirty-six inches will be measured by the judge in the ring. The dog should be prepared for this experience and should be measured two or three times at class until he learns to stand still while this is done. The instructor should have a rule in class that gives a very accurate measurement; every handler should know his dog's height at the withers if he plans to compete in dog shows. The rule shown in the illustration is accurate and was made for me by a friend.

In a show the judge would be using his own ruler which would probably be an ordinary folding rule or steel tape. So, although the instructor uses the accurate ruler to measure the class dogs, he should also measure them with different kinds of rulers so that the dogs will get used to this procedure. Many dogs are nervous about this until they have been measured a few times. In a show it is permissible for the handler to steady his dog with his hands while the judge is measuring him. The instructor should include the measuring routine each week in the Open class lessons.

To quote from the *American Kennel Club Obedience Regulations*:

Every handler should know his dog's height at the withers.

The High Jump shall be jumped clear and the jump shall be as nearly as possible one and one-half times the height of the dog at the withers as determined by the judge, with a minimum height of eight inches and a maximum height of thirty-six inches. This applies to all breeds with the following exceptions:

The jump shall be once the height of the dog at the withers or thirty-six inches, whichever is less, for the following breeds—

  Bloodhounds, Bullmastiffs, Great Danes, Great Pyrenees, Mastiffs, Newfoundlands, St. Bernards

The jump shall be once the height of the dog at the withers or eight inches, whichever is greater, for the following breeds:

Spaniels (Clumber)	Norwich Terriers
Spaniels (Sussex)	Scottish Terriers
Basset Hounds	Sealyham Terriers
Dachshunds	Skye Terriers
Welsh Corgis (Cardigan)	West Highland White Terriers
Welsh Corgis (Pembroke)	Maltese
Australian Terriers	Pekingese
Cairn Terriers	Bulldogs
Dandie Dinmont Terriers	French Bulldogs

The Broad Jump shall consist of four hurdles, built to telescope for convenience, made of boards about eight inches wide, the largest measuring about five feet in length and six inches high at the highest point, all painted a flat white. When set up, they shall be arranged in order of size and shall be evenly spaced so as to cover a distance equal to twice the height of the High Jump as set for the particular dog, with the low side of each hurdle and the lowest hurdle nearest the dog. The four hurdles shall be used for a jump of 52″ to 72″, three for a jump of 32″ to 48″, and two for a jump of 16″ to 28″. The highest hurdles shall be removed first.

When a dog who is on leash is able to clear all the broad-jump hurdles that he will be required to jump in a show, have him try the next step. If there are several handlers who are ready, line them up and let each handler try the jump three times in succession. Then if the dog makes a mistake, it can be corrected immediately. The handler should have his dog sit six feet from and facing the broad jump. He should tell him to "Stay," then walk to the first hurdle. He should then call his dog's name; as the dog responds, the handler should say *hup* and assist him over the jump with the leash. This procedure should be repeated several times until the dog does it well. The next step is to stand in the same position and try this procedure off leash. When the handler gives his dog the command *hup*, he should wave his dog over the jump with his left arm. He should be sure to praise and pet him every time he clears the hurdle. If the dog steps on or in between the hurdles, he should say, "No," quickly put his left index finger in the ring of the dog's collar, run up to the jump with him, and boost him over. As soon as the dog starts to jump, the handler should let go of the collar.

If a dog is stubborn and persists in stepping on or in between the hurdles, try this method: have someone hold the bar from the bar jump on the ground between the first and second hurdles. As the handler runs up to the jump with his dog, the bar should be raised about four inches above the hurdles. The dog will have to clear the hurdles or crash into the bar. If he does crash into it, he will soon learn to pick up his feet and jump clear. This should be tried on leash at first.

Sooner or later a dog will run around the jump instead of jumping over it. When this happens, the handler should say "No," quickly take the dog's collar, run him up to the jump, and assist him over it. The handler should help him this way twice before he lets his dog try it again by himself.

If the class is large, there should be two sets of jumps so that more people can be practicing at one time. When a dog makes an error, the handler should have the dog jump two or three times consecutively, even though he may have to put him on leash or hold his collar. If the handler hasn't practiced at home, he should not try to make up for it by monopolizing the jumps at class.

The Fourth Lesson

The fourth lesson should also start with various kinds of recalls. Another type of drop on recall that can be included in the class routine is one that would be of value to anyone who has had a runoff in a show. For this, the instructor should have his class line up about three feet apart and instruct every second handler to leave his dog. At his command, the handlers should simultaneously call their dogs, using verbal commands or signals, whichever they prefer. The dogs should be dropped at a point designated by the instructor; after a few seconds the instructor should have the handlers call their dogs in and finish. This type of class practice is invaluable because it teaches the dogs to keep their eyes on their own handlers, even though they are all being worked simultaneously.

To teach a dog to be extremely alert in situations like the above, the handler must be very fast to correct his dog when it ignores him. If a dog pretends not to hear a command, the handler should run up to the dog quietly, take his collar, and jerk the dog toward him as he runs backward and says "Come"; if the dog ignores a signal, the handler should not speak but should repeat the signal as he jerks the dog toward him and runs backward. He should stop after backing up about ten feet, tell his dog to stay, and try the exercise over again. This time the dog will have suddenly regained his hearing or eyesight. Of course, when the dog does respond, the handler should praise him in a pleased tone of voice.

Another excellent routine that should be practiced occasionally in the Open class is the following. The instructor should have the class line up, leaving their dogs on a sit-stay. The handlers should stand opposite any dog but their own. The dogs should be called in one at a time with emphasis put on straight sits. Next, the class should repeat this procedure, but everyone should call his dog at the same time. The good workers will have no trouble with this exercise, but the dummies will end up sitting in front of a strange handler. To teach the latter to be more alert, the handlers should go after their dogs and jerk their collars, saying "Come," as they run backwards to their positions in line. This correction will eventually get through to the slower dogs.

The instructor should try to get all the handlers working on the same phase of retrieving. Some handlers will slack off in their training practice at home and will fall behind the others in the class. The instructor can remedy this by taking the handler's dog and giving it a brief lesson so that he can catch up with the others. Every dog can be taught to retrieve; it is sometimes difficult getting the handler to accept this fact. However, once the dog starts to pick up the dumbbell, the handler usually becomes enthusiastic again and will practice harder. It is better for the instructor to take the dog and explain what the handler is doing wrong than it is to let the handler get discouraged. The instructor should watch each of the dogs retrieve so that he can check his progress. It is normal for the dogs to be going out some thirty feet to retrieve their dumbbells at this stage of the training. They may not do it every time, and may need a little encouragement here and there, but they will be doing well. It is always hard for a dog to retrieve in class, where there are many distractions; it is much easier at home.

The dogs that are going out at least ten feet to get their dumbbells should now be taught to retrieve over the high jump. The jumps should be adjusted for each dog so that he will jump one-half his required height. The handler must have his dog on leash in heel position at first, and he should stand about ten feet back from the jump. He should give his dog the command "Stay," and throw the dumbbell, being careful to have it land about ten feet beyond the jump. As he gives his dog the command "Get the dumbbell," he should run up to the jump with him and say "Hup." As soon as the dog has jumped, the handler should go to the dumbbell with him saying "Get the dumbbell," and point to it. When the dog reaches for the dumbbell, the handler should say, "Good, come," and as the dog starts back, the handler should say, "Hup, hold it." If necessary, the handler should guide the dog to the jump with the leash, but the handler should hurry around the jump so that he can turn and be ready to take the dumbbell when the dog brings it in to him after jumping. He should have his dog sit in front of him for a few seconds holding the dumbbell without mouthing it; then he should take it and praise his dog. He should then have his dog finish and praise him again.

At this point the instructor will find that many of the dogs will be ready for the next step. The handler should have his dog sitting at heel position about ten feet from the jump; on command from the instructor, the handler will throw his dumbbell so that it lands a few feet on the other side of the jump. The handler will give his dog the command "Hup," and the dog should run forward and jump over the hurdle. At this point the handler should order his dog to "Get the dumbbell." If the dog makes a move toward picking it up, the handler should praise him with "Good, come," and clap his hands in the air. This will draw the dog's attention to his handler which should make the dog respond by jumping back over the hurdle to get to his handler. The dog should receive assistance from his handler every time he seems in need of it; this might be given by guiding him with the leash, voicing a second command, praising him at the right time, tapping the jump to get him over it, or commanding his attention in some positive way. With all these assists from his handler, the dog will retrieve over the high jump; each successive time he will do a little better. Perfection is just a matter of time and practice.

When the dogs have reached this point in the training, the handlers should take them off leash and try it, but the routine should be slightly different. The handler should stand about fifteen to twenty feet back from the jump (depending upon the size of the dog), with his dog sitting in heel position. He should give his dog the command "Stay," and throw the dumbbell, being careful to have it land about fifteen feet beyond the jump if he has a medium- or large-sized dog. If his dog is small, he should throw the dumbbell at least ten feet beyond the jump. As he gives his dog the command "Get the dumbbell," he should run up to the jump with him to be sure he goes over it. As soon as the dog has jumped, he should command him to "Get the dumbbell," and should point to it. When the dog reaches for the dumbbell, he should be praised; when he starts back, the handler should say, "Hup, hold it." If necessary, the handler should touch the top of the jump with his hands to direct his dog over. As his dog jumps, the handler should step back quickly and stand in his original position. He should have his dog sit straight in front of him and hold the dumbbell a few seconds; then he should take it and praise his dog warmly. Next, he should command him to "Heel," see that he sits straight, and praise him again.

The *AKC Obedience Regulations* state that the dog must clear the High Jump both coming and going. The handler must stand at least eight feet, or any reasonable distance beyond eight feet, from the jump but must remain in the same spot throughout the exercise.

If a dog starts to wander after he jumps, the handler should call him back, make him pick up the dumbbell, jump again, and finish as I have described. If a dog tries to come back around the jump, the handler should quickly block his path, take him back several feet, and insist that he jump. The handler will probably have to hold his collar as he runs up to the jump with him and give him a lift to get him over. The instructor should remind the handler that this is new to his dog and that he should

Hold the end of the dumbbell as you look at the spot where you want
it to land. Then throw it.

He jumps.

He retrieves the dumbbell.

"Come," as he retrieves the dumbbell and heads for the jump.

Step back quickly as he clears the hurdle and you remind him to "Hold it."

He returns to you and sits straight, holding the dumbbell patiently. Then you take it.

be patient with him. It is more difficult for the dog to jump with a dumbbell in his mouth. If he should drop it a few times at first, the handler should tell him to "Get the dumbbell," and should resume the lesson.

The dog goes to heel position and sits straight and you praise him.

Eventually, if not at first, a dog will drop the dumbbell when he comes back to his handler. This is where the step-by-step method of retrieving will be of great value. When the handler tells his dog to "Get the dumbbell," the dog will understand he is to reach down and pick it up again.

The handler should not move out of position himself. When his dog picks it up, he should caution him to "Hold it." The next couple of times he should caution him to "Hold it," as the dog approaches his handler. This command will come in handy many times in the future when the handler wants his dog to hold some object firmly. The dog should never be permitted to chew, mouth, or play with the dumbbell when he is retrieving.

The handler should never step back to get his dog to come in straight to him; this is the wrong psychology. Running backwards to teach a dog to come in fast in the early stages of his training is entirely different. The dog should be taught to come to his handler from any angle, and if he learned his recall lessons well, he should have no problems with sits when he is retrieving. If the sits are poor, the handler should practice angle recalls with him at home.

If a dog is working too slowly, the handler should inspire him by running up to the jump with him, repeating the command "Get the dumbbell" in an excited tone of voice, and clapping his hands when he says, "Hup." Praise will also work magic. It is up to the handler to convince his dog that retrieving is fun. If the handler is lethargic, the dog will act bored or dull. The instructor will have to point this out to the handler.

There is a knack to throwing the dumbbell that the handlers must learn if they are going to place the dumbbells in the best position for their dogs. The dumbbell should never hit the jump, land too far away, or land off to the left or right, thereby making the retrieve unnecessarily difficult. To throw the dumbbell correctly, the handler should grasp one end in his right hand, holding it down by his side. As he throws it, he should flip it up in the air, spinning it toward the spot where he wishes it to land. The dumbbell should stop dead upon landing.

The handler should always stand back far enough from the jump so that his dog can jump gracefully yet come up to him in just a few steps. Once the handler teaches his dog the rhythm of jumping, he will retain it. To teach this properly, the handler must study his dog while the dog is in the act of jumping; he must determine the correct distance from the hurdle that the dog should start to jump. This distance will vary, depending upon the dog's size and jumping style. If the handler is consistently correct in his judgment, his dog will trust him and will jump at his command. When he has learned to coordinate his movements and has the rhythm down perfectly, it will not be necessary for him to cadence his jump.

Oversensitive dogs will sometimes develop a mental block about jumping if they have an unpleasant experience, such as knocking the jump over accidentally. Even though they are physically able, they become afraid to jump. The only way to conquer this fear is to pace them carefully and call "Hup" at the precise moment that they should jump. It will be necessary to start on leash, with the jumps set low. As the dog improves, additional boards can be added until the required height is reached.

If you force a dog to jump higher than he is able to comfortably, you may cause him to strain himself needlessly. A sensitive dog who strains to clear a jump will become afraid to jump. When asked to jump, he will approach the jump and hesitate nervously. Then, when he attempts to jump, he will fling himself into the jump, striking the top. Do not ask your dog to jump more than the required height unless he is a natural jumper, such as a Doberman.

The handlers should conclude this lesson by practicing the broad jump.

The instructor should be watching his handlers carefully to be sure that they correct their dogs for minor errors as well as major ones. He should be quick to point out any lack of precision or timing, failure to praise when deserved, or poor sits. He should notice when a handler is too rough with his dog and when a handler should be more firm. He should also note whether the handler uses his voice to his best advantage in controlling his dog. Most handlers can develop fast reflexes, though with some it is a very slow process.

If there are any handlers who use the verbal command to drop their dogs, the instructor should caution them to use a firm, moderate tone of voice. The majority of people who call "Down" to their dogs do so in a very loud, unpleasant voice. A loud, intimidating tone of voice is as much an error as a hand signal held too long.

When the handlers are working on recalls, they should practice leaving their dogs with just a quiet verbal command "Stay." This should also be practiced as part of any retrieve exercise. Although a handler is permitted to give both the stay signal and the verbal command before he throws his dumbbell, it is more professional to give the dog the quiet verbal command. The instructor should caution the handlers who use both signal and command not to give the signal with the hand that is holding the dumbbell. The handler should learn to control his dog with his voice; this is another sign of expert training. When the handler uses the verbal command to call his dog, he should train his dog to respond to the "Come" portion of the command.

The Fifth Lesson

It is important that the handlers practice a variety of recalls for at least fifteen minutes of each lesson. The instructor should watch his class carefully and point out the dogs that sit crooked. In my classes the handlers have become very conscious of their dogs' sits by the time they have left the Advanced Novice class, so I rarely have to mention them in the advanced classes. The dogs will still sit poorly occasionally, but the handler is quick to correct his dog if this happens.

When a handler has an intelligent dog who tries to please, and when the handler works hard to perfect himself and his dog and is consistent with his praise and corrections, it is very likely that the dog will someday reward the handler's patience by earning one or more perfect scores. Everyone starts out with a perfect score, so it is only natural that a handler would want to work hard to keep as much of it as possible. The instructor will be doing his class a favor if he points out every infraction of the rules that he sees anyone make. It is only by this awareness that they will be able to perfect their work.

The instructor should demonstrate a perfect recall and explain the finer points to the class. This demonstration will be a great help to the handlers, but they will still need individual corrections.

The handler should have his dog sitting at heel position. He should quietly give his dog the verbal command "Stay," leave him, walk about forty feet away, and turn to face him. When he leaves his dog, the handler should not brush past him or bump him, as this might make the dog follow him. When he is ready to leave his dog, the handler should look at his dog to be sure he is sitting straight; if he isn't, he should command his dog to "Sit straight." The handler that leaves his dog sitting crooked is inviting a penalty. The instructor should also explain to the class that Open and Utility dogs may not be guided by the collar or be physically controlled between exercises. This does not, however, mean that the handler may not ask his dog to sit straight if he wishes to.

When leaving his dog, the handler may step off with either his right or left foot. It should not make a particle of difference to a well-trained dog which foot his handler steps off on. The important point here is for the handler to give his dog the stay command before he leaves him. The handler who takes one or more steps forward before giving the stay command is inviting his dog to get up and follow him.

Regardless of the size of the dog, the handler should not bend his body to give a stay signal. This body signal is a sign of inferior handling and training. Small dogs have the ability to turn their heads to watch their handlers given them signals; it is time that handlers realized this and trained their dogs properly.

When the handler has reached the correct distance and is about to turn to face his dog, he should place his hands where he plans to keep them. He should do this now so that he doesn't move his hands after he turns to face his dog. If he moves his hands after he turns around, it might be construed as a signal by his dog. This technique is smooth and natural and another subtle form of expert handling.

The instructor should explain that when he calls his dog verbally, he gives his dog's name first and quickly follows it with the command "Come." His voice is just loud enough for the dog to hear him, and his tone is a pleasant one. If he were to use a signal, it would be given with one hand and arm only. The dog's name may not be used with the signal. It is not permissible to give a head or body signal when calling the dog. A handler who stands with his arms down by his sides should not call his dog, then quickly move his hands to another position as the dog responds; this would be considered an extra signal.

The dog should trot in briskly to the handler, sit straight in front of him, and, upon command, go to heel position promptly, and sit straight. When the handler gives his dog the ve·bal or signal command to finish, he may not turn his head and look to his left. This would be construed as a body signal. If the handler has his hands down by his sides and he gives his dog a signal to come, his hands should be promptly returned to their original position. This procedure should also be followed when the handler gives the finish signal. The dog should sit in front of the handler's feet without touching him, but close enough so that the handler could reach out and touch him. The handler should not stand with his feet wide apart in an unnatural stance. This is sometimes done to signal the dog to sit straight and should be construed as a body signal that would be penalized in a show.

The handlers should all be lined up ten feet apart to practice retrieves on the flat. It is recommended that they practice throwing the dumbbells one at a time until all the dogs are consistently good at retrieving. Many times a handler will start teaching his dog to retrieve and, for one reason or another, will drop out of class for a few weeks. When he comes back, he is apt to hold up the class because he hasn't been practicing. It is best to let the assistant help these handlers. When they have caught up, they can join the others. The dogs should be able to retrieve at any distance now.

Once this point has been reached, it is time to change the routine. The handlers, lined up ten feet apart, should throw their dumbbells about ten

Each handler sends his dog after his own dumbbell.

feet out in a straight line from their dogs. Everyone should send his dog to retrieve at the same time. Next, the handlers should all throw their dumbbells about fifteen feet straight out, but this time the dogs should be sent after their own dumbbells one at a time. This is excellent practice provided that the handlers are careful to throw their dumbbells so that they are all lined up. If the dumbbell goes too far, the handler should run out and place it in line with the others. A dog that tries to pick up someone else's dumbbell should not be allowed to do so. The command to retrieve should be "Get the dumbbell. Get mine." The command should be given quickly and clearly in a moderate tone of voice.

Each week the distance should be increased until the dogs are going out forty feet to retrieve their dumbbells. When they are good enough to do this, the instructor should have them try the supreme test.

The following routine is a perfect one for the dogs who are going on to Utility. Three handlers should throw their dumbbells so that they land close together. The first handler sends his dog after his own dumbbell and has him return it to him. Before the second dog retrieves, the next handler in line throws his dumbbell out, so that there will always be three in the pile close together. It is surprising how quickly some dogs learn to retrieve their own dumbbells; most dogs will do this the first or second time. If a dog starts to pick up the wrong dumbbell, the handler should caution him by saying, "No, get the dumbbell, get mine." He will soon be getting his own.

After all the dogs become proficient at retrieving their own dumbbells, the handlers should stand in a large circle and throw their dumbbells into the center of it. The dogs should be sent out one at a time to find and retrieve their own. The dog that learns to do this in the Open class will have no trouble retrieving the scent articles in the Utility class.

The handlers should take turns practicing the retrieve over the high jump with their dogs. The puppies should practice with the jumps set at half the height they will be required to jump when full grown, but the rest of the exercise should be done with precision. The mature dogs should be jumping the full height as soon as their work warrants it.

The broad jump should be extended as soon as the dogs are ready to try it. It is good practice to teach the puppies to jump half the required distance while they are young. It will make their training that much easier later on.

I do not believe that medium- or large-sized dogs should jump the full height they are required to jump in a show until they are at least ten months old. If they are physically sound, the jumping will not hurt them at this age, provided that the handler will keep the lessons very short. Once a puppy has learned to jump the low hurdles, it is a simple step to raise them when he is mature.

Each dog retrieves his dumbbell from among the others.

The judge asks you if you are ready. If your dog is sitting straight, say "Yes."

Tell your dog to "Stay."

As you stand between the third and fourth hurdle, tell your dog to "Hup."

When your dog is in midair, pivot a quarter turn.

Your dog turns toward you as he lands.

He should sit straight in front of you.

And finish with a perfect sit.

The Sixth and Seventh Lessons

The sixth lesson should be a repetition of the fifth. The instructor should demonstrate with his dog the correct way to do a retrieve on the flat as he gives them some more pointers.

He should stand with his dog sitting straight at heel position. He should explain to the class that he will give his dog the verbal command "Stay" in a quiet tone of voice. The instructor should throw the dumbbell straight ahead of him so that it lands at least thirty feet away. He should then give his dog the verbal command "Get the dumbbell." The dog should trot out briskly, pick up the dumbbell by the middle piece, and return it at a brisk pace. The dog is supposed to trot out briskly and pick up the dumbbell, but it doesn't make any difference whether he picks it up as he is moving forward or turns near the dumbbell and picks it up as he is facing his handler. The important thing is for him to pick it up quickly. He should not go more than five feet or so past the dumbbell and then retrace his steps and pick it up; neither should he stand over the dumbbell for a few minutes before he decides to retrieve it. It is not necessary for him to pick up the dumbbell in the manner of field trial dogs who retrieve live birds by grabbing them quickly as they approach. This is an inert object, and if the dog wishes to pick it up after he turns, or as he is turning, he should not be penalized for doing so.

The dog should come in and sit straight in front of the instructor, without bumping into him but close enough for the instructor to reach him without moving forward. He should carry and hold the dumbbell without mouthing or chewing it and should relinquish his hold on it without any delay. The dog that plays with the dumbbell will be penalized. Many dogs who have been trained incorrectly make a game of retrieving. They will dash out toward the dumbbell, crash into it and make it skid away, chase after it, pick it up, and shake it all the way in to their handlers. This is amusing to the spectators but shows that the handler has no control over his dog.

The dog that drops the dumbbell will be penalized, even though he picks it up immediately and brings it in. The dog that sits so far from his handler that the handler can not reach him will be disqualified.

The handler may give his dog a command or signal to release the dumbbell, but this is one of those instances when the training should be ahead of the obedience regulations. The dog will be quite willing to give it up if he has been trained correctly and will not need any verbal command to do so. The rule permits a command or signal; this means the handler can't give both. (I can't imagine what the signal would be to release a dumbbell.) When the dog sees the handler reaching toward him for the dumbbell, he understands this gesture as a signal to let go of it. So, if the handler were to give the verbal command "Out" at this time, it could be construed as a double command.

The instructor should take the dumbbell from his dog and, after a few seconds, should send him to heel for a straight sit.

The instructor should explain to his class that the reason a dog doesn't come in close enough may be that the handler has been too rough with him. The handler should always be gentle with his dog when he comes in front of him so that the dog will want to continue coming in to him. If the handler has been gentle with his dog and the dog still sits out away from him, he should put his dog on a leash; when the dog stops away from him, the handler should jerk on the leash, releasing it when the dog starts coming toward him. This should be done without any additional command, but when the dog sits in front of him, he should be praised. If the dog is jerked for sitting too far away, he will soon learn to come in all the way. If the dog is doing the recall at the time, the handler could give the verbal command "Come," as he jerks the leash.

If a dog continually drops the dumbbell, the handler should train him to hold it for a few minutes and walk around with it while he is heeling If the dog drops the dumbbell at this time, he should be made to pick it up himself. Once he realizes he will have to pick it up himself if he drops it, he will hang on to it.

The instructor should also demonstrate the correct way for a dog to jump the high jump and the broad jump. He should have his dog sitting at heel position about fifteen feet from the high jump, give him a quiet verbal command "Stay," throw the dumbbell about fifteen feet on the other side of the jump, order his dog to "Get the dumbbell," and return his hands back down by his sides. His dog should jump without touching the hurdle, pick up the dumbbell briskly, return over the jump without touching it, and sit straight in front of his handler. The instructor should take the dumbbell and then have his dog go to heel position and sit straight.

The instructors should advise the handlers to practice throwing their dumbbells over the jump at different angles. Some day in a show the dumbbell might take a weird bounce off to the side, and if the dog hasn't practiced such a retrieve, he might walk around the jump on his way back. By practicing for the unexpected, the dogs will be prepared for anything.

The instructor should leave his dog sitting at least eight feet from the broad jump, take a position between the first and fourth hurdles, and face the jump with his toes about two feet from it. He should give his dog's name and the command "Hup." When the dog is in midair over the jump, the instructor should make a ninety-degree turn to the right in the same spot. His dog should come in briskly and sit straight in front of him. He should then have his dog go to heel for a straight sit.

The instructor should explain these facts to his class: The handler may begin the exercise by standing eight feet or more from the broad jump with his dog sitting at heel position. The exact distance should be determined by the number of steps it takes his dog to reach the broad jump and jump gracefully; this can be determined only by observing the dog during practice. Upon the judge's command "Leave your dog," the handler should stand two feet out from the side of the jump. According to the *AKC Obedience Regulations,* the handler must make a right-angle turn while his dog is in midair, but should remain in the same spot. This is where all the practice work that was done on recalls from odd angles will pay off, as the dog should be used to coming in and sitting straight regardless of the direction the handler is facing. After jumping, the dog should take a few necessary steps, turn, and trot in to his handler. If, in practice, the dog takes a wide turn after jumping, the handler should correct this by calling his dog to him as soon as he lands. Stubborn dogs should be put on leash; when they land, they should receive a sharp jerk and the verbal command "Come." The instructor should notice whether the handlers observe these fine points and give a word of advice to those who forget them.

The Eighth, Ninth, and Tenth Lessons

By the time the handlers have reached the eighth lesson, the dogs should be quite consistent in their work. Each dog should be able to drop on recall, retrieve on the flat, retrieve over the high jump, and clear the broad jump with a certain amount of precision, depending upon the amount of training his handler has given him at home.

The handlers should be able to help each other go through the various exercises while the instructor takes a few of the Advanced Novice handlers and helps them to start teaching their dogs to retrieve.

The last half of the lessons should be devoted to individual work for the Open handlers. Taking one handler at a time, the instructor should have him do an exercise in front of the rest of the class. The class should criticize the work in a constructive way. A dog may appear to be doing very well in the class, but when the handler takes him out on the floor and is not permitted to give him any extra commands or signals, the dog will suddenly fall apart. The dog that looked so promising and the handler that thought he was about ready for a show will find there is still lots of polishing to do before they are ready for Open competition.

The individual work should be conducted the way it would be in a show ring so that the handlers will see how well, or how poorly, their dogs react when they do not receive extra help while working.

The instructor should urge the handlers to try working their dogs in different places so that their dogs will not be distracted or self-conscious when working in strange places.

During the final lesson of the Open series, the instructor should have someone with experience put each handler through all the Open exercises the way he would be in a show. Each handler should be judged according to the *AKC Obedience Regulations,* and the scores they receive should be realistic. I prefer to be strict with the handlers in my classes so that they will find show work easy by comparison. The handlers are always coming back to me after a show to express their thanks for teaching them the finer points of training and handling. Having worked their way through the classes, they are prepared to go out and win—and they enjoy winning.

The exercises and the maximum scores in the Open classes are as follows:

1.	Heel Free	40 points
2.	Drop on Recall	30 points
3.	Retrieve on Flat	20 points
4.	Retrieve over High Jump	30 points
5.	Broad Jump	20 points
6.	Long Sit	30 points
7.	Long Down	30 points
	Maximum Total Score	200 points

I O | *THE UTILITY CLASS*

A ten-week course. The author's
simplified method of teaching the Scent
Discrimination, Directed Retrieve,
Signal, and Directed Jumping
exercises in class.

The First Lesson

The instructor should know at least a week in advance how many handlers he will have in his Utility class, and these people should be asked to procure a set of scent-discrimination articles. The instructor may himself have the Utility articles for sale or advise the handlers where they can buy them or explain how they can make a set of their own. There should be twelve scent-discrimination articles; six of these should be made of leather and six of them should be made of metal. In actual competition, only ten articles will be used—the other two here are just for practice purposes. Both the leather and the metal sets should be numbered consecutively 1 through 5 for easy identification.

Since the *AKC Obedience Regulations* permit a handler to use articles he might find in his home, he doesn't have to buy a set unless he prefers to. When I started in obedience, I made my own articles. Six were one- by four-inch blocks of wood that I covered with leather. For metal articles, I removed the ends of aluminum frozen-fruit-juice cans and flattened them into an oval shape so they wouldn't roll. I have also seen metal salt shakers, leather key cases, baby leather shoes, metal tubing of different sizes and shapes, and leather gloves used successfully. Sets of scent-discrimination articles can be purchased, though, that are attractive and easy to use. These articles are made either in the shape of dumbbells or with two or three bars that are held in place by rigid end pieces. The instructor should inform the handlers that each set of articles they use should be identical and not more than six inches in length. They should also purchase and bring three white cotton work gloves to the first class lesson.

The instructor should advise each of the handlers to keep one metal and one leather article in his pocket for a full week prior to the first Utility lesson. During the course of the week the handlers should take them out frequently and rub them with their hands. The scent on the articles should consist of the handler's hand and clothing scent and nothing else. By the end of the week, the articles will be strongly impregnated with each handler's scent.

The dog is already aware of his handler's scent and could easily find him, if necessary, in a pitch black room among a hundred strangers. A dog will remember his handler's scent longer than any other. Dogs that I have not seen for several years remember me as soon as I offer them my hand to sniff. They catalog different scents in their minds the way we remember the features of our friends. To teach a dog the Scent-Discrimination exercise, all we have to do is teach him to retrieve an article with his handler's familiar scent on it.

Handlers who use shaving lotions on their hands to give them a strong odor are defeating the purpose. The alcohol in the lotion removes most of the handler's scent, and dogs do not like the strong penetrating odor of the perfume. When asked to sniff a bottle of shaving lotion or perfume for the first time, they will snort or sneeze to rid themselves of the offensive odor. The second time they are asked to sniff, they will usually refuse.

At the first class lesson, each handler should have his leather articles. The instructor should have the handlers form two rows about six feet apart, facing away from each other, with their dogs sitting at heel position. The handlers in each row should be ten feet apart so that they will each have a ten-foot area in which to work their dogs without interference. The instructor should explain the first steps to them which they should practice in class and later at home during the week.

With his dog sitting at heel position, the handler should give him the command "Stay," as he throws his scented article about ten feet away. The dog should be sent out to retrieve the article in this manner three or four times. Then, with a pair of sugar tongs, the handler should place an unscented article on the ground about ten feet from his dog. He should

Your dog sniffs the article you have thrown.

As he starts to pick it up, praise him.

throw his scented article out so that it lands about two feet from the other and send his dog after it with the command "Get mine." The dog should be praised if he picks up the right article and discouraged with "No," if he starts to pick up the unscented article. The dog that has already learned to find his handler's dumbbell will have no problem. (The dumbbell routine was practiced in the Open class.)

If the handler accidentally throws the scented article on the unscented one, he should remove it and get another unscented article. A dog with a keen nose will be confused by finding a scent on both articles. If the dog picks up the unscented article, the handler should flick it out of his mouth with one finger and encourage him to get the scented article. Many dogs will learn to distinguish between the two articles right away.

If the dog doesn't seem to understand what his handler wants him to do, the handler should place the scented article near two unscented articles instead of throwing it. Then he should take his dog up to the pile and hold his head over each of the unscented articles, saying, "Get mine." The articles should be about eight inches apart. If the dog tries to pick up the wrong article, his handler should say, "No," and go over to the next article. When he sniffs the scented article, the handler should say, "Good, that's it. Get mine." Then the handler should praise his dog when he picks it up. Later he will be able to help him do this at a distance by using his voice. This method should be practiced until the dog begins sniffing to find his handler's article. At home the handler should continue to use the

The handlers give their dogs the Sit signal.

same scented leather article; when he is not practicing, he should keep it in his pocket and rub his hands on it occasionally.

If the dog is working, the handler should not interfere. When the dog starts sniffing for his handler's article, the handler should step back ten feet and let the dog bring it in to him when he finds it. After this, he should let the dog go to the pile of articles alone, but he should encourage him to keep working and sniffing. If the dog should stop, the handler should take him to the articles and encourage him to look for the scented one.

Many times a dog will give up because he doesn't want to make a mistake. There are also several breeds that are not as keen at scent work as some of the working breeds. When I have one of these to train, I use the following method of starting the scent work. I cut off the shoulder ends of a wire dress hanger and shape them so that each one resembles an inverted U that is four inches long. Then I bend the wire so that it will fit snugly over the article. I start the scent work outdoors on closely cropped grass. I place two unscented leather articles on the grass, fit a wire over each article, and then hammer the excess wire into the ground so that each article is held down securely. When I send my dog out for the scented article, it is the only one that he can retrieve.

Once the dog has started sniffing to locate the scented article, it will not be necessary to use the wires. Until that time the handler should help him by taking him over to each article. The most important point for the class

to remember is to start the training with an article that is heavily impregnated with the handler's scent and to continue using it until the dog is finding it quickly among all the articles. Classes held outdoors should use this method as it is the easiest and the fastest. Handlers should practice this at home during the week and add extra leather articles if their dogs are doing well.

The instructor should now line up the handlers about ten feet apart to practice the Signal exercise. The instructor should explain that the dogs who have been in his Novice and Open classes will understand all the signals except the sit signal. He should demonstrate the Signal exercise with his dog so that the class can observe the order and way in which the signals are given.

Next, the instructor should give them a short heeling routine so that they can utilize the heeling signal several times. The signal which was taught in the Advanced Novice class is to scoop the left hand forward over the dog's head where he can see it. The class should heel briskly and be given several halts so that they can practice the heel signal each time they start. The handlers should try to keep a space of ten feet between them so that it will be easier for the dogs to observe their own handlers.

Now the instructor should order them to "Stand your dogs." For this signal, the handler should quickly bring his right hand down in front of his dog's nose with his fingers outstretched and pointing down. The next signal is "Leave your dogs," the same signal as the Stand but made with the left hand. Here the handler should walk forward about six feet and then turn and face his dog with his hands down by his sides. Upon order from the instructor to "Drop your dog" the handler should then quickly raise his right hand as high as his head. The signal to "Sit your dogs" is given by raising the left hand and arm waist high. This is the signal the dogs have not learned, so each handler must repeat the signal as he approaches his dog and lifts him into a sitting position with his collar. The handlers should then step back, and upon the order "Call your dogs," signal their dogs to come to them by sweeping the right hand out sideways and then in to the chest. When the dogs come in, the handlers must be sure that they sit straight in front of them. When the instructor calls "Finish," the handlers should signal their dogs to finish by sweeping their left hands back by their sides and then placing their hands down by their sides.

The handlers should begin the series of signals with their hands down by their sides and after each signal they should return their hands to the same position. If they follow this procedure in all the exercises, their entire performance will be smooth, natural, and integrated. The instructor should mention that this is a routine that should be used consistently throughout the Novice, Open, and Utility exercises; at this

"Stand."

"Down."

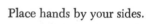

"Stay."

Place hands by your sides.

"Sit."

"Come."

Place hands down by your sides.

He sits straight in front of you.

"Heel." Dog turns toward you into heel position.

And returns to heel position for a straight sit.

point the handlers are probably doing it so smoothly that they are not even thinking about it.

In the beginning it may be necessary for the handlers to give their dogs the verbal commands along with the signals in order to make them respond more quickly. The signals should be exaggerated and held longer in the early stages of the training.

A handler who has not taught his dog any signals will have to keep his dog on leash until he has learned all of them. The handler should be especially patient with him when teaching him the sit signal; it generally takes a dog longer to learn this signal than the others. If he seems a little slow to grasp the idea, the handler should put him on leash; as he gives the signal, he should lift him up with the leash. He should praise his dog each time he sits. If the handler has his dog off leash and he fails to respond to the sit signal, he should say "Sit" as he runs up and lifts him into a sitting position with his collar. He should encourage him by praising him as he carries out the signal.

Since the dogs will learn the signals only by constant repetition, the handlers should be instructed to practice them at home for at least fifteen minutes a day. The class should practice these signals until the instructor feels that each handler understands what his dog is supposed to learn and is able to give his dog the correct signals in the proper sequence.

The balance of the first lesson should be spent in teaching the Directed Retrieve exercise. The handlers should line up about ten feet apart with their dogs sitting at heel position. The instructor should give them the command "Quarter turn to the left," and the handlers should order their dogs to "Heel," as they pivot to the left for a quarter turn. Then, the instructor should call "Quarter turn to the right," and the handlers should pivot and take a short step while remaining in the same spot as their dogs go to heel position on command. The class should practice these turns for a short time while the instructor helps anyone who is making errors or having difficulty. Since this routine was learned in the Advanced Novice class, most of the handlers will be doing it easily.

Next the instructor should have the handlers give their dogs a stay command and instruct them to place their gloves about forty feet in front of their dogs. At this stage of the training, each handler will be using just one glove. The instructor should then demonstrate the correct signal for getting the glove. It is given by stretching the left hand and arm out toward the glove, with the handler bending his knees and body to do so if desired but not sitting on his heels, when the verbal command "Get the glove" is given. The handler may give the command to retrieve either simultaneously with or immediately following the giving of the direction. To be sure the dog is looking in the right direction it is wisest to give him the signal and then the verbal command.

After you turn with your dog to face the glove, signal the direction with your left hand and arm as you give the verbal command "Get it," either simultaneously with, or directly after, the signal.

The dog retrieves the correct glove.

He sits straight in front of you holding the glove patiently.

At first the handler should exaggerate the signal, placing his arm alongside his dog's head as he points to the glove. Since the dog has watched the handler place the glove down and he knows how to retrieve, he will no doubt trot out after the glove. If he doesn't, the handler should repeat the signal. If he still doesn't move, the handler should scoot him out by the collar.

If there is a dog who doesn't want to pick up the glove, the handler should start by handing the glove to his dog saying, "Get the glove," and when he does, he should say, "Hold it." If he doesn't take it readily, the handler should place it in his mouth and make him hold it for a few seconds. He should repeat this until his dog does it correctly.

If the dog doesn't run out in a straight line, the handler should run after him, take him by the collar, and run with him up to the glove. The dog should not be permitted to wander from a straight line.

The instructor should have the class practice this at home by working on one glove at first. The handler should place his glove about forty feet from his dog, then turn his dog toward the glove, and send him after it. The dog should have the practice of turning toward the glove without receiving additional help from his handler other than the verbal command. He should get used to going after the glove once he has turned. When giving the verbal command, "Get the glove," the handler should name the article to be retrieved so that the dog will learn the name of one more article to be used in the Working Class Vocabulary exercise.

The Second Lesson

It is unlikely that all the handlers in the Utility class will be able to keep up with each other. The instructor will find that while some have fallen behind in the work, requiring individual attention, others are way ahead of everyone else and anxious to teach their dogs new steps. A good way to cope with this is to devote a certain period of time to one exercise during which the instructor can help everyone that needs assistance.

The dogs that have started sniffing for the scented article should be working on all leather articles, the number of which should be increased until the dog is working with five of them. When a dog reaches this point, the handler should try using the metal articles in the same manner he has taught his dog to find the leather.

There could be any number of reasons for a dog's not sniffing for the article. The handler may not have kept his article in his pocket where it would acquire a strong scent. He may not be encouraging his dog to pick up the correct article by praising him. He may be discouraging his dog by shouting at him and confusing him. He may not be training him at home. The dog may lack confidence and be afraid to sniff around for fear he will make a mistake. The handler may not be using the wires on the articles when they work outdoors. The handler should continue using the prescribed method until his dog starts to sniff for the article. The instructor should watch the handler practice to be sure he is following his instructions.

This method is an excellent one; a dog can be taught to retrieve articles in two days, and this includes young puppies.

The instructor should now give the handlers some Directed Retrieve practice. He should have the handlers line up with their dogs at heel

The handler gives his dog the signal and command, "Get the glove."

The dog retrieves the glove . . .

. . . and returns it to his handler.

position about twenty feet apart. The handlers will work in groups of two. Only every second person in line will be working at the same time, but two handlers will be working their dogs in one area. If there is an odd number of handlers, the last three in line can work together.

Both handlers should place their gloves about thirty feet in front of their dogs. The handler on the right of each twosome should send his dog out first to retrieve the glove that is directly in front of him. He must be sure that his dog goes straight to his own glove and retrieves it. After he retrieves it, the handler must put his glove back where it was so that there will always be two gloves visible. Now the handler on the left should send his dog in the same manner. If the dogs do this well, the handlers should switch the gloves. Now the handler on the right will make a left turn with his dog, sending him out to get the left glove. The handler on the left will make a quarter turn to the right with his dog, sending him to get the glove on the right.

Teaching this step will consume a considerable amount of time and training as the dogs will not always go out straight or pick up the correct glove.

If a dog starts for the wrong glove, the handler should run after him and stop him before he gets to it. He should bring him back to the starting point and send him over again, only this time he should take his collar in his left hand and run him toward the glove. If his dog is headed for the glove, he should let go of his collar and let him continue on alone, but he should praise him encouragingly. When the dog reaches the correct glove and picks it up, the handler should praise his dog in an excited tone of voice and clap his hands so that he will return quickly.

Since it is natural for a dog to go in a straight line if he sees the object that he is to retrieve, be sure the dog always sees the glove. If necessary, the handler may prop it up by placing a rock or something similar under it. If a handler has a dog that is hard-headed and refuses to go out in a straight line, he should put him on a twenty-foot leash, send him out with the signal and verbal command, and follow behind him so that he can jerk him into line if he swerves off. He will have to repeat this dozens of times with this type of dog. If a dog refuses to go out after the signal is given, his handler should scoot him out by the collar and run with him in the direction of the glove.

The handlers should be instructed to practice at home with two gloves placed thirty feet apart at a distance of thirty feet.

The handlers should practice the Signal exercise quite a few times in class. As soon as the dogs are responding to the signals, the distance between the dogs and their handlers should be increased.

The class should now practice the Directed Jumping exercise. For this,

Run out with the dog on leash as you signal and
command him to "Go."

When you are twenty feet beyond
the jumps, call the dog's name and,
as he turns, say, "Sit."

Praise him for sitting.

Give the dog the Go signal off leash.

If the dog doesn't go straight, run out with him as you repeat the command and signal.

At first, stand near the jump when you signal and command "Hup."

Later you should stand midway between the jumps.

The dog should jump without touching the bar.

The handler sends the dog out again and has him sit.

He is given the signal to jump the high jump.

When the dog is in midair over the jump, turn in his direction.

the bar jump and the high jump should be placed twenty feet apart but set lower than the dog is required to jump in a show. The handler should stand twenty feet back from the jumps and centered between them. When he says, "Go," to his dog, he should run with him to a point that is halfway between the jumps but twenty-five feet beyond them; as he calls "Sit," he should have his dog about turn and sit. When he runs out, the handler should try to keep his dog running straight ahead of him, even though he may find it necessary to put his dog on leash. At this stage of the training, the emphasis should be placed on the directed jumping; thus this send-out should be performed very quickly with the handler running the dog out straight, keeping him under control all the way. When the dóg is sitting, the handler should order him to "Stay," and walk to a point five feet back from the jumps, and stand opposite his dog. As he gives his dog a signal by raising his right arm and pointing to the right jump, he should say, "Hup." As the dog stands up, the handler should move toward the right jump and repeat the signal and the verbal command. If necessary, the handler should move quickly behind the jump and place his hand on it to encourage his dog to jump. The dog should be given as many extra commands and signals as it takes to get him to jump over the hurdle. Once he does, he should repeat this whole routine, changing hurdles each time. The handler and his dog should have at least three practice jumps before the next handler tries it so that the dog will retain the lesson.

This work is so time-consuming that the handlers must do most of their practicing at home if they expect to make any progress. The instructor should encourage them to do this so that the handlers in the class will keep up with each other.

The whole class should practice the Group Examination exercise each week. The handlers should stand their dogs side by side in a comfortable square stance; that is, so that their weight is evenly distributed on all four feet. The handlers are permitted to pose their dogs by hand. When all the dogs are standing, the instructor should order the handlers to "Leave your dogs." After giving their dogs a quiet verbal command "Stay," and the stay signal if they wish, the handlers should walk forward together about twenty feet, about turn, and face their dogs. It is permissible for the handlers to stand with their arms folded, or in any other position that is comfortable for them. In a show they should never signal or correct their dogs from a distance. After a minute or so, the instructor, or someone on the sidelines, should approach each dog and examine it. The examiner should run his hands over the dog's head, body, legs, hindquarters, and tail. After a few minutes the handlers should return to their dogs by walking around them into heel position. They should not pet their dogs until the instructor calls "Exercise finished." The class should practice this stand for up to five minutes, even though in a show, the stand would probably last only three minutes, which is ample time for an efficient judge to examine fifteen dogs.

Try placing a white rock out beyond the jumps. This encourages the dog to go out straight.

If a dog breaks his position, sits, sniffs the ground or another dog, or lies down, the handler should hurry back to him and correct him. The correction for a Utility dog should generally consist of a verbal "No, shame, bad dog" and a little jerk on his collar. The dog that goes over to another dog and growls at him should receive a sharp tap on the nose in addition to the verbal reprimand. The dogs should be cautioned to stay while the handlers return until they become steady enough to be trusted. The dog that moves his feet to shift his weight should practice very brief stands at first. The handler should return to his dog several times during the duration of the class stand. When the dog gets used to standing for thirty seconds without moving, the handler can gradually increase the time.

The instructor examines the dogs during the Group Stand.

The Third Lesson

The instructor should start the lesson by having all the handlers practice scent discrimination with their dogs. He will find that some of the handlers are slower than others in teaching their dogs to find the scent articles. This is normal; it just means that the instructor will have to spend extra time with the handlers who are not following his instructions at home. If he will show them how to do it correctly by demonstrating with the handler's dog, it is quite possible that the dog will start sniffing for the scented article right then and there. Once this step is reached, the rest is just practice.

The dogs who are sniffing for the scented leather article among four or five other leather articles should now be ready to try the same procedure with the metal articles.

The handlers who have trained their dogs to find both the leather and the metal articles can go on to the next step. The dogs should be placed at heel position with their backs to the articles and standing about fifteen feet away from them. A stranger should place five leather articles and one metal article on the ground about six inches apart so that the dog will get used to finding a different scent on the other articles. The handler should rub his hand scent on the metal article, tell his dog to "Stay," and place the scented article near the other articles. As the handler pivots to the right, he should give his dog the order "Get mine." As his dog trots out briskly to the articles and searches for the scented one, the handler should remain in the same spot. If the dog refuses to go out, goes in a wide arc, goes out slowly, or goes just part way, the handler should bring him back and try it again. This time he should hold the dog's collar as he turns and scoot him out in a direct line for the articles.

Your dog turns with you as you pivot. You should not move more than one step toward the articles as you do this. Send your dog after the article with the command or signal to retrieve.

Without stopping, your dog hurries out to retrieve the scented article.

Your dog picks the correct article from the pile.

He selects the correct metal article.

Hammer the articles into the ground with a U wire.

I started this method of turning back in 1950 with Topper because it was faster and looked smoother. A handler may give his hand scent to his dog before turning, and he may order his dog to heel, make a right about turn, sit, and then send him for the article. A dog may fail this exercise unless his handler has practiced turning and sending his dog in every conceivable direction hundreds of times. It will be at the judge's discretion where he will place the articles in his ring. A handler who has very little time to practice but who wishes to get his titles quickly would be wise to send his dog out to retrieve after they have turned and his dog has sat. This way the dog will see the articles in front of him.

If the handler will combine the two sets of articles gradually, he will not have any difficulty. If he works with the nine articles at once, the dog might get discouraged if he does not find the scented article immediately and lose his self-confidence. The handlers should take it easy, be patient, and let their dogs gradually build up confidence in their own ability. If the handler lays a good foundation, his dog will become a consistent worker.

The instructor should watch the handlers carefully when they reach this stage of their training. He should be ready to advise them when he sees them making a move that would be penalized in a show. He should remind them that when the handler turns with his dog, he should not bend his body over or take any steps forward. Instead, he should pivot or take small steps while remaining in the same spot. Excessive body movements are made by handlers to encourage their dogs to go out faster. This practice is fine in training, but will draw a penalty in a show. He should also remind them to give quiet verbal commands to their dogs. The handler who gives his dog verbal commands in a voice louder than his normal speaking voice is inviting a penalty. Loud commands are particularly obnoxious when used in advanced classes, especially when the dog is beside the handler at the time they are given.

From now on the handlers should take turns practicing the directed retrieve. With his dog at heel position the handler should stand with his back to the gloves. Someone should place the three gloves seventeen feet apart and twenty-five feet away from him. If possible, each handler should have at least three practice retrieves. A dog will become confused and fail to get the correct glove if his handler gives him a poor signal. The instructor should demonstrate the two ways a handler could teach his dog to take the direction. He should observe the handlers when they are practicing and be ready to assist them.

The handlers should be reminded that they may bend their knees and bodies to get down to their dog's height to give the signals. If the handler chooses to give the signal by swishing his hand and arm in the direction of the glove as he gives his dog the verbal command "Get the glove," he may do so. The method one chooses should depend upon the dog's personality, and generally speaking this method is best for the eager retriever.

I feel the second way of giving the direction will make a dog become more reliable. When giving the direction to his dog, the handler should hold his forearm motionless alongside his dog's head so that he can sight down his arm toward the glove; when the dog looks at the correct glove he should be given the command to retrieve. If the dog is looking at the wrong glove when his handler commands him to retrieve, the dog will get the wrong glove.

If the handler gives his dog the direction by holding his left hand or arm alongside his dog's head, then motions the dog to retrieve as he gives the verbal command, he will be disqualified. This would be considered a double command.

The handler who elects to give the signal by motioning with his left hand and arm toward the glove as he gives the command to retrieve must first keep his left hand in back of his dog's head. This is an important point to remember.

The instructor should caution the handlers not to turn too far when they face the gloves. The dog and handler must be facing the glove when they turn toward it. Since glove 3 is the most difficult to retrieve, the handlers should practice this one the most. I would suggest that the handlers take a right turn for gloves 1 and 2, and take a left turn for glove 3. These turns must be practiced consistently day after day.

The Signal exercise should be practiced now at a distance of twenty feet. If a dog doesn't respond to his handler's signals, the handler should rush up to the dog, repeat the signal, and make him respond immediately. This is the same correction a handler would use if the dog were to pretend not to notice the signal. Instead of waiting for the dog to look at him or calling the dog's name, the handler should rush up to his dog, repeat the signal en route, and make him obey. The handler should not give his dog the verbal command. If the handler will follow this procedure, the dog will soon keep his eyes riveted on him and start responding to the signals immediately and from any distance.

When a dog is only partially trained to do the Signal exercise, he may become a little anxious and anticipate the signals. If the dog goes down before the handler has had the chance to give him the signal, the handler should go back, stand his dog, and leave him. As he is walking away, he should keep one eye on his dog so that he can correct him if he drops again. The handler should try to control his dog with his voice by telling him to stay as he walks away with his back to his dog and by repeating the stay command while he is standing opposite him. Often a word of

A good square stance.

praise will be just as effective. The handler should try not to give the signals with precisely the same time intervals between them when he is training his dog; instead, he should let his dog wait a few extra seconds between signals to teach him to wait for them. With a little more experience, the dog will learn to watch his handler and obey the signals. In the interim the handler should not get upset and be rough with his dog, for he should remember that the dog is still learning.

In the Directed Jumping exercise the handlers should be practicing by running their dogs out beyond the jumps and having them turn and sit. Then they should teach them to jump on the signal and verbal command

The wrong stance, feet not together.

"Hup." In the ensuing lessons, the handlers should gradually increase the distance between their dogs and themselves until they are standing about forty feet apart. The handler should remember to call cadence at the right moment as his dog approaches either the high jump or the bar jump; this will teach him to jump gracefully. The instructor should remind the handlers that if their dogs were to climb the high jump or knock off the bar jump in a show, they would be disqualified.

If a dog starts for the wrong jump, the handler should say "No," and walk toward the correct jump as he repeats the signal and again gives the command "Hup." The handler should never let his dog take the wrong jump even though he may have to run up and block his path to stop him.

Now when the dog is in midair over the jump, the handler should turn in the direction in which he will come in and the dog should come in, sit straight in front of his handler, and finish in the usual manner. Again praise is important in this exercise, for a word spoken at the right moment will bring the dog in quickly after he jumps. The handlers should learn to use praise wisely, for the dog that is praised intelligently will be a happy worker eager to please his handler.

The class should end the lesson by practicing the Group Examination with each handler taking turns examining all the dogs.

The Fourth Lesson

By this time all the dogs in the class should be retrieving the scent-discrimination articles quite consistently. When the dogs have reached this plateau, it is time to start using clean articles. The handler should scour the articles he has been using with hot water and soap, rinse them thoroughly to remove all the scent, and let them air for three days. Thereafter, it will be necessary only to run hot water over the scented articles and to air them overnight. The first few times the handler uses all clean articles, he should be sure to rub them well to give them a strong scent. After his dog is doing well, he should reduce the time he rubs his hand scent on the articles to a few seconds.

It is quite possible for the handlers to practice this exercise by themselves, but if there is a second person present, he should be asked to place the articles in the pile. This person should handle each unscented article and place the scented article in the pile with a pair of sugar tongs.

The handler should practice this exercise in different locations, indoors and outdoors, until the dog is very steady and consistent in his work. If the dog starts to slow down, his handler is either making the work tedious or not encouraging him enough. It is better to take four weeks to teach him this exercise than to dampen his spirits by long, monotonous lessons. Make the lessons short but pleasant and to the point. Whether practicing in class or at home, the handler should stop when his dog has gotten each article correctly twice. Any longer period of practice would be boring for the dog.

The other exercises should be practiced in the same way they were in the third lesson.

The Fifth, Sixth, and Seventh Lessons

The handlers should continue to practice the Scent-Discrimination exercise and should help each other to place the articles. When the dogs have reached this stage, it doesn't take very long to practice with them.

The handlers should continue to practice the Directed Retrieve exercise alone. It would be beneficial to everyone concerned to practice this routine with the bar jump and high jump in position about nineteen feet apart. The handler with his dog at heel position should stand in line with, and halfway between, the jumps with his back to the gloves. In this exercise the dog is supposed to see the gloves when he turns to face them. Be sure that he does by bending down to the dogs height to observe them.

The instructor should watch each handler give the direction to his dog and advise him when his signal confuses him. More people fail this exercise from poorly given signals than for any other reason.

The handlers should practice the Signal exercise together. This makes practice more difficult, but the dog that watches his handler and responds to his signals is the dog that will be steady. The instructor should give the heeling pattern, having the handlers leave their dogs at a different distance each time. The dogs shouldn't get used to one certain routine. The reason that many obedience dogs work like robots is that the handlers never give them any variety.

The handlers could start sending their dogs out between the jumps. The Directed Retrieve exercise should be helpful there. If the handlers have practiced at home sending their dogs out forty feet to get the center glove, the dogs by now will be used to going out.

The handler should be standing back about twenty feet from the jumps and halfway between them with his dog sitting at heel position. The first time he should send the dog out after the center glove. The next time a small white rock should be placed in the center instead, and the dog should be sent toward that. When the dog gets near the rock, the handler should order him to "Sit." It is unlikely he will sit, so the handler should make him sit. The next time the dog is sent out with the command "Go," the handler should follow him quietly and be ready to make him sit when he orders him to do so.

At home also, the handler should use a small white rock and place it about twenty-five feet past the jumps and centered between them. If his dog doesn't go out far enough, which is normal, the handler should run out with his dog and make him go all the way. The command "Go" and the signal with the left arm should be repeated as often as it is necessary.

In the beginning when the dog has found that he is not going to retrieve anything, he may start to wander to the left or to the right. To correct this, the handler will have to turn after him and send him out straight by running along with him.

If the handler were to start this exercise at home each time by doing the center glove, the dog would get the idea quicker. It shouldn't be practiced more than once, though, or the dog might expect to retrieve every time. This exercise takes a great deal of practice at home; the instructor should advise the handlers to work on it at least half an hour per day.

The class should end every practice session with the Group Examination exercise.

The Eighth and Ninth Lessons

By now all the dogs should understand the Scent-Discrimination exercise and should be working with a full set of articles. The instructor should try to get strangers to place the articles down so that every article is touched except the scented ones. He should put these down with a pair of tongs.

Once a dog can consistently find his handler's scented article, it just remains to perfect the dog's performance. The handler should get his dog to turn and go out briskly, search continuously until he finds the scented article, carry it without dropping, mouthing, or chewing it, return briskly, and sit straight in front and at heel position. The instructor should remind the handlers that a dog will be penalized if he makes any of these errors or picks up the wrong article, even though he drops it immediately and chooses the correct one.

Each handler should practice the Directed Retrieve exercise by himself. When the handler turns to face the gloves, glove 1 is on his left, glove 2 is in the center, and glove 3 is on his right. The instructor should call out the glove he wants the handler's dog to retrieve. In a show this is what the judge would do, and it is excellent experience for the handler to get used to this procedure at this time. The instructor should warn the handlers that they will not be able to touch their dogs to get them to turn and should remind them to train their dogs to work at a brisk pace.

The handlers should now start working their dogs on the signals at a distance of forty feet. If the dogs have become fairly consistent, the increased distance will not make much difference. The instructor should give the class a little heeling routine before he has them stand their dogs and practice the signal sequence.

It is normal for a dog to begin anticipating the signals once he has learned them. To correct this, the handler should work in closer to the dog, or he should make his dog wait an extra few seconds after a signal before he gives him the next one. The down signal is the one most dogs anticipate; a handler can correct this habit by leaving his dog standing, and instead of dropping him, by walking back to him.

The Directed Jumping exercise cannot be perfected unless the handler is willing to spend a great deal of time practicing it with his dog. However, any handler who has the time and space to practice the jumping phase of this exercise at home should have his dog responding to the correct signal to jump in two weeks or less. When the handler gives his dog the signal to jump, he should simultaneously give the verbal command "Hup." If a dog is very eager to respond to the jump signal his name should be omitted before the verbal command. If there is no problem of the dog anticipating then the handler should give his dog's name before the command and signal.

When the instructor feels that a handler and his dog understand the jumping signals and the work is fast and precise, it is time to make it more difficult. The handler should be instructed to place his dog way off center behind the bar jump, go back to the send-out position, and give his dog the signal to jump the high jump. He should be prepared to correct or help his dog immediately if he starts for the wrong jump. By practicing the signals in various and awkward positions, the dog will become adept at obeying his handler's signal and jumping the correct hurdle.

Now it is time to combine the two phases of this exercise. If the handler started the send-out portion of this exercise by giving the dog the exaggerated directed retrieve signal, the dog should be going out by himself. It is normal at some point for the dog to lie down when he goes out. If this error is corrected immediately, the dog will soon start sitting on command.

Handlers should be reminded to make their dogs go out twenty-five feet beyond the jumps and not be satisfied with anything less. If the handlers insist upon good work habits, the dogs will soon be responding to the send-out command. When learning this exercise a dog will eventually veer off to the left or right. The handler should always be quick to correct his dog and never let him get away with this.

The instructor should point out to the class that a dog will fail the exercise if he anticipates the handler's command to go out or to jump, does not go out between the jumps and a substantial distance beyond, does not stop on command, does not jump as directed, knocks the bar off, climbs the high jump, or uses the high jump for aid in going over. The dog must do it right or he will fail. Therefore, the handler must practice with his dog consistently.

The Tenth Lesson

Very few handlers will be ready for Utility competition in ten weeks, but it will be good practice for them to go through the exercises individually so that they can see how their dogs are coming along.

The instructor should put each handler through as though it were show work. The handlers are apt to forget many of the finer points that the instructor has mentioned over the weeks, and this is a good time to bring them to everyone's attention.

A handler should not enter the Utility class until he feels his dog is ready. Since more failures occur in this class than in any other, it is wise to try the dog in several club matches and regular matches before entering him in point shows.

Handlers should practice the Utility exercises in the following order. The maximum scores are as follows:

1. Signal Exercise	40 points
2. Scent Discrimination Article One	30 points
3. Scent Discrimination Article Two	30 points
4. Directed Retrieve	30 points
5. Directed Jumping	40 points
6. Group Examination	30 points
Maximum Total Score	200 points

11 THE SUBNOVICE CLASS

The Subnovice class is a competitive nonregular class that is quite popular at AKC-Sanctioned Obedience Matches. All the work in this class is done on leash, and the exercises included are Heeling on Leash, Figure Eight on Leash, Stand for Examination, Recall, Long Sit for one minute, and Long Down for three minutes. The maximum score in this class is 155 points.

This class is excellent practice for handlers in the Beginners' class as it gives them the actual experience of competing in obedience. Many times this introduction to dog shows will be all the incentive they need to continue training their dogs and obtain their obedience titles. Even if the handlers and their dogs make mistakes they will have fun competing and, after all, this is what it is all about. The Subnovice class should be included in club practice matches and should be open to any handler who is just beginning.

The Subnovice class should be restricted to beginners. Handlers who show their dogs in this class should not be permitted to show the same dogs in another class. If a handler has a dog ready for the Novice class, that is where he should compete, not in a class so elementary as the Subnovice class.

I 2 | THE GRADUATE NOVICE CLASS

The Graduate Novice class is a competitive nonregular class and is open to any dog or bitch who has not gained a leg toward the CDX title. This class is not provided at every obedience trial, but is generally included at obedience specialty shows sponsored by training clubs. No credit is given toward any obedience title.

This class should be provided at club practice matches and at regular AKC-Sanctioned Matches as it gives the dogs another chance to gain experience at these shows.

Dogs in this class may be handled by the owner or any other person. A person may handle more than one dog in this class, but each dog must have a separate handler for the Long Sit and Long Down exercises when judged in the same group. Dogs entered in this class may also compete in Open. Judging shall be the same as in the regular classes, except that the Figure Eight is omitted from the Heel on Leash, a Drop on Recall is included, and the Long Sit and Long Down are the same as in the Open classes.

The exercises, maximum scores, and order of judging are as follows:

1. Heel on Leash (no Figure Eight)	30 points
2. Stand for Examination	30 points
3. Open Heel Free	40 points
4. Open Drop on Recall	40 points
5. Open Long Sit	30 points
6. Open Long Down	30 points
Maximum Total Score	200 points

13 | *THE BRACE CLASS*

The Brace class is a competitive nonregular class offered at Obedience Trials. Competition in a Brace class is open to any brace of dogs or bitches, or combination of both, of the same breed. It is not a regular class, and no credit toward any obedience title will be given. This class is generally found at obedience trials sponsored by a training club.

Brace work is very interesting and a great deal of fun. If the handler has trained two dogs that work equally well, he has good material for a brace. They should work at about the same speed and should sit quickly. Their response to commands should be identical. This type of obedience work is not worth watching unless it is nearly perfect. Precision and teamwork must be in evidence. To call the dogs, it is wise for the handler to use one name for both dogs, such as "Boys, come," or the word "Come" alone, or signal them to come.

While there will be very few people who are interested in working a brace of dogs in a class, I believe the instructor should know all the answers to the questions an interested person might want to ask. He should know the best training method so that the dogs will not have to be trained with a hit-and-miss routine. In my classes, I encourage handlers who have trained two dogs of the same breed to try the brace work because it is so much fun. I suggest that they work their dogs in my regular Novice classes to see how they make out at first; then if they do well, they are invited to join the Advanced Novice class.

The Novice routine is employed, and a tandem chain is used to clip the two dogs together. This is a short chain, about ten inches long, with a clip at both ends. The handler can make one himself or buy one. He should not buy one that is too long, or it will be a nuisance.

The dog that works the fastest—or the one that heels the closest—should be on the outside since he will have to hurry on the turns. The other dog will work the inside position next to the handler. The first exercise is Heeling on Leash with the slow, normal, fast, halt, about turn, left turn, and right turn commands given at different intervals. The Figure Eight is employed, but the stewards will stand farther apart since two dogs will require more room to turn.

During the Stand-for-Examination exercise, the judge will examine each dog individually by touching his head, back, and croup. This is done off leash.

Heeling on leash. A beautiful brace. Leash should be attached to collar of the dog nearest to the handler.

The Stay signal and verbal command as the dogs walk into a perfect stance.

Heeling off Leash should be done with the same precision as the Heeling on Leash.

The Recall exercise is next. Here the dogs are expected to come in at a trot and sit straight in front of the handler. Upon command, they should go to heel smartly.

The Long Sit for one minute and the Long Down for three minutes will be executed with the braces lined up together in a row on one side of the ring. At the judge's command, the handlers will leave their dogs, cross the ring, turn to face their dogs, and stand there for the allotted time. When the judge orders the handlers to "Return to your dogs," they will do so.

The brace that works with the most precision stands the best chance of winning. It is desirable that the dogs work as if they were one, keeping in step at all times while heeling, making turns, sitting, etc.

Straight sits in front after a recall.

Heeling on Leash: The handler should use just one leash, clipping it to the collar of the dog nearest him. He should practice the regular Novice heeling, and on the turns, call the name of the dog that lags, telling him to heel. If one dog forges ahead, he should reach down and jerk him back by using the tandem chain. The dog doing it correctly should not be jerked; he should be praised. If both dogs are perfectly trained, the only problems will be to keep them in step and to see that they sit at the same time. If one sits more slowly than the other, he should be tapped to make him sit faster. Praise should be given at every opportunity so that they will think it is fun and will enjoy working together.

Figure Eight: The handler will have to watch the outside dog on the Figure Eight and make him hurry around the outside turn. When working the inside turn, caution the dogs with the word "Easy." The dog that tries to crowd too close to the handler should be tapped lightly on the side of his cheek.

Stand for Examination: For this off-leash exercise, the handler may pose his dogs singly or walk them into the pose and stand them with a hand signal. The latter looks smoother and more impressive; it is a sign of expert handling. If the dogs are heeling with precision, they will stop in step with each other. The handler should practice until he has this down perfectly. Whether the dogs are still attached with the tandem chain or not is up to the handler. If the tandem chain is used in one exercise off leash, it must be used in all exercises off leash. I prefer to use the tandem chain as it gives the handler more control over his dogs.

Heeling off Leash: This exercise is not very difficult for trained dogs. The handler must watch carefully to see that every change of pace, every turn, and every sit is performed with precision. Too often in brace work a handler will do a fast pantomime instead of really running. With practice one can teach his dogs to do the fast pace with as much precision as the normal pace.

Be careful that the dogs do not weave in and out as they are heeling. They should not be wide one minute and crowd the next. Practice to attain precision, and be quick to correct the dog that is making the mistake. Be equally fast with a word of praise when it is earned.

The Recall exercise: This exercise is done off leash. When the handler calls his dogs, he should say "Boys, come," using the name first. If one lags behind, he should be urged to come in faster. As they come in, the handler should be sure that they sit directly in front of him. He should practice the finish the dogs know, and repeat it until they can do it smoothly together. One dog will learn to wait for the other, and they will become adjusted to working shoulder to shoulder.

The Long Sit and the Long Down exercises: These exercises are performed exactly the same way as they were in the Novice class, except that the dogs are close together. They may or may not be connected with the tandem chain, depending upon the handler's choice in the Stand-for-Examination exercise.

The handler will find this training most helpful if he owns two dogs. If he can handle both dogs at the same time, it will be no problem to take them places together. By teaching them the brace work, the handler will gain more control over them and they will be better behaved. The training will teach them to get along well together, to give a thought to each other, and to learn the technique of keeping in step.

It is heart-warming to handle a brace of dogs that has been precision trained. The pleasure you get from watching them respond is worth all the work that is put into it.

14 | THE TEAM CLASS

If an obedience club or training class has a very active group of handlers, there might be five or six people who would be interested in getting a team together. Team work is a nonregular class, and no credit toward any obedience title will be given. This class is generally found at obedience trials sponsored by a specialty club or training club.

The four people on the team should be approximately the same height, and the dogs should preferably be the same breed although this isn't absolutely necessary. The handlers should work at the same speed since they must keep in step with each other. The dogs should be taught to work at the same speed, for one slow worker in the group will spoil the whole team. If these handlers have all worked under one instructor, the chances are good that they will work alike. I have found that 95 percent of the handlers who graduate from my Advanced Novice class work alike and control their dogs in the same manner because every week they have been seriously training them to attain the precision and perfection necessary to be "in the ribbons." The dogs are not bored with this routine because the direct method we use appeals to them.

To be successful, a team must train and practice under one qualified instructor. The members must be congenial and willing to forego other pleasures in order to practice regularly, to work hard, and to take orders from one member of the team. The friction starts when one team member is repeatedly late for practice, always out of step, too slow on turns, too fast to start out, too quick to stop, or in any other way out of step with the rest of the team. In order to maintain precision and accuracy, the members must work together, which means they must think of themselves as a group and not as individuals.

The captain of the team must be a person who knows what he is doing, has a top working dog, and is tactful, good-natured, and able to give orders pleasantly. He should have a team composed of handlers who are willing to follow his instructions and to accept constructive criticism. It is up to the individual handlers to train their dogs to work with precision and willingness. Any handler who has worked in a fast-moving training class will know how to make turns correctly and should be able to do so smoothly.

The team should follow the pace set by the captain. The heeling work should be done at a normal pace, which is a brisk walk, and the handlers should always march with their heads up and their arms held in the same positions. Here is where a continuity of handling is important. If the handlers on a team carry the left arm folded in front with the leash held in the left hand and the right arm swinging, they should keep these same positions when the dogs are working off leash. When doing the drop on recall the handlers should place their arms down by their sides, and should give the same type of signal when dropping their dogs. The whole performance from start to finish should be smooth, coordinated, natural, and integrated.

The four handlers should move forward on the last word of the captain's command such as, "Forward, march," or "About turn." When stepping off with their left feet to make a right turn, the handlers should pivot a quarter turn and step off with their left feet. On left turns the handlers should bring their feet together and step off on their left feet. On about turns the handlers should take a couple of small steps with their feet close together as they turn and step off with their left feet. On every halt, the handlers should take one forward step with each foot and halt. Normally when a halt is called, the handler is about to complete a step, so he should complete that one, take one more step, bring his feet together, and stop. This is not difficult, but when it is done by a team, it requires practice.

The team should practice heeling behind each other with emphasis being placed upon keeping in step and keeping the same distance between handlers. When the handlers are moving in line four abreast, there should be one yard, or about an arm's length, between them. The captain should call the turns and direction as necessary, and each handler should keep one eye on the captain as he keeps an eye on all of them.

One of the important points for a team to remember is to keep moving at a brisk pace. The handlers should not stop on the turns or move around slowly. All the work should be done at this pace except the fast or slow paces in the heeling routines.

The judging of this class should start after the judge asks the team captain whether his team is ready to start the Heeling on Leash. Prior to that time it is up to the captain to see that he gets his team to the starting point with the precision of a drillmaster. This preliminary marching, the precision marching to move into position for the start of each exercise, and the exit march should be done with a flourish, for although the team is not judged for this, these finishing touches give the team finesse and appeal.

Heeling on Leash: The team should practice this exercise by employing different patterns each time it tries it. In this way the team can be prepared for the unexpected. The captain or alternate member of the team should call the orders to see how the team performs. When the judge calls the orders "Fast, slow, normal," the handlers should react as though he were saying "Fast pace, slow pace, normal pace" and should move on the word *pace*. This way the team will keep their precision.

Figure Eight on Leash: This will require five stewards in line with each other eight feet apart. Each dog and handler shall face in the same direction and stand between two stewards. The captain will have his handlers march up to their respective set of stewards and halt. On order from the judge the handlers will start heeling briskly to the left and maintain the same pace around the Figure Eight turns. The handlers should keep their eyes left so that they take the turns at precisely the same time.

Stand for Examination: The captain should have his team pass their dogs' leashes to him. The handlers may stand their dogs by walking them into a stance or by posing them. It looks more impressive to walk the dogs into a stance, give them the stay signal, and leave them simultaneously. The handlers then walk out about six feet from their dogs, as they would in the Novice class. When the judge orders them to "Return to your dogs," the handlers should move back on the last word of the command. The captain should then take his team back to the position where they started the Heeling on Leash.

Heeling off Leash: This exercise is similar to the Heeling on Leash. Again, the handlers should start forward briskly on the imagined second word of the command such as "Forward, *march*."

Drop on Recall: The captain should march his team to a place designated by the judge as the starting point. Upon order from the judge, "Leave your dogs," the handlers should march abreast to a point about forty feet from their dogs, about turn, and halt. When the judge orders

"Call your dogs," each handler should call his dog to him separately, but each dog will be dropped when he is halfway to his handler. The dogs should be dropped in line with each other, which will take a great deal of practice. When all the dogs are down, the judge will give the order "Call your dogs,' 'and the handlers will do so simultaneously. Then upon the judge's order, the dogs will be sent to heel at the same time.

At the conclusion of the exercises, the captain will march his team out of the ring.

When each of the teams has been judged individually, they must all return to the ring to do the Long Sit and the Long Down exercises. The judge will probably limit the class to four teams at a time. The captains should march their teams into the ring and to the side the judge has indicated he will use for these exercises. The handlers of each team should stand about one yard apart, but the teams should be about two yards apart. The captain should give his team the nod when the judge orders "Leave your dogs," and the handlers should give their dogs a quiet stay command simultaneously. The teams should then march across the ring uniformly.

When the judge orders the team to "Down your dogs," in preparation for the Long Down exercise, the captain should again give a nod to his team and they should all give their dogs the down signal simultaneously. This should be practiced so that the dogs will drop immediately. Again when the judge orders "Leave your dogs," the handlers should give the quiet stay command and march forward in step to the other side of the ring, about turn, and stand with arms folded. The return to their dogs should also be made with precision. After the judge says "Exercise finished," the handlers should pet their dogs quietly and then march with precision from the ring.

Team work is very interesting to watch when the handlers present an attractive appearance by dressing in outfits that match, when the dogs are alert and well trained, and when the team displays precision and spirit. Such a team has every right to be proud of its accomplishments.

The exercises and maximum scores are:

1.	Heel on Leash	160 points
2.	Stand for Examination	120 points
3.	Heel Free	160 points
4.	Drop on Recall	120 points
5.	Long Sit	120 points
6.	Long Down	120 points
	Maximum Total Score	800 points

15 | *THE WORKING CLASS*

An exciting group of exercises to
challenge every handler who has trained
a Utility Dog.

The Working class should be included in an obedience club's curriculum,
and the instructor should be familiar with the exercises involved, even
though at this writing the Working class is a nonregular class. However,
since obedience enthusiasts have wanted an advanced class beyond the
Utility class for many, many years, it might conceivably become a regular
class some day if there are enough skilled handlers and dogs around to
warrant it.

This class can only be staged outdoors as it requires a one-hundred- by
fifty-foot ring, an excellent footing for the dogs, and a barrier jump that is
pegged down to prevent it from moving. The ring should be set up on
turf as this gives the dogs the best footing for takeoffs and cushions them
when they land. When the grass is wet, the dogs should not jump as they
might slip. A club could solve this problem by covering the thirty-foot
takeoff path ahead of the long jump and the landing area beyond it with
a strip of tarpaulin to keep it dry when the jump is not being used. This
idea could also be utilized during home practice sessions so that a handler
could practice with his dog regardless of the weather.

It is impractical to incorporate these exercises with the Open or Utility
exercises. The best plan is to hold the training class at the location of the

A ring ready for the Working class.

jumps. If the instructor, or someone in the club, has the space to accommodate this equipment, the training lessons could be given there. It is quite likely that the number of people interested in this class will be small, so the instructor should be able to handle them easily.

The construction and measurements for the jumps are illustrated; any handyman should be able to build them. The Working class ring is also illustrated, and I would advise that it be set up for the practice sessions also. The handlers may practice many phases of these exercises at home, but the class practice should provide the dogs and their handlers with the correct ring size and regulation jumps so that they will have the experience of working with the proper equipment.

If the instructor has a dog that can perform the exercises, he should give a demonstration to his class; if not, he should get a film of a dog doing these exercises. He should ask his handlers to read the Working class chapter in my book *Expert Obedience Training for Dogs,* which contains instructions and illustrations for the different exercises.

I have conceived these exercises exclusively for obedience enthusiasts. They are new and exciting and a challenge to every handler and every dog. All the dogs we have trained love this new work. Spectators find every exercise fascinating to watch. A handler can train his dog successfully by using my method, a little patience, and a great deal of praise. Even though today it is not uncommon in the other fields of training for trainers to use shock collars, spike collars, and shock sticks, such equipment will be completely unnecessary in teaching dogs these obedience exercises. The only equipment needed is a nylon or chain choke collar and a leash.

The new jumps can be homemade or made to order for about seventy

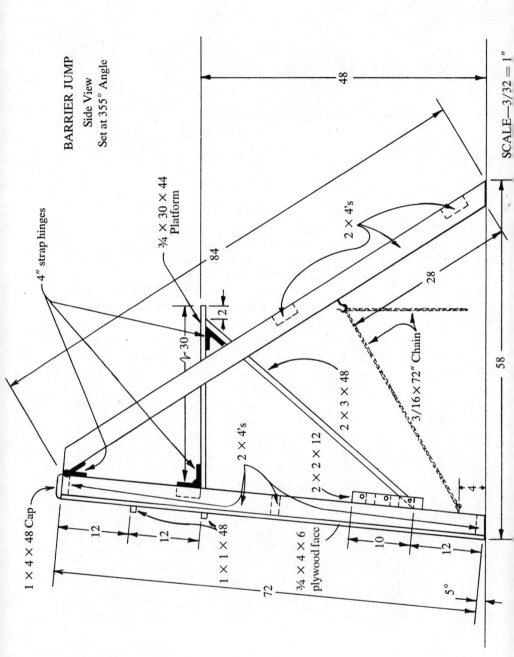

BARRIER JUMP
Side View
Set at 355° Angle

SCALE—3/32 = 1"

4" strap hinges

1 × 4 × 48 Cap

¾ × 30 × 44
Platform

84

30

2

2 × 4's

2 × 4's

2 × 2 × 12

2 × 3 × 48

3/16 × 72" Chain

28

58

48

4

12

12

1 × 1 × 48

72

¾ × 4 × 6
plywood face

10

12

5°

BARRIER JUMP
Back View

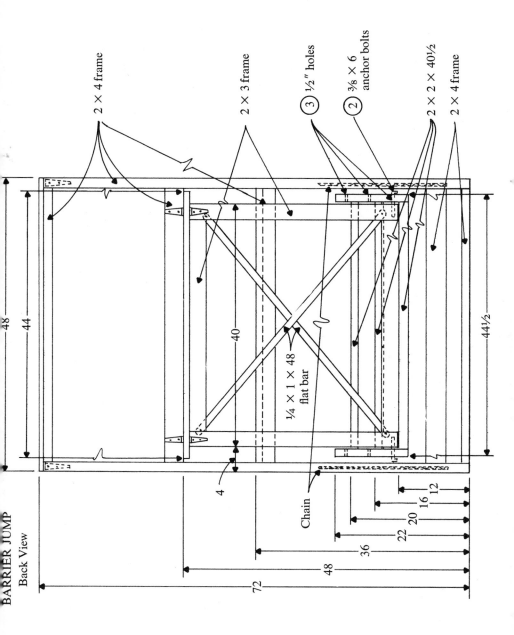

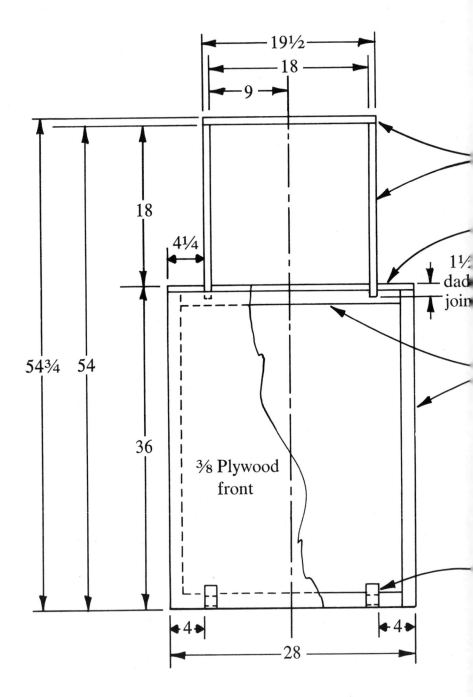

19½
18
9
18
4¼
1½
dad
join
54¾   54
36
⅜ Plywood
front
4
28
4

FRONT VIEW

ale 3/32 = 1 inch

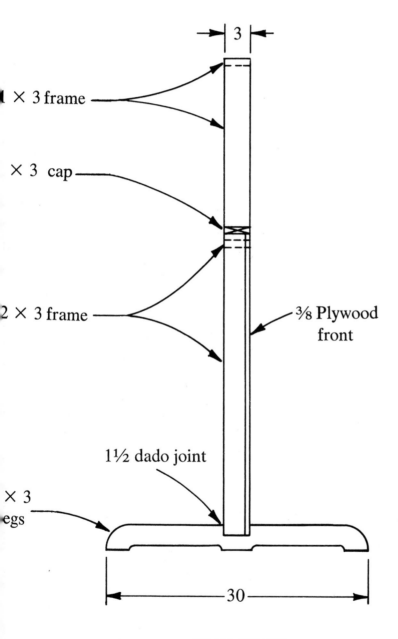

3

1 × 3 frame

× 3 cap

2 × 3 frame

⅜ Plywood
front

1½ dado joint

× 3
egs

30

SIDE VIEW

LONG JUMP

Front View of Long Jump

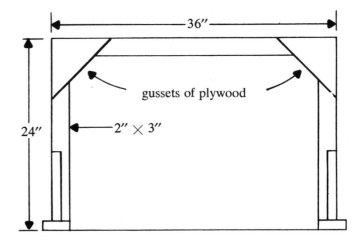

36″

24″

gussets of plywood

2″ × 3″

Side View of Long Jump

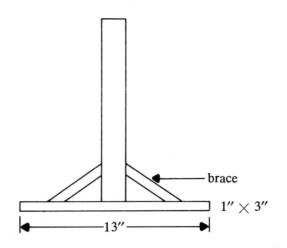

brace

1″ × 3″

13″

dollars. The jumps that I have designed are simple in principle and safe to use. Since they don't require a dog to clear more than a three-foot jump, he will not acquire the habit of climbing these jumps. For instance, if a handler has a German Shepherd he wants to continue showing in both Open B and Utility but would love to try this new class, this work will improve the other. The high jump, bar jump, and window jump are each three feet high and must be cleared. The barrier, though, must be climbed, so a dog must learn to differentiate between them. I designed the barrier with a platform on the back to break the dog's jump to the ground so that breed champions could compete without the danger of injuring themselves. The largest dogs will be jumping down from a height of four feet, which is not difficult for a physically sound dog. The long jump is designed to improve a dog's jumping ability. The individual hurdles will fall over if a dog does not clear them, which is a good reminder for him to pick up his feet.

Not every dog will be able to do these exercises. Only the most intelligent and the most agile will succeed. But to those who meet the mental and physical requirements, here is a new challenge.

In conceiving these exercises, I studied them from the point of view of the trainer, the dog, the handler, the judge, and the audience. I have found that they are more fun, although more difficult, to teach than any others I have taught before. The dogs seem to love them, and the spectators are extremely enthusiastic about them. I wanted to create exercises that were completely new, exciting to learn or watch, interesting for everyone, and difficult enough to bring out the latent talent a dog may possess.

The exercises and maximum scores in the Working class are as follows:

1. Control exercise	40	points
2. Vocabulary exercise	40	points
3. Search exercise	40	points
4. Agility exercise	40	points
5. Long Jump exercise	40	points
Total score	200	points

The Control Exercise

The handler will stand with his dog sitting at heel position, and upon an order from the judge to "Start," the handler will give his dog the following commands which the dog will execute at a brisk pace: "Go, Sit, Come, Down, Crawl, Stand, Stay, Come, Heel." The handler may give his dog either a verbal command or a signal each time, but not both. The dog must Go out about sixty feet, Sit, Come half the distance, Down promptly, Crawl about ten feet, Stand, Stay, Come the remaining distance to the handler and sit straight in front of him, and Finish smartly with a straight sit.

The dog that fails to execute any one portion of the exercise on the first command or signal or that anticipates a command will fail the entire exercise. Substantial deductions will be made for the dog that doesn't go out far enough or that doesn't crawl the required distance. Minor penalties will be given for slow responses to commands, excessively loud commands, poor sits, or no sits in front or at heel position.

To teach a dog to go out sixty feet is not particularly difficult, provided that the handler insists his dog go out that distance each time he sends him. After a dog has been practicing this distance for a couple of weeks, his instinct will tell him how far he should go. A dog can be amazingly accurate in determining the distance he is supposed to go out. After trying them in a familiar place for a couple of weeks and then trying them in a completely different location, I have found upon measuring the course that the dog has stopped instinctively at sixty feet. Many times a dog's instinct has been more accurate than my eye.

To teach a dog to go the full distance, place a small white object on the ground sixty feet in front of the handler. This object should become visible to the dog after he has covered the first thirty feet. If the dog stops, the handler should run up to him and send him out again. When the dog reaches the correct distance, the handler should command or signal him to sit. The dog should never be permitted to pick up the white object; this is placed there to help the dog orient himself, it teaches him to go sixty feet, and it helps him to go out straight. With repetition he will eventually learn to go this distance without this aid.

The trained Utility dog knows how to sit, come, and down. The next step is to teach the dog to crawl. This is done separately until the dog understands both the crawl command and the signal. Then this phase of the exercise is combined with the rest of it. To teach a dog to crawl, the handler should have his dog on leash and should give him the down signal. He should call his dog to him as he pulls the leash a little, holds the down signal, and controls him by saying "Down, crawl." He should make him crawl about ten feet, then have him stand as he praises and pets him. When he says "Stand" to his dog, he should give him the stand signal. Starting with his hands down by his sides he should swiftly move his right hand back to start the signal, then sweep it up toward his dog, bending his elbow to do so, and finish by swinging his hand out to his right side waist high, showing his dog the palm of his right hand all the

Pull your dog toward you as you give the Down signal and say, "Down, crawl."

Give your dog the Crawl signal as you say, "Crawl."

while. This should be done in a continuous sweeping motion. Then he should give him the verbal command "Stay," and the stay signal.

As soon as it is feasible, the handler should combine the crawl signal with the verbal command *crawl*, even though he still has to use the down command and signal to keep his dog down. To execute the crawl signal, the handler should hold his right hand down by his side with the back of his hand toward his dog and flick his hand back and forth twice by bending his wrist. He should then return his hand to its original position.

The handler should be patient but firm; he shouldn't let his dog get up and walk one step when he tells him to crawl. A verbal correction should be all that is necessary to teach a dog this exercise. The handler's dog may be taken off leash when he feels he has sufficient control over him to guide him with the verbal command "Crawl," or the crawl signal.

Now the handler can combine the whole exercise in the proper sequence. It will be just a matter of practice before the dog does the entire routine without making mistakes. In fact, the dog will reach a point where he will want to keep on crawling and will ignore any signals or commands to make him stand. Not only does a dog like to continue crawling, but he will go so fast that he will be oblivious to what the handler is doing. To correct this the handler must rush up to his dog, take him by the collar, and jerk him up on his feet as he says "Stand, stay." The handler might also find that his dog will try to substitute a sit for a stand-stay. The handler should be quick to correct this by having his dog do several stands from a down position to show the dog that he must stand when he is ordered to do so.

The handler must train his dog to execute the command quickly. When the dog is coming to the handler, the dog should move at a brisk pace.

Vocabulary Exercise

Many people think that their dogs understand every word they say to them, but this is not actually the case. Dogs do not learn the names of objects the way humans do, but associate words or names by performing some act that is connected with it. Practically every word or phrase that is used in dog training means action of some kind to the dog with the exception of words of praise. Some dogs who have been taught to entertain people in shows appear to have a large vocabulary, but while their handlers are making a spiel, the dogs are picking up key words that mean a certain action which they must perform. The routines are always the same and the dog learns his lessons by repetition.

If a handler has trained his dog by my methods, his dog will now understand the words *dumbbell, glove,* and *leash.* If the handler has not trained his dog by my method, his dog will be familiar with some of these articles but will have no idea which one to get when he is sent after a specific article.

The handler who has trained his dog to retrieve by naming the specific article may now place the four articles on the ground, eight inches apart, twenty feet in front of his dog and send his dog after one of them. The dog may trot right out and pick up the correct article as he is already used to the names of three of them. He might, however, momentarily forget when he reaches the pile and need some assistance. If he seems utterly confused, the handler should start with just two articles and gradually work up to four.

The handler who has never taught his dog the names of the articles should start with just two articles. For instance, if he uses the glove and the basket first, he should keep working on these until his dog will retrieve either one without difficulty. When he reaches this point, the handler should use one of the articles, such as the basket, which his dog can now retrieve by name, and add a new one to it, such as the leash. He will understand that if you do not say "Basket," you must want him to retrieve the other object. When he has this down, try the leash with the dumbbell. Never work with more than two articles at the same time until he is proficient at retrieving any one of the four articles in this set of two.

Now the handler may work with any three articles in different combinations, but including each of the four articles at one time or another. If the dog makes a mistake and selects the wrong article, such as a glove when he has been sent for a leash, the handler should say "No, drop it, get the leash" and put his hand on the leash. The dog should be praised immediately when he gets the leash.

When the dog has reached the point where he will retrieve a specific object each time he is given the verbal command, the handler may add the fourth article. At this point some dogs will still be having trouble choosing the correct article from the pile of four. Although a dog is remotely familiar with the names of all the articles, he may not be able to concentrate enough to retain that one name from the time the handler gives him the command to the time he gets to the pile of articles. In this case, the dog's ability to remember a set routine will enable the handler to teach him the names of the articles. The dog should first be sent out to get the basket, the dumbbell, the glove, and the leash four times a day for two weeks. At the end of this time the handler will be pleased at how easily the dog does this.

You will be standing with your dog at heel position while the judge

Joll correctly selects the basket after his handler has given him the verbal command to do so.

places your four articles on the ground eight inches apart and twenty feet in front of you. The judge will tell you to send your dog. Your dog will make four separate retrieves in this order: the basket, the dumbbell, the glove, and the leash. You will give your dog the verbal command for each article by naming the article, then ordering him to get it. It will be like this, "Basket, get the basket." Your tone of voice must be moderate as any loud tones will be penalized. Your dog should trot out briskly, choose the correct article, return it to you at a brisk pace, and sit straight in front of you without mouthing or playing with it. When the judge orders you to "Finish" your dog should do so in the proper manner. Then your dog must retrieve the remaining three articles in the aforementioned order.

The dog will fail if he returns with the wrong article, fails to retrieve, or does not retrieve on the first command. A substantial penalty will be incurred if the dog chooses the wrong article, even though he drops it and picks up the correct one. Minor penalties will be given for slowness in working, mouthing, chewing, poor sits, or no sits or finish.

The Search Exercise

For the Search exercise, the handler will stand with his dog sitting at heel position, and on order from the judge, will execute such portions of the Heel Free exercise as the judge may direct. Upon order from the judge, the handler will surreptitiously drop a small key case that is dark brown in color and about two inches by three inches in size. The judge will have the handler and his dog continue heeling until they are at the opposite end of the ring at which time he will give them an order to "Halt." While the handler and his dog have their backs turned, the judge will place his own key case about two feet from that which the handler dropped. The judge's case will be the same size and color. The judge will then direct the handler to "About turn and halt." On order from the judge to "Send your dog," the handler will give his dog the command or signal to "Search mine." If the handler elects to use a signal, it must be made with one hand and arm only; body signals will be penalized. The handler must remain in the same spot and may not turn toward the key case.

The dog may check the judge's case by sniffing it, but will be failed if he returns it to his handler. A substantial deduction will be made if the dog picks up the wrong case, even though he drops it and retrieves the correct one. He should trot out briskly, search until he finds his handler's key case, and return with it at a brisk pace. He should return the case to his handler without mouthing or playing with it, and should relinquish it immediately when the handler reaches for it. His sit in front should be straight, and his finish should be precise.

Minor penalties will be given for heeling imperfections, slowness, no sits, poor sits, and mouthing or playing with the case. The dog that does not return his handler's case to him will be failed.

This is a practical exercise which has a twofold purpose. It teaches a dog to distinguish between his master's belongings and those of a stranger, and it teaches him to be useful in finding lost articles. A key case is a small object to find in a large ring.

To practice this exercise, the jumps should be set up in the practice area. With his dog sitting at heel position, the handler should offer him the key case saying "Get it." When he takes it, the handler should say,

Joll finds a key case and sniffs it to be sure it belongs to his handler.

"Hold it," and after a few seconds take it from him. If his dog does not take the case when he is commanded to do so, the handler should open his dog's mouth, and put the case in it as he tells him to "Hold it," and immediately praise him. His dog will probably take the case the next time he orders him to do so. Now he should throw the case on the ground in front of him and tell his dog to "Get it." He should discourage him from mouthing or playing with it when he gets it by saying "No, hold it."

The handler should have two key cases, one of which carries his scent. The other should be handled from time to time by some member of his family, and be kept in a plastic bag or an airtight jar to preserve the scent. If the cases are identical, the handler should put a mark on his so that he can quickly identify it.

Now the handler should place both cases on the ground about twenty feet in front of his dog. At first he should work his dog close to him so that he can correct him immediately if he tries to pick up the foreign case. The handler should practice this in different places in the ring. Since the dog is already familiar with the Scent-Discrimination exercise, he will catch on very quickly.

When the dog understands this phase of the exercise, the distance should be increased between the dog and the cases. The handler should pretend to be excited when his dog finds his case so that the dog will be anxious to find it quickly each time. As his dog improves, the handler should make the search a little more difficult. An assistant should be present to place the foreign case two feet from the handler's case, and he should tell the handler immediately if his dog picks up the wrong case.

The handler should include a heeling routine in this exercise as soon as his dog is searching continuously for his case. After a short heeling routine, he should drop his key case surreptitiously, each time in a different place to accustom his dog to searching for it. His assistant should be ready to place the foreign case near the handler's case when the dog is not watching. If the handler is alone, he should carry the foreign case in a small plastic bag. After he has dropped his own case, he should heel his dog to the opposite end of the ring and leave him on a stay command with his back to the case while he drops the foreign case near it. He should always make his dog keep searching for the case. If he stops because he cannot find it, the handler should run out immediately and encourage him to keep working. If necessary, he should show him the case and keep repeating the command "Search mine," every time his dog hesitates. Learning this exercise is only a matter of repetition; the dog will quickly learn the exercise if the handler is patient with him.

When a dog is learning this exercise, he may become discouraged if he doesn't see the case after glancing around once or twice and he may lie down. When this happens, the handler should walk his dog by the collar for a few steps as he leads him toward the case. As he approaches the case, he should let his dog go out ahead of him so that his dog will think that he found it himself, for which he should be praised. The handler should then run backward as he says "Come," and should praise his dog as he responds. If the dog drops the case, the handler should say, "No, get it," and when his dog picks it up again, he should caution him to "Hold it."

This is another difficult exercise but one that any alert dog can learn. The dog that will fail this exercise is the one that searches diligently for the case, spots one of them, and picks it up quickly without checking. The important thing is to keep the dog working fast by encouraging him, and as he improves, keep making it harder to find the case. If the handler makes a game of it, his dog will be eager to learn.

The Agility Exercise

The Agility exercise requires four hurdles that are placed ahead of each other but directly in line. By running and jumping, the dog must be able to clear all four hurdles in succession. The hurdles will be set up in this order: the high jump, the bar jump, the window jump, and the barrier. The jumps will be placed eighteen feet apart, and they will be painted a flat white. The width of each jump shall be four feet, with the exception of the window jump, which is twenty-eight inches wide. The inside measurement of the window is eighteen by eighteen inches.

For all dogs twenty-two inches or over at the withers, the height of the high jump, bar jump, and window jump will be three feet, and of the barrier, six feet. For all dogs fifteen through twenty-one inches at the withers, the first three jumps will be set at thirty inches and the barrier at five feet. For all other dogs, the first three jumps will be set at two feet, and the barrier will be at five feet.

The first two jumps must be jumped clear. The dog must then jump through the window portion of the third jump without touching the hurdle with his feet or any other side with his body. The barrier must be climbed on the dog's first attempt.

To begin, the handler will be standing with his dog at heel position facing the high jump, which is eighteen feet in front of them. When the judge instructs the handler to leave his dog, he will give his dog the signal or verbal command to stay and take his position between the window jump and the barrier, standing about five feet out from them and facing them. Upon order from the judge to "Send your dog," the handler may give his dog a verbal command or signal to jump. When the dog has jumped three hurdles, the handler will make a right-angle turn but remain in the same spot. After the dog has jumped all the hurdles, he will sit straight in front of the handler and then finish smartly upon command or signal.

This exercise was designed to make full use of a dog's jumping ability. The hurdles are narrower than the Utility jumps, which makes building, storing, and moving them much easier; the new width also makes the test more difficult for a dog. The window jump is a challenge because it is purposely narrower than the others in order to tempt a dog to go around it. The dog must gauge himself carefully in order to clear it without touching any portion of it. This newly acquired skill will help him to jump the other hurdles more gracefully. The barrier is an exciting new test of the dog's agility.

This exercise is very beautiful to watch when a dog does it perfectly. In order for a dog to perform this exercise correctly, he must quickly consider each hurdle as he approaches it so that his timing and movements will be coordinated.

The dogs in the class should line up and take turns jumping. Since the dogs already know how to jump the high jump and the bar jump, the first

Joll jumps through the window hurdle without touching it.

Joll jumping through the window jump after clearing the other two hurdles.

lesson will be to teach them to jump the window jump. Each handler should, in turn, stand behind the window jump, but a little off to the side, so that he can place his hand on the bottom section of the window when he asks his dog to jump. By placing his hand there, his dog will understand that he is to jump through the opening. This practice should be repeated until each dog jumps smoothly without touching the lower portion of the window with his feet. This jump is very valuable in that it corrects many jumping problems. Many dogs arch their backs as they are jumping, which will cause them to hit the top of the window with their backs. They will correct themselves when they do this, and after a few attempts, will jump without touching it.

When the dog has learned the window jump, the handler should stand off to the side, give his dog the command "Hup," and praise him when he jumps. He should not let his dog go around the jump at any time; the handler should be fast with his corrections if the dog doesn't jump or if he tries to climb it.

As soon as the dog is jumping smoothly, the handler should combine the first three hurdles. The handlers should practice these until their dogs will take all three in succession on one command. At first a handler may have to give his dog several commands and signals, but with practice, his dog will soon be doing it on just one command.

The next step is to teach the dogs to climb the barrier. This can be done in two stages. The barrier should be set up apart from the other hurdles, the side brackets should be adjusted so that the jump is slanted at a 350-degree angle, and when the platform in the back is also adjusted, the height of the jump should be about four feet. With a little spring, the dog will practically be able to walk over it. The handler should have his dog on leash, and as he runs up to the jump with him, he should say "Hup, climb." He should move over behind the jump quickly so that he can teach his dog to step onto the platform before he jumps to the ground. This will have to be repeated a few times before he is ready for the next step. Some dogs may balk when they see this barrier and refuse to try it; such a dog should be pulled over the jump with the leash while someone else gives him a boost from the rear. If the handler stands on the platform and pulls his dog up with the leash while he encourages him with his voice, the dog will want to try it himself the next time. The dog doesn't understand that he can climb the barrier; until he is forced to try it, he will refuse to attempt it himself. It is important here that the person who is giving the dog a boost from the rear simply support him. He should *not* lift the dog at any time, for the dog must realize that he has to scramble up the jump by himself. The person helping him can guide him, though, by placing his paws on the horizontal strips of wood that are nailed to the barrier for that specific purpose.

Joll learning to climb the six-foot barrier with the jump in the Number Three Position. He is on leash and the author is standing by ready to assist him if necessary.

Joll scales the barrier with the jump in the Number Two Position.

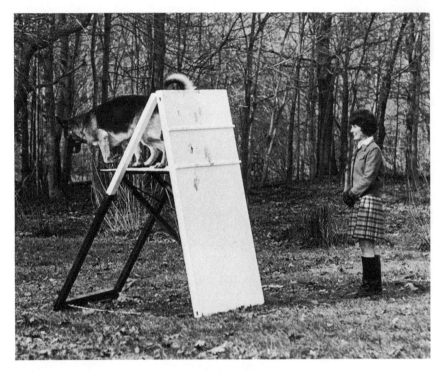

Joll jumps to the platform and then to the ground.

Now that he has learned to jump all four hurdles, they are combined. The barrier is in the Number One or Vertical Position. On one command or signal Joll takes the four hurdles in succession, sits straight in front of the author, then goes to heel upon command. Everyone seems to enjoy this exercise more than any other.

When the dog is climbing the barrier willingly, the handler may set it at the show position, which is a 355-degree angle and a height of six feet. The handler should be sure the jump is strong and steady by testing it with his hands. His dog realizes at this point that he must climb the barrier, so the handler should run him up to the jump as he says "Climb." If his dog balks, he should try it again, encouraging him with his voice. Most dogs will attempt the high barrier once they have learned to do it at a lower level. For a stubborn dog the handler may have to keep lowering the barrier until his dog will get up enough courage to try it. If a dog starts to slide back when he attempts to jump, the handler should quickly support him so that the dog can scramble over it. When the dog climbs the barrier, the handler should praise him excitedly, for the dog will be proud of himself and should be praised. Dogs enjoy climbing, for it is more natural for them than jumping. It is not really a difficult exercise. I have taught six of my dogs to do this in just one lesson.

Once the dogs have acquired the knack of climbing the barrier, the instructor should combine all four hurdles. At first when a handler is training his dog, he should run alongside the jumps and call "Hup," as his dog takes each jump in succession. If the handler praises his dog as he jumps each hurdle, the dog will think it is great fun. Eventually the handler will be able to stand alongside the jumps, and when he calls "Hup," his dog will jump all four hurdles in succession.

There will be times when a dog will try to go around a particular hurdle; these times the handler should stop, take his dog back, and make him jump before going on to the next one.

It is not difficult for the dogs to learn to jump these hurdles. It is more difficult to teach a dog to jump them smoothly, without hesitation, and to climb the barrier without stopping in front of it. A dog should take all three jumps smoothly and with perfect rhythm and continue over the barrier, even though he will probably change his stride the last six feet so that he can be prepared to crouch, leap, and climb in one fast motion which will propel him over the barrier. It is a beautiful jump to watch when it is done right.

As with the other jumping exercises, the handlers should take turns practicing these hurdles with their dogs.

The Long Jump Exercise

Taking the measurements at the top of the hurdles, the Long Jump will be seven feet long for dogs twenty-one inches or over at the withers, six feet long for dogs sixteen through twenty-one inches at the withers, and five feet long for all other dogs. There will be five individual hurdles spaced an equal distance apart to reach the required length. The jump will be three feet wide and two feet high for all dogs over fifteen inches high and one foot high for all other dogs.

With his dog sitting at heel position, the handler will stand thirty feet from the Long Jump but directly in line with it. On order from the judge to "Leave your dog," the handler will give his dog the stay signal or command, take a position three feet beyond and one foot from the side of the Long Jump, and face it.

Or order from the judge to "Send your dog," the handler will give his dog a verbal command or signal to jump. When the dog is landing, the handler will take a right-angle turn and the dog will come and sit in front of the handler. Upon order from the judge to "Finish," the handler will command or signal his dog to do so. The judge must take a position near the bar jump and must not move until the dog is sitting in front of his handler. The stewards must be near the entrance outside the first perimeter of the ring.

The dog that does not clear the jump, does not jump on the first command, knocks one of the hurdles over, or does not return and sit in front of his handler will be failed. The dog that touches a hurdle or anticipates the jump command or signal will receive a substantial point deduction. Minor deductions will be made for a poor sit or finish or no sit or finish.

This is a difficult hurdle to jump, but it can be mastered if the handler will teach his dog to do it in easy stages. There are three reasons why this

Joll clears the Long Jump, which is eight feet in length.

hurdle is difficult and why it is a challenge. First, it is a long jump. Second, although it is two feet high (or one foot high, depending upon the size of the dog), the dog must jump considerably higher than that in order to clear the full length. Third, it is what I call a blind jump because a dog will be able to see only a quarter of it until he is in the air. This means he must learn to gauge his distance by his handler's position.

The first lesson should be an introduction to this type of jump. The handlers should line up and take turns jumping their dogs. Each handler should have his dog jump over one hurdle, then two, and then three, stretching out the hurdles until his dog is jumping half of the required length. As the dog approaches the jump, the handler should run up to the hurdles with him and say "Hup," praising his dog every time he jumps them. He can build up his dog's confidence at this time and let his dog think this new jump is easy and great fun.

A Utility dog should be able to do this easily off leash, but if a dog balks, try him on leash. The dog should be jumping half the required distance off leash before the next step is attempted.

Now the handler should add another hurdle. Leaving his dog on a sit stay about twenty feet from the jump, he should take a position about two feet beyond the Long Jump. He should then call his dog by name, and when he gets to the most advantageous position for a takeoff, say "Hup." If his dog clears the jump, the handler should add another hurdle, spacing them an equal distance apart so that his dog will now be clearing three quarters of the required jump. The handlers should work on this length for at least a week.

Now the handler should have his dog try a longer jump. This type of hurdle demands a running jump and should be taken with the dog moving at a fast trot or gallop. The dog must build up enough momentum in his dash to the jump and his subsequent leap into the air to clear the hurdles. The principle is the same as that employed by a pole-vaulter taking a fast sprint to clear a jump. For at least three weeks, the handler should start his dog each day at three-quarters of the required length and work up to the full length. He should continue this practice until he is quite certain that his dog can clear the full length on his first attempt. If, for some reason, a handler isn't able to work with his dog for more than a week's time, he should go back to using three-quarters of the required distance when he resumes his training.

The handler should not rush his dog into this, but should play it safe and give his dog the chance to build up his confidence in his jumping ability. Remember, too, that a dog must get in condition gradually to be able to jump this distance. An athlete always builds himself up gradually before he is ready to make an all-out effort.

When the handlers have reached this stage in class, each should be given all the space he needs so that his dog can be given the opportunity to concentrate on his jumping. A dog that is distracted by another dog or a person moving nearby might crash into the jump. This is one jump that should be practiced under ideal conditions. Later when the dog is fully trained, distractions will not disturb him, for he will realize he must keep his mind on his jumping in order to do it.

Above all, remember that this a difficult jump that will require considerable practice and patience. Do not practice this jump unless the dog is in top condition and the ground is clean, is free of small stones, and provides a dry, firm footing for the takeoff and landing. The ideal place to practice is on a level stretch of lawn as the grass will cushion the dog's landing. Never practice when there is any danger of a dog slipping.

16 | *THE VERSATILITY CLASS*

This is a nonregular class that is found at obedience specialty trials. A dog may be handled by his owner or another person and should be capable of doing the Novice, Open, and Utility exercises. The handler must bring his dumbbell, scent-discrimination articles, and directed retrieve gloves into the ring with him. The high jump, bar jump, and broad jump will be set up in the ring.

The handler will select a card from the judge that will tell him what exercises his dog will perform from the Novice, Open, and Utility exercises. There are several different combinations, and it is a matter of luck whether the handler chooses a card that contains the most difficult exercises or the easiest ones. If the dog knows the individual exercises from all three classes, he will have no problem.

The order of judging and maximum scores are as follows:

1.	Novice exercise	25 points
2.	Novice exercise	25 points
3.	Open exercise	35 points
4.	Open exercise	35 points
5.	Utility exercise	40 points
6.	Utility exercise	40 points
	Maximum Total Score	200 points

17 | *THE TRACKING CLASS*

The American Kennel Club will issue a Tracking Dog certificate to a registered dog, and will permit the use of the letters "T.D." after the name of each dog that has been certified by two judges to have passed a licensed or member Tracking Test in which at least three dogs actually competed.

Tracking is becoming a popular sport, and there is no reason why an obedience club shouldn't conduct tracking classes if they have an instructor who is qualified to teach them.

A Tracking Test is conducted by an accredited obedience training club, but there are very few tests in one area during the course of a year. Each month the Tracking Tests are listed in the leading dog publications. Not many handlers train their dogs to track because it is time-consuming, there are very few qualified trainers who can help them, and it is becoming increasingly difficult each year to find fields one can use for practicing.

Several large fields are required for a Tracking Test. Each contestant will work a track that is not less than 440 yards nor more than 550 yards long. It is easy to see why Tracking Tests are not held at dog shows. The scent left by the track-layer should be at least half an hour old but no more than two hours old. The length of the leash used in tracking must be twenty to forty feet, and the dog must work at this length with no help from the handler.

Two judges will judge the Tracking Test and keep duplicate charts of each track, showing the length in yards of each leg, major landmarks, and boundaries. The course the dog pursues is to be marked on the charts, and both judges will forward a signed copy of this to the American Kennel Club with a notation "Passed" or "Failed" on each copy.

If the dog is not tracking and taking the turns correctly, he will not be marked "Passed," even though he may come upon the article while he is wandering around. The object of the test is for the dog to follow the track-layer's scent as closely as weather conditions permit.

The instructor should check the dates of the Tracking Tests scheduled in his area so that he may plan to have his handlers ready for it. He must plan about six months ahead in order to be ready. To enter a Tracking Test, the handler's entry must be accompanied by a certificate signed by a qualified Tracking judge, stating that the dog is considered ready for such a test. The American Kennel Club will furnish the instructor with the names of the Tracking judges in his area. The judge will want to see the handler and his dog work an actual track first to determine whether the dog is ready for a test.

Tracking is not the great mystery that many people claim it to be. The dog simply follows a scent that has been left by someone walking over the ground. Some of this scent clings to the ground, some is airborne and is wafted away on the wind currents and deposited on anything in its path. The scent is carried on air currents, and if the handler will study these, he will have a good idea of the way the scent is carried along. A handler doesn't have to be a meteorologist or have any special scientific knowledge in order to teach his dog to track. All it requires is a little common sense.

When I go walking in the woods after a rainstorm, the scent all around me is very strong and pungent; this is a sharp contrast to the light fragrance I enjoy on a sunny day. My common sense tells me, when I am tracking, that the scent is stronger on wet grass, low boggy areas, shady spots, sheltered valleys, and the leeward side of the hills. These, then, will be the easiest places for the dog to pick up the scent.

If the handler will notice how the air currents carry smoke, he will get an idea what they could do with scent. When the wind changes capriciously, the smoke is tossed around helplessly. It is no wonder a dog will work off the track on a windy day, and it is a matter of common sense to train a dog to work as close to the actual track as possible.

While training, it is wiser for the handler to keep bringing the dog back to the track by guiding him with the leash than to let him follow the scent which is being scattered by the wind. If the handler will do this the first month or so, his dog will get in the habit of working close to the track.

The training method that I used in 1952 to earn my first two Tracking Dog titles is basically the same one I use today. By observing and studying my dogs I have concluded that this method is a sound one.

Any opinions I have on tracking have been formed as a result of watching my dogs; I'm sure if anyone were to observe his own dog he would reach the same conclusions.

It is perfectly natural for a dog to use his nose in the same manner in which humans use their eyes. A person is never satisfied to have something described to him, he must see for himself. A dog is never satisfied to look at something, he wants to sniff it. A dog sees with his nose. Dogs do not accept what they see; they believe what they smell. They use their noses throughout their lives to help them make decisions. A dog will catalog a person's scent in his mind for years and eventually when he meets this old friend or foe he will recognize him by scent alone.

Dogs differentiate between members of a family by scent alone. Even when one tries to fool a dog by having two members of a family exchange clothes the dog finds it a very elementary test to distinguish between them. Everyone has a different scent just as everyone has a different set of fingerprints.

When following a trail, a dog is following a total scent. In other words, the scent of crushed vegetation and the track-layer's clothing, personal articles, body odor, hair, and breath are mingling together. The dog will follow this scent in two ways: by finding it on the ground and by sniffing it in the air.

With a no-wind condition scent will remain in the air for hours at a time. I have noticed this many times and the following incident is just one example. One morning when my dog and I were visiting my mother I called a friend and asked him to stop by my home at noontime and pick up some papers I needed. That evening when I returned and opened the door my dog dashed through the house barking angrily. It gave me a start at first until I realized he had picked up the scent of my friend who had stopped in earlier. The person was a stranger to the dog and his scent was that of an intruder. No one had been in the house all day so the scent remained undisturbed.

I believe that scent flies off a person whether he is sitting or walking. I have seen a dog go up to a chair where a friend of his was sitting an hour earlier and start wagging his tail. He hadn't known that his friend was visiting us until he came in the house later and smelled the chair.

When a person is walking scent particles fly out from him in all directions. The heaviest of these particles fall close to him and those that are of medium weight fly out from him and settle to the ground a little farther away. The lightweight scent particles are airborne for different lengths of time depending upon the weather conditions at the time. It is my opinion that the scent that a dog picks up on the ground is a combination of the total scent that I mentioned earlier and not just a shoe or foot odor scent. It has never seemed to make any difference to a good tracking dog what kind of footwear, if any, the track-layer wore. I found a dog would follow a scent even if the track-layer wore plastic bags over his shoes. The dog appeared to be following the total scent which was present both on the ground and in the air.

The scent that is in the air is the same as that on the ground. To believe this one must realize that a moving body is enveloped by an air current and as one strides along the body, arms, and legs create a certain amount of turbulence. I believe that the body creates small parallel shoulder vortices that are agitated by the arms swinging back and forth. The amount of turbulence caused by every stride forces the scent particles that are flying out from the body, and up from the ground, to be tumbled around in the air. The scent is therefore scattered along a track that could be twenty or more feet wide. Wind currents play a part here in depositing the scent particles on anything in their path. The scent that lasts the longest is that that falls to the ground or adheres to some stationary object. The lightweight scent particles never reach the ground but remain airborne until they fade away or are dispersed by wind currents or weather conditions. It is my opinion that different kinds of vegetation absorb the heavy scent particles more than others. Dogs very often will take more time to sniff certain weeds as if the scent is stronger on them than others.

When tracking on snow I found that the dog would always follow the air scent and give little regard to the prints that were visible in the snow. He always depended upon his nose and never used his eyes. In the warm weather the dog would have difficulty tracking over a freshly plowed field. The scent didn't seem to stay very long and although I could see the footprints of the track-layer, the dog would be using the air scent to run the track. Here the convection currents present in a freshly plowed field were carrying the scent particles up into the air.

The older the track the harder it is for the dog to find it. This might be for several reasons. Heavy rain will wash out a track but a light drizzle, humidity, or early morning fog will preserve it. Direct sunlight seems to dry up the scent just as an exposed drop of perfume will fade away quickly in the sun. A strong wind seems to eradicate the air scent in a short time.

The best way to teach a dog to track at the very beginning is to have someone he loves lay the track, leave his glove, and hide either on the ground or behind some object about twenty feet beyond the end of the track. The dog will be so anxious to find his friend that he will start working naturally with little urging.

The instructor should have his handlers work in groups of two. Each handler will lay the track for his own dog, but his partner will work the dog on the actual track.

The instructor should find good open fields where the grass is about eight inches high and there are no burrs or thorns. If it is possible, the tracks should be laid out in the open away from natural boundaries. The practice sessions should take place early in the morning or late in the evening when it is less windy. Each handler should take his dog out to the tracking field on leash; he should not put his dog's tracking harness on him until his dog is ready to work on the track. In the beginning the handler should use a twenty-foot leash and clip it to his dog's harness.

The handler should make his dog sit where he can see him laying the track. Before he starts, he should pet his dog and tell him to be a good boy, or say something he understands to arouse his interest. At the start of the track, the handler should plant a stake in the ground, scuff his feet for the first twenty feet, and then plant another stake. He should then walk in a straight line about two hundred feet, plant another stake, continue on for another ten feet, and then take a slight turn to the right, like the hands of a clock pointing to five past six. He should go straight for fifty feet, drop the glove, continue straight on for twenty feet to a hiding place, lie down, and wait for his partner to work his dog on the track.

When the handler is laying the first two hundred feet of track, he should stop occasionally to wave to his dog and say something to get the dog excited, such as "Good-by, Hussan," using his dog's name. His dog will be sure he is missing something and want to follow him.

In order for the track-layer to walk a perfectly straight track, he should keep his eye on some tree or object on the horizon and walk toward it. If he looks down at the ground, his track will weave all over the place. The track-layer's job is important—he should always do it correctly.

After waiting five minutes, the partner should take the handler's dog up to the first stake, make him lie down with his nose close to the scuffed earth, point to the spot without putting his hand in front of the dog's nose, and say excitedly, "See, track." As soon as the dog takes a good sniff, he should let him start tracking. The dog will be very interested in finding his handler and should need little urging to stay out at the end of the leash and pull. If he should hesitate for any reason, he should be told to "Track," and the partner could point to the trail as he gives him the order. When the dog reaches the glove, he should pick it up and return it to the

Point to the scuff mark, or the starting point, but do not put your hand ahead of your dog's nose where he would get your scent.

partner, who should praise him. The dog should then be sent out again to find his handler who is still hiding. The handler should make a big fuss over him. If the dog is not interested in returning the glove to the partner, he should carry it to his handler.

I believe it is best to start a dog tracking after he has learned to retrieve, but it isn't absolutely necessary. Even if a dog has had no obedience training at all, he should be able to comprehend the tracking lessons and go on to earn his tracking title.

By working on tracks of this kind, with either a left or right turn, for a few days, the dog will think it is great fun. It is not necessary to give the dog food as a reward when using this method; he has all the incentive he needs—he is finding someone he loves.

Now the handler should lay a track with a slightly sharper turn; one that resembles the hands of a clock pointing to ten past six. Repeat this track several times, until the dog does it well. The next day try some tracks with the turn to the left, resembling the hands of a clock pointing to ten minutes to six. The track-layer should not scuff the track now.

The handlers should try these tracks with each other's dogs, getting in as much practice as they can. The tracks should be aged for five minutes in the beginning; as the dogs become proficient, the age of the track

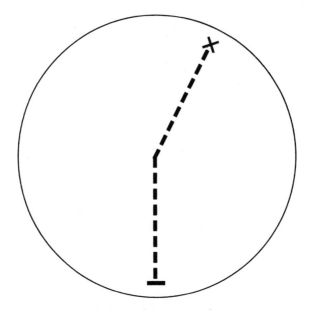

Slight angle turn to right.

should be increased to ten minutes and then to fifteen minutes. By this time the dogs will understand that they have to follow a certain scent if they are going to find the gloves and their handlers. It is at this point that each handler should start working with his own dog. The partners should lay the tracks from now on.

Now the dog should be ready to try his first right-angle turn, which on the clock would be fifteen minutes past six. The handler should encourage his dog to work at the end of the leash. When he approaches the corner, the handler should be prepared to give him enough leash so that he can overrun the turn, come back, circle around until he finds the track, and continue on. The handler should never let his dog pass him and start backtracking to the starting point. If the handler stands about twenty feet from the turn, his dog will have plenty of room to circle and pick up the track. The turns should always be made at least ten feet beyond a stake so that the dog doesn't get wise about turning when he sees a stake.

The handler should notice how his dog takes a turn; later, when he is following a blind trail, he will recognize a turn by the individual manner in which his dog searches for it. Dogs differ a great deal in this respect. The handler should study his dog so that he can eventually recognize a turn by the signal he gives him. A dog may whine, lift his head, drop his tail, circle, or give some other indication of a change of direction. The dog should be praised every time he takes a turn correctly.

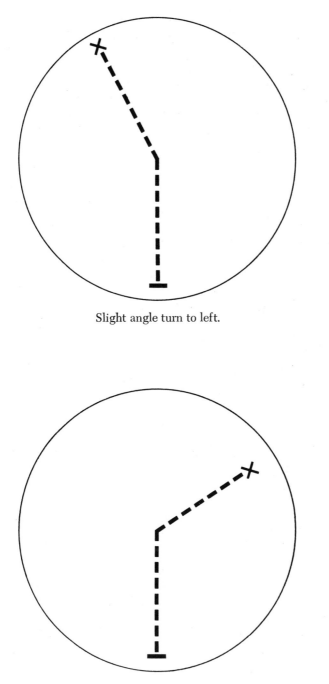

Slight angle turn to left.

Sharper turn to right.

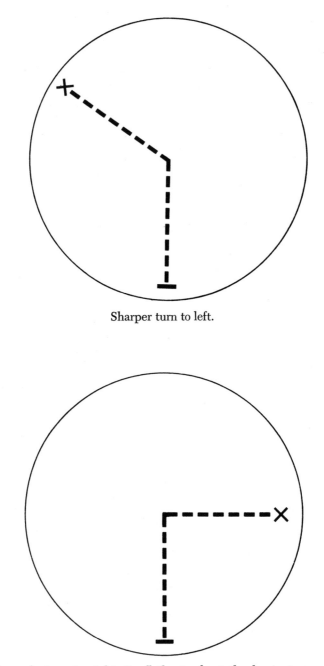

Sharper turn to left.

Right-angle turn to right. Scuff the track at the beginning and at the center turn.

The handler should not expect his dog to make a turn at the exact point. Most dogs overrun the turn about twenty feet before they realize they are no longer on the track. Then they return to the turn and start checking before striking out again on the right track. If the wind is blowing toward the handler, his dog will probably pick up the turn before actually reaching it and will then work parallel to the actual track; then, when the dog is opposite the track-layer's wallet or glove, he will pick up the scent in the air and make a turn toward it. If there is a cross wind, the

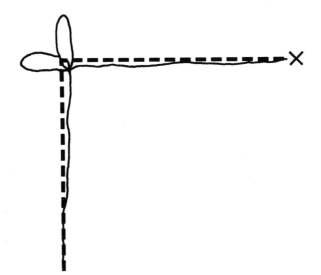

A dog may overrun the turn, come back to it, then strike out in another direction before he again returns and finds the track.

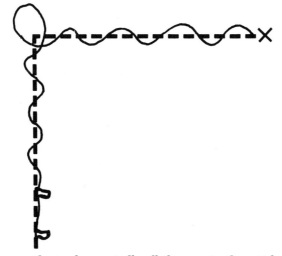

A dog may cross the track repeatedly all the way to the article.

Wind. Some of the track-layer's scent is still on the actual track, but most dogs will follow the scent that the wind has carried some distance from it.

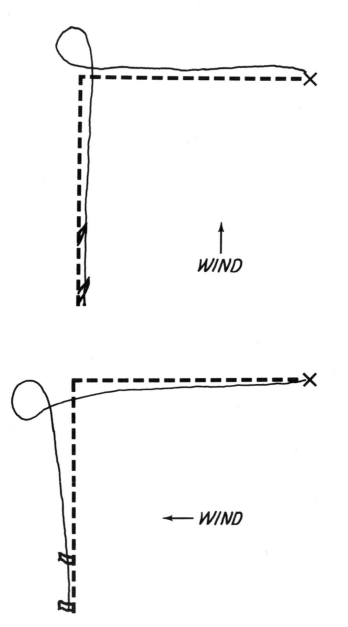

dog will work alongside the actual track; the distance from the track will vary depending on the wind direction, wind velocity, and terrain. If the dog has his tail to the wind, he will stay close to the track.

The exception to the above is the perfect tracking dog that keeps his nose down on the track every inch of the way. Wind makes no difference to this dog, for he is working close to the ground with his nose in the grass. I have seen dogs such as this take right-angle turns without any hesitation whatever. The work was so flawless that they did not have to stop at any point to double-check. Trackers like this are few and far between.

Dogs can be taught to work close to the ground by starting them on closely cropped grass and by working them on a ten-foot lead. When the dog has become accustomed to keeping his nose to the ground, the tracks can be laid in fields where the grass is longer. The leash should be played out gradually, until he is working on a thirty-foot leash. The important thing is to wait until the dog is doing an excellent track on the ten-foot lead.

When the handler feels certain that his dog has mastered the ninety-degree turn to the right, he should follow the same procedure to teach him the ninety-degree turn to the left. The handler should practice these turns a week or more, or until he is certain his dog understands them. If the dog gets them down perfectly before he goes on to the next step, it will save the handler a lot of trouble later on. These tracks should be practiced when they have aged five minutes, ten minutes, and fifteen minutes.

From now on the tracks should be three hundred yards in length and should incorporate at least three turns. The handler should use different turns each time. He should start practicing with his dog when the track is five minutes old and gradually work up to a track that has aged twenty minutes. He should now use a forty-foot leash with a knot at twenty feet and one at thirty feet. He should try to work at thirty feet, holding the rest in reserve in case he needs it on a turn.

The handler should discuss the track with the track-layer before he starts. If there are any landmarks, such as a tree, shrub, large boulder, etc., that are visible at a distance, he should use them for turning points instead of stakes. Use stakes only when there is nothing else to mark the turn. Never make the turn precisely at the landmark as the dog will get wise to this. The turns should be made about twenty feet past the landmark; if this is done, the handler will be able to guide his dog correctly. The dog must be convinced that his handler knows exactly where the track leads, for this will encourage him to try harder. If the dog has any notion that his handler doesn't know where the track is and is relying on

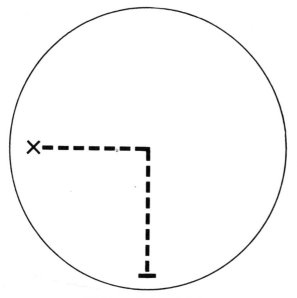

Right-angle turn to left.

him to find it, he might get fresh and start wandering off the track. Nothing prompts a dog to be disobedient quicker than the realization that he has the upper hand. A tracking lesson is not the time to foster such notions.

A dog will occasionally go off the track. It is up to the handler to show him where it is, by pointing to a portion of the track that is heavy with scent. Since the dog will depend on his handler to help him when he gets confused, it is of the utmost importance that the handler always know where the track lies, where each turn should be made, and when to find the glove.

At the start of each track, there should be two flags, spaced thirty yards apart. The track-layer should scuff the ground lightly near the first flag. The dog should be encouraged to take the scent at the first flag and keep his nose to the ground up to the second flag. This distance should be sufficient for the dog to retain the scent enough to follow the trail. A dog will be permitted to return to the first flag to take the scent again, provided that he has not gone beyond the second flag. The dog should not be permitted to play with the flag or retrieve it.

I have noticed many handlers fail in Tracking tests because they did not keep their dogs on a short lead between the two flags. The dog immediately wandered off the track without picking up the scent; he didn't have the remotest idea what he was looking for and wandered around aimlessly. If the handler had held his dog on the track, which is a

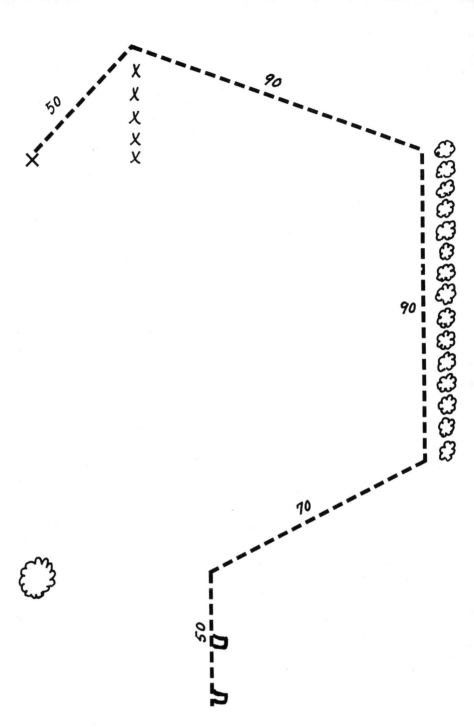

A simple track that you can use at the beginning. When laying a track along a boundary, such as a row of trees, do not work within fifty feet of it.

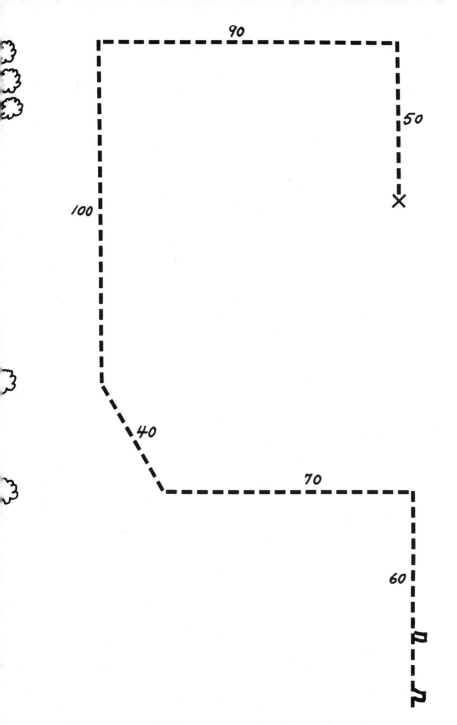

Another practice track that is easy to plan. You will note the turns are made opposite trees, a row of shrubbery, or weeds. When you lay a track, walk toward a distant tree or object and it will keep your line straight.

straight path to the second flag, his dog might have picked up the scent and passed the test. At the second flag, the handler should stand and let his lead play out to twenty feet or more. Every handler has two chances to let his dog pick up the scent between the two flags but very few handlers take advantage of this.

When the dog is doing well, the handler should increase the length of the track to 550 yards and incorporate seven or eight turns. The track-layer will have to plan the track carefully so that he will end up near an exit from the field. He should never become so engrossed in laying the track that he finds himself stuck in a corner of the field with no way out except over the freshly laid track. He should never make a turn sharper than ninety degrees or the dog will cut across to the other portion of the track. The objective is to keep the dog as close to the actual track as possible; avoid laying any tracks that prevent this.

Since tracking fields are generally to be found in the country, it is quite probable that the dog will flush a pheasant or some other game while he is tracking. The handler should caution him to "Track," and insist that he continue to work and ignore the interruption. The handler should try to give his dog the experience of working near cows or horses. Some tracks are laid in fields that adjoin cow pastures. If there are cows or horses grazing in a nearby field, they will all come over to the fence to watch the dog track. They are naturally inquisitive, and they will clop noisily up and down along the fence or stick their heads over and create a general commotion. A dog must be well trained to resist the temptation to dash over and inspect them; it is good experience for him to get this kind of distraction during a practice session. The dog that can work under trying conditions is the dog that will pass.

The dog should now be working on thirty-minute tracks, and the handler must still be absolutely certain where the track is laid. The dog does not realize that the handler cannot smell the track and fully expects help when he misses a turn. At first the handler should encourage him with his voice and guide him with the leash. However, as the dog becomes interested in tracking, the handler should gradually fade into the background and let the dog take the initiative. The handler's part will be to interpret the dog's signals correctly and to try to prevent his dog from tracking too fast. A good tracker gets excited when he knows he is on the trail and is apt to want to rush ahead exuberantly. The dog's speed should be checked from the beginning so that he will not overrun the turns.

Different dogs track different ways. Some zigzag across the track; some work with their noses close to the ground; others work with their heads held so high that one wonders whether they are following the scent at all. Some dogs work so slowly that it is incredible they pass, and some go so

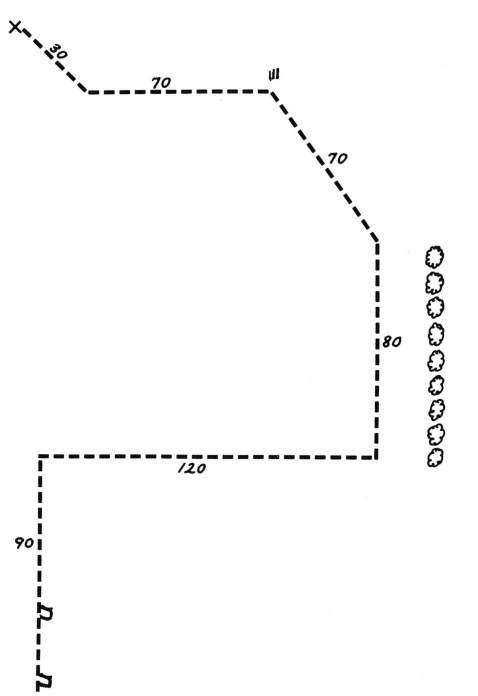

460 yds.

Another example of a well-planned track. This is the type of track you might find at a Tracking Test.

Play out your leash slowly, and hold your dog back so that he will take the time to keep his nose to the ground and get a strong scent.

fast that their handlers have to run around the entire track. What I like to see is the dog who tracks steadily with his nose about six inches from the ground; this is the dog who knows what he is doing.

When the handler checks the wind direction, he should be sure to do so at the dog's level and not his own. Unevenness of terrain cuts down the wind velocity. Test this fact by standing in a field on a windy day and noting the degree of wind at your height; then lie down and note the amount of wind at your dog's height. Most dogs will be taking the scent at a height of fourteen inches or less from the ground.

When the dogs have reached the thirty-minute track and are tracking well, it is time for them to practice with different track-layers. It is important that each track-layer leave his own glove or wallet that carries his

Stand at the second flag and let twenty feet of your leash play out. Place a knot in your leash at thirty feet also so that you may hold the remainder in abeyance until you need it.

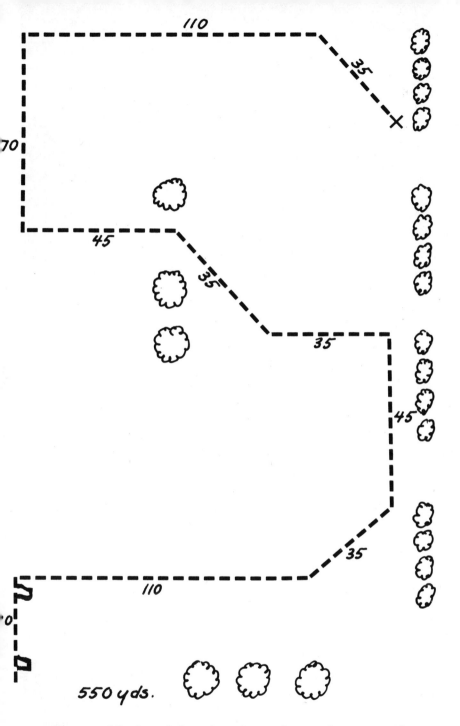

This is a difficult track but planned according to the terrain. When you and your dog can follow a blind track like this you are ready for a Tracking Test. The actual test will be much easier than this.

The leash will be taut like this when your dog is working on the track.

scent. The tracks should be sixty minutes old now, and the dog should practice four days per week.

The final stage is to have an experienced track-layer lay at least five tracks a week for you, without your observing him. The handler must now get used to relying on his dog's nose. The track-layer may follow the handler at a discreet distance and advise him if his dog goes astray. When the handler and his dog have reached this point, they are ready for a Tracking Test.

The instructor should caution his handlers to leave the tracking to the dogs on the day of the test. Since the handler will not be able to see the track, he should make up his mind that he will trust his dog and let him do the work. Many dogs have failed Tracking Tests because their handlers thought they were making the wrong turns and pulled them off the right track.

Judges plan the tracks the day before the Tracking Test, using tracking poles on the turns and at the end of the track. On the day of the test, the poles are removed in numerical order by the track-layer as he lays the actual track. It takes a great deal of time and effort on the part of the judges to prepare a Tracking Test. Therefore, the instructor should be quite sure that his handlers are ready before he advises them to enter.

The Tracking method described here will enable anyone to pass an AKC Tracking Test and get his Tracking title. I have earned the Tracking title with several dogs and have helped dozens of other people get the coveted "T." This is the method that helped each dog pass. The work that is involved is up to the handler; a Tracking title means practice, practice, practice.

18 | *THE JUDGE'S SIDE*

In writing this book I have presented one side of the picture—that of preparing a handler–dog team for competitive obedience trials through expert class instruction and correct practice at home. Up to now the instructor and the handler have been doing all the work, trying to mold an untrained dog into one who is expertly trained for two reasons—to be well mannered at home, and to perform certain obedience exercises as perfectly as possible with the utmost willingness.

In order for an instructor or a handler to excel at this sport, he must have a thorough knowledge of the *American Kennel Club Obedience Regulations* and be able to visualize a handler–dog team giving a perfect performance in each exercise. To better evaluate a dog's ring performance, we should, in all fairness, look at it from the judge's point of view. Here are many of the things a judge must look for in judging each of the exercises, plus the factors that decide the winner.

HEELING ON LEASH

Does the handler start by having his dog sit straight? Do they start heeling at precisely the same time? Is the leash slack at all times? Are the commands given in a soft, authoritative tone of voice? Is the dog watching the handler attentively? Does the dog keep his shoulder in line with his handler's left leg? Does the handler move briskly during the normal pace? Does the dog change pace with the handler? Do they make turns in a natural manner without hesitating? Do they work together smoothly as a team? Does the dog sit straight each time the handler stops? Is the handler gentle with his dog? On the negative side, does the dog lag occasionally? Does the handler give extra body signals, extra signals with his fingers, fumble with the leash, or adapt his pace to that of his dog?

If there are two or three very good dogs, the winner will be the dog–handler team that moves briskly and works with precision and accuracy, displaying the zeal that is evident when there is rapport between dog and handler. Rapport can be recognized by the many outward signs the dog gives to express his feelings; these might be the erect way he walks, the proud manner in which he holds his head, the happy expression on his face, the gleam in his eye, the swish of his tail, or the attentive manner in which he watches his handler. These signs should not be confused with any momentary signs given by the dog that has been trained with force methods, such as when the dog wags his tail in relief when the handler gives a feigned "Good dog" for the benefit of the judge. The dog's deportment during the exercise will betray his true feelings, which are those of uneasiness and distrust. His ears will be held back close to his head, his eyes clouded over with apprehension, his body in a semicrouch ready to jump aside, and his expression, while working, one of forced resignation and obedience rather than willingness. A keen judge will differentiate between these two dogs and penalize the latter. By recognizing and penalizing a dog who has been trained with force, we can eventually eradicate this cruel practice.

FIGURE EIGHT

Does the dog start heeling on the command "Heel"? Does he keep his shoulder in line with his handler continually? Does the handler stay close to the posts, and does he keep the leash slack at all times? Does the dog have straight sits? On the negative side, does he crowd his handler on the inside turn or lag behind on the outside turn? Does the handler give his dog extra signals when he feels the judge can't see him?

The important factor here is the dog's ability to keep his shoulder in line with his handler's left leg without crowding or going wide. I would consider it a bad fault if I saw a dog heeling behind his handler's left leg on turns, for it could only mean that the dog had been poorly trained.

STAND FOR EXAMINATION

Does the handler stand and leave his dog quickly? Does he turn his back and walk away from his dog, and does he stand about six feet from him? Does the handler give the stay command in a gentle, authoritative voice?

The dog is expected to stay without moving his feet and should show no shyness or resentment when the judge examines him.

HEEL FREE

The judge will be looking for the same errors that might be made in the Heeling-on-Leash exercise.

Again the factors to be considered between the top workers would be precision, rapport, accuracy, gentleness, and smoothness of handling.

RECALL

Does the handler give his dog a quiet "Stay" command? Does the dog respond to his handler's commands quickly and move briskly? Does the dog have three straight sits?

The obedience regulations state that the dog should move at a brisk pace, so this is all that should be required of him. The judge should not expect all breeds of dogs to run every time they are executing a command. Running may be natural for some breeds, but it is certainly not desirable for most of them. A dog is moving at a brisk pace when he is trotting.

LONG SIT AND LONG DOWN

Does the handler give his dog a quiet stay command? Does the dog stay in position quietly until the handler returns? Does the dog drop on the handler's command and/or signal without crawling? Does the dog remain in position when the handler returns?

DROP ON RECALL

Does the dog stay in position when he is told? Does the dog drop instantly when given the command or signal? Does the handler give the verbal command in a moderate tone of voice? Does the dog respond immediately to the handler's command or signal to come? Is the dog working at a brisk pace? Does the dog sit straight? On the negative side, does the handler hold the signal too long? Does the dog slow down in anticipation of a drop?

The main factor here is the dog's instant response to the *down* and the *come* commands.

RETRIEVE ON THE FLAT

Does the handler control his dog with a quiet, authoritative tone of voice? Does the dog move out briskly to retrieve the dumbbell, pick it up immediately, and return with it at a brisk pace? Are the three sits straight?

The judge would like to see a dog trot out briskly and retrieve the dumbbell without hesitation. He should appear to be enjoying the work.

RETRIEVE OVER THE HIGH JUMP

Does the handler give the stay command in a moderate tone? Does the dog move briskly, jump gracefully, and clear the jump both ways? Does he pick up the dumbbell without hesitating? Does the dog carry the dumbbell without mouthing, playing, chewing, or dropping it? Are the sits straight? They should be at least eight feet or more from the high jump, and the handler should not move.

The judge would like to see the dog jump gracefully without any hesitation, pick up the dumbbell immediately, and return it to his handler at a brisk pace.

THE BROAD JUMP

Does the handler leave his dog sitting at least eight feet from the broad jump? Does he stand two feet out from the side of the jump, taking a ninety-degree turn when his dog is in midair while remaining on the same spot? Does the dog respond immediately and jump straight over the middle section of the hurdles? Does he land, take the necessary steps to slow him down, return to his handler, and sit straight? Does the handler use any body signals?

The main factors here are for the dog to jump gracefully, turn promptly, and sit straight.

SIGNAL EXERCISE

Is the heeling worthy of a dog in the Utility class? Does the handler–dog team work with coordination, precision, and accuracy? Does the handler give the signals without any excessive body movements? Does the dog respond to each signal immediately, and does he watch his handler attentively? Does the dog work at a brisk pace throughout the whole exercise? Are the sits straight?

A judge would expect a Utility dog to be able to heel perfectly. The dog should respond to the signals immediately without moving out of position. The dog should be very alert and attentive, and the handler should give signals that are made with one hand and arm only.

SCENT DISCRIMINATION

Does the handler give his dog the command or signal to retrieve without bending his body, waving his arms, nodding his head, stepping forward, or screaming at his dog? Does the handler apply his scent to the article quickly? Does the dog move forward briskly, keep working until he finds the article, and return without mouthing, chewing, or dropping it? Does he sit close enough to the handler? Does he relinquish the article without any further commands? Are the three sits straight for each retrieve?

DIRECTED RETRIEVE

Does the dog turn and sit straight on the handler's command? Does the handler give the signal and command without sitting on his ankles to do it? Does the dog go out straight, move briskly to pick up the glove, and retrieve it without hesitating, mouthing, or playing with it? Are the sits straight? Does the handler who gives the direction to his dog immediately follow it with the command? And does the handler who elects to give his dog the direction by motioning toward the glove as he simultaneously gives the command keep his hand in back of his dog's head before he motions? Does the handler give his dog the direction in seven seconds or less?

The main factors here are the dog's ability to turn with precision, the handler's smooth signal to his dog, and the dog's willing and accurate retrieve.

DIRECTED JUMPING

Does the dog go out straight for at least twenty feet beyond the jumps? Does he sit on command? Does he respond promptly to his handler's signal to jump? Does he jump gracefully without touching either jump? Does the handler turn when his dog is in midair? Does the dog have six perfect sits?

The dog's precision is the main factor here. His straight send-out, prompt response to commands, graceful jumping, and quick returns are all to be considered when evaluating this exercise.

If a dog works perfectly, he deserves to receive a perfect score. Only a judge with a limited amount of personal experience would say, "No dog deserves a perfect score." Because he has never attained this achievement is no reason that he should deny a perfect score to the handler–dog team which earns one. It takes a great deal of time and work to bring a dog to the point of perfection. Although every perfect score is a new thrill, the handler will derive most of his pleasure from watching his dog respond to his commands in his individual way. Many intelligent dogs who are capable of working perfectly become self-conscious when they compete in shows, and it takes a great deal of time and experience for them to overcome this feeling. Often a dog that acts up in a show is not doing so because he is deliberately being disobedient; he is reacting the way a small child would when asked to perform before strangers.

Throughout this book I have given the instructor and the handler–dog team very sound advice so they could develop the skills necesary to become good trainers and expert handlers. The *AKC Obedience Regulations* have been fully covered so that the instructors and handlers will be as familiar with them as the judges. Despite all this, when the handler–dog teams are competing in shows, there will be days when the dogs goof for one reason or another, or the handlers commit errors because they are nervous or momentarily forget the rules. This is to be expected occasionally, but what a handler will find discouraging is having his dog fail because the judge didn't interpret the rules correctly or for one reason or another caused the handler's' dog to fail.

It is a privilege to be licensed by the American Kennel Club to judge obedience trials. Obedience judges should acknowledge this by employing a standard of ethics that places them above pettiness, favoritism, or egoism. The vast majority of judges are sincere, hardworking, knowledgeable people who were handlers or instructors at one time. Handlers find it a pleasure showing their dogs under judges such as these.

A cross section of handlers were asked what they admired or disliked about obedience judges and the following comments are the result of this survey.

Handlers admire the efficient judge who is in full command of his ring. This judge makes sure the ring is the correct size; is kept free of trash, such as paper articles that might blow into the ring; insists that the grass is short; and keeps spectators, dogs, and children several feet away from the ring while he is judging.

He starts his class on time, and if, for some valid reason, he is not judging in catalog order, he advises his steward to notify each handler when it will be his turn in the ring.

Without appearing to hurry, he judges efficiently without any lost motion. He lets the handlers wait outside the ring until he is ready to judge and greets everyone with a smile.

During the heeling routines in Novice, Open, and Utility, this considerate judge will keep his distance when judging because he is capable of seeing any errors without interfering with the dog's performance. Handlers dislike the way some judges walk beside them when they are heeling, run beside them when they go fast, and jump around the handlers when they stop to study the sits. The efficient judge is able to make an honest appraisal of the handler–dog team without such antics. The ideal handler–dog team should work in a natural manner. One can guess how completely unnatural this type of behavior would seem to a dog, and how it might interfere with his work.

This same objection applies to the judge who stands too close to the dog when he is performing an exercise. This could apply to the Recall, Drop-on-Recall, or Retrieve exercises. Handlers prefer the judge who gives them quiet, unobtrusive signals for the Recall, Drop-on-Recall, and Signal exercises that do not attract the attention of their dogs.

They admire the judge who doesn't permit his stewards to interfere with the handler–dog team. He cautions them to sit down or stand near the ring entrance when the handler is working near the judge's table.

His exemplary procedure in judging the Scent-Discrimination exercise includes advising his steward not to touch the two working articles or over-handle the remaining articles as he is placing them down, and to be sure the handler–dog team watches him do this. It is a nice gesture when the steward places the two working articles in a plastic bag after the exercise is finished.

The point was raised that handlers object to Novice dogs executing the Recall exercise at the ring entrance. Similar objections were raised to the positioning of a dog so that he must go toward the ring entrance when executing the retrieve or the broad jump. These situations are probably an oversight on the judge's part and not intentional.

Handlers admire the judge who designates different glove numbers for successive dogs as they enter his ring. This seems to be a very fair way of officiating. The judge who suddenly disregards this practice to give a particular handler glove 3 is obviously hoping the dog will fail. Such pettiness is unbecoming to a licensed judge.

The handlers also stressed their preference for the knowledgeable judge who directed them to stand about twenty feet from the jumps in the Directed Jumping exercise, and not thirty feet because the ring was oversized.

It was also acknowledged that the judge who examined the dogs in the Group Examination in a straightforward manner without trying any cute tricks to get the dogs to move was their idea of an excellent judge.

In summary, everyone prefers those judges who understand the rules thoroughly and are considerate in their interpretation of them.

AMERICAN KENNEL CLUB OBEDIENCE REGULATIONS

PURPOSE

Obedience trials are a sport and all participants should be guided by the principles of good sportsmanship both in and outside of the ring. The purpose of obedience trials is to demonstrate the usefulness of the pure-bred dog as a companion of man, not merely the dog's ability to follow specified routines in the obedience ring. While all contestants in a class are required to perform the same exercises in substantially the same way so that the relative quality of the various performances may be compared and scored, the basic objective of obedience trials is to produce dogs that have been trained and conditioned always to behave in the home, in public places, and in the presence of other dogs, in a manner that will reflect credit on the sport of obedience. The performances of dog and handler in the ring must be accurate and correct and must conform to the requirements of these regulations. However, it is also essential that the dog demonstrate willingness and enjoyment of its work, and that smoothness and naturalness on the part of the handler be given precedence over a performance based on military precision and peremptory commands.

CHAPTER I
GENERAL REGULATIONS

Section 1. **Obedience Clubs.** An obedience club that meets all the requirements of The American Kennel Club and wishes to hold an Obedience Trial at which qualifying scores toward an obedience title may be awarded, must make application to The American Kennel Club on the form provided for permission to hold such trial. Such a trial, if approved, may be held either in conjunction with a dog show or as a separate event. If the club is not a member of The American Kennel Club it shall pay a license fee for the privilege of holding such trial, the amount of which shall be determined by the Board of Directors of The American Kennel Club. If the club fails to hold its trial at the time and place which have been approved, the amount of the license fee paid will be returned.

Section 2. **Dog Show and Specialty Clubs.** A dog show club may be granted permission to hold a licensed or member obedience trial at its dog show, and a specialty club may also be granted permission to hold a licensed or member obedience trial if, in the opinion of the Board of Directors of The American Kennel Club, such clubs are qualified to do so.

Section 3. **Obedience Classes.** A licensed or member obedience trial need not include all of the regular obedience classes defined in these Regulations, but a club will be approved to hold Open classes only if it also holds Novice classes, and a club will be approved to hold a Utility class only if it also holds Novice and Open classes. A specialty club which has been approved to hold a licensed or member obedience trial, if qualified in the opinion of the Board of Directors of The American Kennel Club, or an obedience club which has been approved to hold a licensed or member obedience trial may, subject to the approval of The American Kennel Club, offer additional nonregular classes for dogs not less than six months of age, provided a clear and complete description of the eligibility requirements and performance requirements for each such class appears in the premium list. However, the nonregular classes defined in these Regulations need not be described in the premium list. Pre-Novice classes will not be approved at licensed or member obedience trials.

Section 4. **Tracking Tests.** A club that has been approved to hold licensed or member obedience trials and that meets the requirements of The American Kennel Club, may also make application to hold a Tracking Test. A club may not hold a tracking test on the same day as its show or obedience trial, but the tracking test may be announced in the premium list for the show or trial, and the tracking test entries may be included in the show or obedience trial catalog. If the entries are not listed in the catalog for the show or obedience trial, the club must provide, at the tracking test, several copies of a sheet, which may be typewritten, giving all the information that would be contained in the catalog for each entered dog. If the tracking test is to be held within 7 days of the obedience trial the entries must be sent to the same person designated to receive the obedience trial entries, and the same closing date should apply. If the tracking test is not to be held within 7 days of the obedience trial the club may name someone else in the premium list to receive the tracking test entries, and may specify a different closing date for entries at least 7 days before the tracking test.

The presence of a veterinarian shall not be required at a tracking test.

Section 5. **Obedience Trial Committee.** If an obedience trial is held by an obedience club, an Obedience Trial Committee must be appointed by the club, and this committee shall exercise all the authority vested in a dog show's

Bench Show Committee. If an obedience club holds its obedience trial in conjunction with a dog show, then the Obedience Trial Committee shall have sole jurisdiction only over those dogs entered in the obedience trial and their handlers and owners; provided, however, that if any dog is entered in both obedience and breed classes, then the Obedience Trial Committee shall have jurisdiction over such dog, its owner, and its handler, only in matters pertaining to the Obedience Regulations, and the Bench Show Committee shall have jurisdiction over such dog, its owner and handler, in all other matters.

When an obedience trial is to be held in conjunction with a dog show by the club which has been granted permission to hold the show, the club's Bench Show Committee shall include one person designated as "Obedience Chairman." At such event the Bench Show Committee of the show-giving club shall have sole jurisdiction over all matters which may properly come before it, regardless of whether the matter has to do with the dog show or with the obedience trial.

Section 6. **Sanctioned Matches.** A club may hold an Obedience Match by obtaining the sanction of The American Kennel Club. Sanctioned obedience matches shall be governed by such regulations as may be adopted by the Board of Directors of The American Kennel Club. Scores awarded at such matches will not be entered in the records of The American Kennel Club nor count towards an obedience title.

All of these Obedience Regulations shall also apply to sanctioned matches except for those sections in which it is specified that the provisions apply to licensed or member trials, and except where specifically stated otherwise in the Regulations for Sanctioned Matches.

Section 7. **American Kennel Club Sanction.** American Kennel Club sanction must be obtained by any club that holds American Kennel Club obedience trials, for any type of match for which it solicits or accepts entries from nonmembers.

Section 8. **Dog Show Rules.** All the Dog Show Rules, where applicable, shall govern the conduct of obedience trials and tracking tests, and shall apply to all persons and dogs participating in them except as these Obedience Regulations may provide otherwise.

Section 9. **Identification.** No badges, club jackets, coats with kennel names thereon or ribbon prizes shall be worn or displayed, nor other visible means of identification used, by an individual when exhibiting a dog in the ring.

Section 10. **Immediate Family.** As used in this chapter, "immediate family" means husband, wife, father, mother, son, daughter, brother, or sister.

Section 11. **Pure-Bred Dogs Only.** As used in these regulations the word "dog" refers to either sex but only to dogs that are pure-bred of a breed eligible for registration in The American Kennel Club stud book or for entry in the Miscellaneous Class at American Kennel Club dog shows, as only such dogs may compete in obedience trials, tracking tests, or sanctioned matches. A judge must report to The American Kennel Club after the trial or tracking test any dog shown under him which in his opinion appears not to be pure-bred.

Section 12. **Unregistered Dogs.** Chapter 16, Section 1 of the Dog Show Rules shall apply to entries in licensed or member obedience trials and tracking tests, except that an eligible unregistered dog for which an ILP number has been issued by The American Kennel Club may be entered indefinitely in such events provided the ILP number is shown on each entry form.

Section 13. **Dogs That May Not Compete.** No dog belonging wholly or in part to a judge or to a Show or Obedience Trial Secretary, Superintendent, or veterinarian, or to any member of such person's immediate family or household, shall be entered in any dog show, obedience trial, or tracking test at which such person officiates or is scheduled to officiate. This applies to both obedience and dog show judges when an obedience trial is held in conjunction with a dog show. However, a tracking test shall be considered a separate event for the purpose of this section.

No dogs shall be entered or shown under a judge at an obedience trial or tracking test if the dog has been owned, sold, held under lease, handled in the ring, boarded, or has been regularly trained or instructed, within one year prior to the date of the obedience trial or tracking test, by the judge or by any member of his immediate family or household, and no such dog shall be eligible to compete. "Trained or instructed" applies equally to judges who train professionally or as amateurs, and to judges who train individual dogs or who train or instruct dogs in classes with or through their handlers.

Section 14. **Qualifying Score.** A qualifying score shall be comprised of scores of more than 50% of the available points in each exercise and a final score of 170 or more points, earned in a single regular or nonregular class at a licensed or member Obedience Trial or Sanctioned Match.

Section 15. **When Titles Are Won.** Where any of the following sections of the regulations excludes from a particular obedience class dogs that have won a particular obedience title, eligibility to enter that class shall be determined as follows: a dog may continue to be shown in such a class after its handler has been notified by three different judges of regular classes in licensed or member trials, that it has received three qualifying scores for such title, but may not be entered or shown in such a class in any obedience trial of which the closing date for entries occurs after the owner has received official notification from The American Kennel Club that the dog has won the particular obedience title.

Where any of the following sections of the regulations require that a dog shall have won a particular obedience title before competing in a particular obedience class, a dog may not be shown in such class at any obedience trial before the owner has received official notification from The American Kennel Club that the dog has won the required title.

Section 16. **Disqualification and Ineligibility.** A dog that is blind or deaf or that has been changed in appearance by artificial means (except for such changes as are customarily approved for its breed) may not compete in any obedience trial or tracking test and must be disqualified. Blind means having useful vision in neither eye. Deaf means without useful hearing.

When a judge finds any of these conditions in any dog he is judging, he shall disqualify the dog marking his book "Disqualified" and stating the reason. He shall not obtain the opinion of the show veterinarian.

The judge must disqualify any dog that attempts to attack any person in the ring. He may excuse a dog that attacks another dog or that appears dangerous to other dogs in the ring. He shall mark the dog disqualified or excused and state the reason in his judge's book, and shall give the Superintendent or Show or Trial Secretary a brief report of the dog's actions which shall be submitted to AKC with the report of the show or trial.

When a dog has been disqualified under this section as being blind or deaf or having been changed in appearance by artificial means or for having attempted to attack a person in the ring, all awards made to the dog at the trial shall be cancelled by The American Kennel Club and the dog may not again compete unless and until, following application by the owner to The American Kennel Club, the owner has received official notification from The American Kennel Club that the dog's eligibility has been reinstated.

Spayed bitches, castrated dogs, monorchid or cryptorchid males, and dogs that have faults which would disqualify them under the standards for their breeds, may compete in obedience trials if otherwise eligible under these regulations.

A dog that is lame in the ring at any obedience trial or at a tracking test may not compete and shall not receive any score at the trial. It shall be the judge's responsibility to determine whether a dog is lame. He shall not obtain the opinion of the show veterinarian. If in the judge's opinion a dog in the ring is lame, he shall not score such dog, and shall promptly excuse it from the ring and mark his book "Excused—lame."

No dog shall be eligible to compete if it is taped or bandaged in any way or if it has anything attached to it for medical or corrective purposes. Such a dog must be immediately excused from the ring, and under no circumstance may it be returned later for judging after the tape, bandage or attachment has been removed.

With the exception of Maltese, Poodles, Shih Tzu and Yorkshire Terriers, which may be shown with the hair over the eyes tied back as they are normally shown in the breed ring, no dog shall be eligible to compete if it appears to have been dyed or colored in any way or if the coat shows evidence of chalk or powder, or if the dog has anything attached to it for protection or adornment. Such a dog may, at the judge's sole discretion, be judged at a later time if the offending condition has been corrected.

An obedience judge is not required to be familiar with the breed standards nor to scrutinize each dog as in dog show judging, but shall be alert for conditions which may require disqualification or exclusion under this section.

Section 17. **Disturbances.** Bitches in season are not permitted to compete. The judge of an obedience trial or tracking test must remove from competition any bitch in season, any dog which its handler cannot control, any handler who interferes willfully with another competitor or his dog, and any handler who abuses his dog in the ring, and may excuse from competition any dog which he considers unfit to compete, or any bitch which appears so attractive to males as to be a disturbing element. If a dog or handler is expelled or excused by a judge, the reason shall be stated in the judge's book or in a separate report.

Section 18. **Obedience Ribbons.** At licensed or member obedience trials the following colors shall be used for prize ribbons or rosettes in all regular classes and for the ribbon or rosette for Highest Scoring Dog in the Regular Classes:

First Prize . . . . Blue
Second Prize . . . . Red
Third Prize . . . . Yellow
Fourth Prize . . . . White
Qualifying Prize . . . . Dark Green
Highest Scoring Dog in the Regular Classes . . . . Blue and Gold

and the following colors shall be used for nonregular classes:

First Prize . . . . Rose
Second Prize . . . . Brown
Third Prize . . . . Light Green
Fourth Prize . . . . Gray

Each ribbon or rosette shall be at least two inches wide and approximately eight inches long, and shall bear on its face a facsimile of the seal of The American Kennel Club, the words "Obedience Trial," the name of the prize, the name of the trial-giving club, the date of the trial, and the name of the city or town where the trial is given.

Section 19. **Match Ribbons.** If ribbons are given at sanctioned obedience matches they shall be of the following colors and shall have the words "Obedience Match" printed on them, but may be of any design or size:

First Prize . . . . Rose
Second Prize . . . . Brown
Third Prize . . . . Light Green
Fourth Prize . . . . Gray
Qualifying Prize . . . . Green with Pink edges

Section 20. **Ribbons and Prizes.** Ribbons for the four official placings and all prizes offered for competition within a single regular or nonregular class at licensed or member trials or at sanctioned matches shall be awarded only to dogs that earn qualifying scores.

Prizes for which dogs in one class compete against dogs in one or more other classes at licensed or member trials or at sanctioned matches shall be awarded only to dogs that earn qualifying scores.

Prizes at a licensed or member obedience trial must be offered to be won outright, with the exception that a prize which requires three wins by the same owner, not necessarily with the same dog, for permanent possession, may be offered for the dog with the highest qualifying score in one of the regular classes, or the dog with the highest qualifying score in the regular classes, or the dog with the highest combined qualifying scores in the Open B and Utility classes.

Subject to the provisions of paragraphs 1 and 2 of this section, prizes may be offered for the highest scoring dogs of the Groups as defined in Chapter 2 of the Dog Show Rules, or for the highest scoring dogs of any breeds, but not for a breed variety. Show varieties are not recognized for obedience. In accordance with Chapter 2, all Poodles are in the Non-Sporting Group and all Manchester Terriers in the Terrier Group.

Prizes offered only to members of certain clubs or organizations will not be approved for publication in premium lists.

Section 21. **Highest Scoring Dog in the Regular Classes.** The dog receiving the highest qualifying score in the regular classes shall be awarded the ribbon and any prizes offered for this placement, after the announcement of final scores of the last regular class to be judged. The Superintendent or Show or Trial Secretary shall mark the catalog to identify the dog receiving this award.

In case of a tie between dogs receiving the highest qualifying score in two or more regular classes, the dogs shall be tested again by having them perform at the same time some part or parts of the Heel Free exercise. The judge for the run-off shall be designated by the Bench Show or Obedience Trial Committee from among the judges of the obedience trial. When the run-off has been completed, the judges shall record the results on a special sheet which shall identify the dogs taking part in the run-off by catalog number, class and breed. When the judge has marked and signed the sheet, it shall be turned over to the Superintendent or Show or Trial Secretary who shall mark the catalog accordingly and forward the sheet to The American Kennel Club as part of the records of the trial.

Section 22. **Risk.** The owner or agent entering a dog in an obedience trial does so at his own risk and agrees to abide by the rules of The American Kennel Club and the Obedience Regulations.

Section 23. **Decisions.** At the trial the decisions of the judge shall be final in all matters affecting the scoring and the working of the dogs and their handlers. The Obedience Trial Committee, or the Bench Show Committee, if the trial is held by a show-giving club, shall decide all other matters arising at the trial, including protests against dogs made under Chapter 20 of the Dog Show Rules, subject, however, to the rules and regulations of The American Kennel Club.

Section 24. **Dogs Must Compete.** Any dog entered and received at a licensed or member obedience trial must compete in all exercises of all classes in which it is entered unless disqualified, expelled, or excused by the judge or by the Bench Show or Obedience Trial Committee, or unless excused by the official veterinarian to protect the health of the dog or of other dogs at the trial. The excuse of the official veterinarian must be in writing and must be approved by the Superintendent or Show or Trial Secretary, and must be submitted to The American Kennel Club with the report of the trial. The judge must report to The American Kennel Club any dog that is not brought back for the Group exercises.

Section 25. **Judging Program.** Any club holding a licensed or member obedience trial must prepare, after the entries have closed, a program showing the time scheduled for the judging of each of the classes. A copy of this program shall be mailed to the owner of each entered dog and to each judge, and the program shall be printed in the catalog. This program shall be based on the judging of no more than 8 Novice entries, 7 Open entries, or 6 Utility entries, per hour during the time the show or trial will be open as published in the premium list, taking into consideration the starting hour for judging if published in the premium list, and the availability of rings. No judge shall be scheduled to exceed the rate of judging. In addition, one hour for rest or meals must be allowed if, under this formula, it will take more than five hours of actual judging to judge the dogs entered under him. No judge shall be assigned to judge for more than eight hours in one day under this formula, including any breed judging assignment if the obedience trial is held in conjunction with a dog show.

If any nonregular class is to be judged in the same ring as any regular class, or by the judge of any regular class, the nonregular class must be judged after the regular class.

Section 26. **Limitation of Entries.** If a club anticipates an entry in excess of its facilities for a licensed or member trial, it may limit entries in any or all regular classes, but nonregular classes will not be approved if the regular classes are limited. A club may limit entries in any or all regular classes to 64 in a Novice class, 56 in an Open class, or 48 in a Utility class.

Prominent announcement of such limits must appear on the title or cover page of the premium list for an obedience trial or immediately under the obedience heading in the premium list for a dog show, with a statement that entries in one or more specified classes or in the obedience trial will automatically close when a certain limit or limits have been reached, even though the official closing date for entries has not arrived.

Section 27. **Additional Judges, Reassignment, Split Classes.** If when the entries have closed, it is found that the entry under one or more judges exceeds the limit established in Section 25, the club shall immediately secure the approval of The American Kennel Club for the appointment of one or more additional judges, or for reassignment of its advertised judges, so that no judge will be required to exceed the limit.

If a judge with an excessive entry was advertised to judge more than one class, one or more of his classes shall be assigned to another judge. The class or classes selected for reassignment shall first be any nonregular classes for which he was advertised, and shall then be either the regular class or classes with the minimum number of entries, or those with the minimum scheduled time, which will bring the advertised judge's schedule within, and as close as possible to, the maximum limit. If a judge with an excessive entry was advertised to judge only one class, the Superintendent, Show Secretary, or Obedience Trial Secretary, shall divide the entry as evenly as possible between the advertised judge and the other judge by drawing lots.

The club shall promptly mail to the owner of each entry affected, a notification of any change of judge. The owner shall be permitted to withdraw such entry at any time prior to the day of the show, and the entry fee shall then be refunded. If the entry in any one class is split in this manner, the advertised judge shall judge the run-off of any tie scores that may develop between the two divisions of the class, after each judge has first run off any ties resulting from his own judging.

Section 28. **Split Classes in Premium List.** A club may choose to announce two or more judges for any class in its premium list. In such case the entries shall be divided by lots as provided above. The identification slips and judging program shall be made up so that the owner of each dog will know the division, and the judge of the division, in which his dog is entered, but no owner shall be entitled to a refund of entry fee. In such case the premium list shall also specify the judge for the run-off of any tie scores which may develop between the dogs in the different divisions, after each judge has first run off any ties resulting from his own judging.

Section 29. **Split Classes, Official Ribbons, Prizes.** A club which holds a split class, whether the split is announced in the premium list or made after entries close, shall not award American Kennel Club official ribbons in either division. The four dogs with the highest qualifying scores in the class, regardless of the division or divisions in which such scores are made, shall be called back into the ring and awarded the four American Kennel Club official ribbons by one of the judges of the class. This judge shall be responsible for recording the entry numbers of the four placed dogs in one of the judges' books.

If a split class is announced in the premium list, duplicate placement prizes may be offered in each division. If prizes have been offered for placements in a class that must be split after entries close, duplicate prizes or prizes of equal value may be offered in the additional division of the class.

Section 30. **Stewards.** The judge is in sole charge of his ring until his assignment is completed. Stewards are provided to assist him, but they may act only on the judge's instructions. Stewards shall not give information or instructions to owners and handlers except as specifically instructed by the judge, and then only in such a manner that it is clear that the instructions are those of the judge.

Section 31. **Ring Conditions.** If the judging takes place indoors the ring should be rectangular and should be about 35′ wide and 50′ long for all obedience classes. In no case shall the ring for a Utility class be less than 35′ by 50′, and in no case shall the ring for a Novice or Open class be less than 30′ by 40′. The floor shall have a surface or covering that provides firm footing for the largest dogs, and rubber or similar non-slip material must be laid for the take off and landing at all jumps unless the surface, in the judge's opinion, is such as not to require it. At an outdoor show or trial the rings shall be about 40′ wide and 50′ long. The ground shall be clean and level, and the grass, if any, shall be cut short. The Club and Superintendent are responsible for providing, for the Open classes, an appropriate place approved by the judge, for the handlers to go completely out of sight of their dogs. If inclement weather at an outdoor trial necessitates the judging of obedience under shelter, the requirements as to ring size may be waived.

Section 32. **Obedience Rings at Dog Shows.** At an outdoor dog show a separate ring or rings shall be provided for obedience, and a sign forbidding anyone to permit any dog to use the ring, except when being judged, shall be set up in each such ring by the Superintendent or Show Secretary. It shall be his duty as well as that of the Show Committee to enforce this regulation. At an indoor show where limited space does not permit the exclusive use of any ring for obedience, the same regulations will apply after the obedience rings have been set up. At a dog show the material used for enclosing the obedience rings shall be at least equal to the material used for enclosing the breed rings. The ring must be thoroughly cleaned before the obedience judging starts if it has previously been used for breed judging.

Section 33. **Judge's Report on Ring and Equipment.** The Superintendent and the officials of the club holding the obedience trial are responsible for providing rings and equipment which meet the requirements of these regulations. However, the judge must check the ring and equipment provided for his use before starting to judge, and must report to The American Kennel Club after the trial any undesirable ring conditions or deficiencies that have not been promptly corrected at his request.

CHAPTER 2

REGULATIONS FOR PERFORMANCE AND JUDGING

Section 1. **Standardized Judging.** Standardized judging is of paramount importance. Judges are not permitted to inject their own variations into the exercises, but must see that each handler and dog executes the various exercises exactly as described in these regulations. A handler who is familiar with these regulations should be able to enter the ring under any judge without having to inquire how the particular judge wishes to have any exercise performed, and without being confronted with some unexpected requirement.

Section 2. **Standard of Perfection.** The judge must carry a mental picture of the theoretically perfect performance in each exercise and score each dog and handler against this visualized standard which shall combine the utmost in willingness, enjoyment and precision on the part of the dog, and naturalness, gentleness, and smoothness in handling. Lack of willingness or enjoyment on the part of the dog must be penalized, as must lack of precision in the dog's performance, roughness in handling, military precision or peremptory commands by the handler. There shall be no penalty of less than ½ point or multiple of ½ point.

Section 3. **Qualifying Performance.** A judge's certification in his judge's book of a qualifying score for any particular dog constitutes his certification to The American Kennel Club that the dog on this particular occasion has performed all of the required exercises at least in accordance with the minimum standards and that its performance on this occasion would justify the awarding of the obedience title associated with the particular class. A qualifying score must never be awarded to a dog whose performance has not met the minimum requirements, nor to a dog that shows fear or resentment, or that relieves itself at any time while in an indoor ring for judging, or that relieves itself while performing any exercise in an outdoor ring, nor to a dog whose handler disciplines or abuses it in the ring, or carries or offers food in the ring.

In deciding whether a faulty performance of a particular exercise by a particular dog warrants a qualifying score, the judge shall consider whether the awarding of an obedience title would be justified if all dogs in the class performed the exercise in a similar manner. The judge must not give a qualifying score for the exercise if he decides that it would be contrary to the best interests of the sport if all dogs in the class were to perform in the same way.

Section 4. **Judge's Directions.** The judge's orders and signals should be given to the handlers in a clear and understandable manner, but in such a way that the work of the dog is not disturbed. Before starting each exercise, the judge shall ask "Are you ready?" At the end of each exercise the judge shall say "Exercise finished." Each contestant must be worked and judged separately except for the Group exercises, and in running off a tie.

Section 5. **No Added Requirements.** No judge shall require any dog or handler to do anything, nor penalize a dog or handler for failing to do anything, that is not required by these regulations.

Section 6. **A and B Classes and Different Breeds.** The same methods and standards must be used for judging and scoring the A and B Classes, and in judging and scoring the work of dogs of different breeds.

Section 7. **Interference and Double Handling.** A judge who is aware of any assistance, interference, or attempts to control a dog from outside the ring, must act promptly to stop any such double handling or interference, and shall penalize the dog substantially or, if in the judge's opinion the circumstances warrant, shall give the dog a score of zero for the exercise during which the aid was received.

Section 8. **Rejudging.** If a dog has failed in a particular part of an exercise, it shall not ordinarily be rejudged nor given a second chance; but if in the judge's opinion the dog's performance was prejudiced by peculiar and unusual conditions, the judge may at his own discretion rejudge the dog on the entire exercise.

Section 9. **Ties.** In case of a tie any prize in a Novice or Open class, the dogs shall be tested again by having them perform at the same time all or some part of the Heel Free exercise. In the Utility class the dogs shall perform at the same time all or some part of the Signal exercise. The original scores shall not be changed.

Section 10. **Judge's Book and Score Sheets.** The judge must enter the scores and sub-total score of each dog in the official judge's book immediately after each dog has been judged on the individual exercises and before judging the next dog. Scores for the group exercises and total scores must be entered in the official judge's book immediately after each group of dogs has been judged. No score may be changed except to correct an arithmetical error or if a score has been entered in the wrong column. All final scores must be entered in the judge's book before prizes are awarded. No person other than the judge may make any entry in the judge's book. Judges may use separate score sheets for their own purposes, but shall not give out nor allow exhibitors to see such sheets, nor give out any other written scores, nor permit anyone else to distribute score sheets or cards prepared by the judge. Carbon copies of the sheets in the official judge's book shall be made available through the Superintendent or Show or Trial Secretary for examination by owners and handlers immediately after the prizes have been awarded in each class. If score cards are distributed by a club after the prizes are awarded they must contain no more information than is shown in the judge's book and must be marked "unofficial score."

Section 11. **Announcement of Scores.** The judge shall not disclose any score or partial score to contestants or spectators until he has completed the judging of the entire class or, in case of a split class, until he has completed the judging of his division; nor shall he permit anyone else to do so. After all the scores are recorded for the class, or for the division in case of a split class, the judge shall call for all available dogs that have won qualifying scores to be brought into the ring. Before awarding the prizes, the judge shall inform the spectators as to the maximum number of points for a perfect score, and shall then announce the score of each prize winner, and announce to the handler the score of each dog that has won a qualifying score.

Section 12. **Explanations and Errors.** The judge is not required to explain his scoring, and need not enter into any discussion with any contestant who appears to be dissatisfied. Any interested person who thinks that there may have been an arithmetical error or an error in identifying a dog may report the facts to one of the stewards or to the Superintendent or Show or Trial Secretary so that the matter may be checked.

Section 13. **Compliance with Regulations and Standards.** In accordance with the certification on the entry form, the handler of each dog and the person signing each entry form must be familiar with the Obedience Regulations applicable to the class in which the dog is entered.

Section 14. **Handicapped Handlers.** Judges may modify the specific requirements of these regulations for handlers to the extent necessary to permit physically handicapped handlers to compete, provided such handlers can move about the ring without physical assistance or guidance from another person, except for guidance from the judge or from the handler of a competing dog in the ring for the Group exercises.

Dogs handled by such handlers shall be required to perform all parts of all exercises as described in these regulations, and shall be penalized for failure to perform any part of an exercise.

Section 15. **Catalog Order.** Dogs should be judged in catalog order to the extent that it is practicable to do so without holding up the judging in any ring.

Judges are not required to wait for dogs for either the individual exercises or the group exercises. It is the responsibility of each handler to be ready with his dog at ringside when required, without being called. The judge's first consideration should be the convenience of those exhibitors who are at ringside with their dogs when scheduled, and who ask no favors.

A judge may agree, on request in advance of the scheduled starting time of the class, to judge a dog earlier or later than the time scheduled by catalog order. However, a judge should not hesitate to mark absent and to refuse to judge any dog and handler that are not at ringside ready to be judged in catalog order if no arrangement has been made in advance.

Section 16. **Use of Leash.** All dogs shall be kept on leash except when in the obedience ring or exercise ring. Dogs should be brought into the ring and taken out of the ring on leash. Dogs may be kept on leash in the ring when brought in to receive awards, and when waiting in the ring before and after the Group exercises. The leash shall be left on the judge's table or other designated place, between the individual exercises, and during all exercises except the Heel on Leash and Group exercises. The leash may be of fabric or leather and, in the Novice classes, need be only of sufficient length to provide adequate slack in the Heel on Leash exercise.

Section 17. **Collars.** Dogs in the obedience ring must wear well-fitting plain buckle or slip collars. Slip collars of an appropriate single length of leather, fabric or chain with two rings, one on each end are acceptable. Fancy collars, or special training collars, or collars that are either too tight or so large that they hang down unreasonably in front of the dogs, are not permitted. There shall not be anything hanging from the collars.

Section 18. **Heel Position.** The heel position as used in these regulations, whether the dog is sitting, standing, or moving at heel, means that the dog shall be straight in line with the direction in which the handler is facing, at the handler's left side, and as close as practicable to the handler's left leg without crowding, permitting the handler freedom of motion at all times. The area from the dog's head to shoulder shall be in line with the handler's left hip.

Section 19. **Hands.** In all exercises in which the dog is required to come to or return to the handler and sit in front, the handler's arms and hands shall hang naturally at his sides while the dog is coming in and until the dog has sat in front. A substantial deduction shall be made if a handler's arms and hands are not hanging naturally at his sides.

Section 20. **Commands and Signals.** Whenever a command or signal is mentioned in these regulations, a single command or signal only may be given by the handler, and any extra commands or signals must be penalized; except that whenever the regulations specify "command and/or signal" the handler may give either one or the other or both command and signal simultaneously. When a signal is permitted and given, it must be a single gesture with one arm and hand only, and the arms must immediately be returned to a natural position. Delay in following a judge's order to give a command or signal must be penalized, unless the delay is directed by the judge because of some distraction or interference.

The signal for downing a dog may be given either with the arm raised or with a down swing of the arm, but any pause in holding the arm upright followed by a down swing of the arm will be considered an additional signal.

Signaling correction to a dog is forbidden and must be penalized. Signals must be inaudible and the handler must not touch the dog. Any unusual noise or motion may be considered to be a signal. Movements of the body that aid the dog shall be considered additional signals except that a handler may bend as far as necessary to bring his hand on a level with the dog's eyes in giving a signal to a dog in the heel position, and that in the Directed Retrieve exercise the body and knees may be bent to the extent necessary to give the direction to the dog. Whistling or the use of a whistle is prohibited.

The dog's name may be used once immediately before any verbal command or before a verbal command and signal when these regulations permit command and/or signal. The name shall not be used with any signal not given simultaneously with a verbal command. The dog's name, when given immediately before a verbal command, shall not be considered as an additional command, but a dog that responds to its name without waiting for the verbal command shall be scored as having anticipated the command. The dog should never anticipate the handler's directions, but must wait for the appropriate commands and/or signals. Moving forward at heel without any command or signal other than the natural movement of the handler's left leg, shall not be considered as anticipation.

Loud commands by handlers to their dogs create a poor impression of obedience and should be avoided. Shouting is not necessary even in a noisy place if the dog is properly trained to respond to a normal tone of voice. Commands which in the judge's opinion are excessively loud will be penalized.

Section 21. **Additional Commands or Signals.** If a handler gives an additional command or signal not permitted by these regulations, either when no command or signal is permitted, or simultaneously with or following a permitted command or signal, or if he uses the dog's name with a permitted signal but without a permitted command, the dog shall be scored as though it had failed completely to perform that particular part of the exercise.

Section 22. **Praise.** Praise and petting are allowed between and after exercises, but points must be deducted from the total score for a dog that is not under reasonable control while being praised. A handler shall not carry or offer food in the ring. There shall be a substantial penalty for any dog that is picked up or carried at any time in the obedience ring.

Section 23. **Handling between Exercises.** In the Novice classes the dog may be guided by the collar between exercises and to get it into proper position for an exercise. No other physical guidance, such as placing the dog in position with the hands or straightening the dog with the knees or feet, is permitted and shall be substantially penalized even if occurring before or between the exercises.

In the Open and Utility classes there shall be a substantial penalty for any dog that is physically guided at any time or that is not readily controllable.

Posing for examination and holding for measurement are permitted. Imperfections in heeling between exercises will not be judged. Minor penalties shall be imposed for a dog that does not respond promptly to its handler's commands or signals before or between exercises in the Open and Utility classes.

Section 24. **Orders and Minimum Penalties.** The orders for the exercises and the standards for judging are set forth in the following chapters. The lists of faults are not intended to be complete but minimum penalties are specified for most of the more common and serious faults. There is no maximum limit on penalties. A dog which makes none of the errors listed may still fail to qualify or may be scored zero for other reasons.

Section 25. **Misbehavior.** Any disciplining by the handler in the ring, any display of fear or nervousness by the dog, or any uncontrolled behavior of the dog such as snapping, barking, relieving itself while in the ring for judging, or running away from its handler, whether it occurs during an exercise, between exercises, or before or after judging, must be penalized according to the seriousness of the misbehavior, and the judge may expel or excuse the dog from further competition in the class. If such behavior occurs during an exercise, the penalty must first be applied to the score for that exercise. Should the penalty be greater than the value of the exercise during which it is incurred, the additional points shall be deducted from the total score under Misbehavior. If such behavior occurs before or after the judging or between exercises, the entire penalty shall be deducted from the total score.

The judge must disqualify any dog that attempts to attack any person in the ring. He may excuse a dog that attacks another dog or that appears dangerous to other dogs in the ring.

Section 26. **Training on the Grounds.** There shall be no drilling nor intensive or abusive training of dogs on the grounds or premises at a licensed or member obedience trial or at a sanctioned match. No practice rings or areas shall be permitted at such events. All dogs shall be kept on leash except when in the obedience ring or exercise ring. Special training collars shall not be used on the grounds or premises at an obedience trial or match. These requirements shall not be interpreted as preventing a handler from moving normally about the grounds or premises with his dog at heel on leash, nor from giving such signals or such commands in a normal tone, as are necessary and usual in everyday life in heeling a dog or making it stay, but physical or verbal disciplining of dogs shall not be permitted except to a reasonable extent in the case of an attack on a person or another dog. The Superintendent, or Show or Trial Secretary, and the members of the Bench Show or Obedience Trial Committee, shall be responsible for compliance with this section, and shall investigate any reports of infractions.

Section 27. **Training and Disciplining in the Ring.** The judge shall not permit any handler to train his dog nor to practice any exercise in the ring either before or after he is judged, and shall deduct points from the total score of any dog whose handler does this. A dog whose handler disciplines it in the ring must not receive a qualifying score. The penalty shall be deducted from the points available for the exercise during which the disciplining may occur, and additional points may be deducted from the total score if necessary. If the disciplining does not occur during an exercise the penalty shall be deducted from the total score. Any abuse of a dog in the ring must be immediately reported by the judge to the Bench Show or Obedience Trial Committee for action under Chapter 2, Section 29.

Section 28. **Abuse of Dogs.** The Bench Show or Obedience Trial Committee shall investigate any reports of abuse of dogs or severe disciplining of dogs on the grounds or premises of a show, trial or match. Any person who, at a licensed or member obedience trial, conducts himself in such manner or in any other manner prejudicial to the best interests of the sport, or who fails to comply with the requirements of Chapter 2, Section 26, shall be dealt with promptly, during the trial if possible, after the offender has been notified of the specific charges against him, and has been given an opportunity to be heard in his own defense in accordance with Chapter 2, Section 29.

Any abuse of a dog in the ring must be immediately reported by the judge to the Bench Show or Obedience Trial Committee for action under Chapter 2, Section 29.

Article XII Section 2 of the Constitution and By-Laws of The American Kennel Club Provides:

Section 29. **Discipline.** The Bench Show, Obedience Trial or Field Trial Committee of a club or association shall have the right to suspend any person from the privileges of The American Kennel Club for conduct prejudicial to the best interests of pure-bred dogs, dog shows, obedience trials, field trials or The American Kennel Club, alleged to have occurred in connection with or during the progress of its show, obedience trial or field trial, after the alleged offender has been given an opportunity to be heard.

Notice in writing must be sent promptly by registered mail by the Bench Show, Obedience Trial or Field Trial Committee to the person suspended and a duplicate notice giving the name and address of the person suspended and full details as to the reasons for the suspension must be forwarded to The American Kennel Club within seven days.

An appeal may be taken from a decision of a Bench Show, Obedience Trial or Field Trial Committee. Notice in writing claiming such appeal together with a deposit of five ($5.00) dollars must be sent to The American Kennel Club within thirty days after the date of suspension. The Board of Directors may itself hear said appeal or may refer it to a committee of the Board, or to a Trial Board to be heard. The deposit shall become the property of The American Kennel Club if the decision is confirmed, or shall be returned to the appellant if the decision is not confirmed.

(See Guide for Bench Show and Obedience Trial Committees in Dealing with Misconduct at Dog Shows and Obedience Trials for proper procedure at licensed or member obedience trials.)

(The Committee at a Sanctioned event does not have this power of suspension, but must investigate any allegation of such conduct and forward a complete and detailed report of any such incident to The American Kennel Club.)

CHAPTER 3
NOVICE

Section 1. **Novice A Class.** The Novice A class shall be for dogs not less than six months of age that have not won the title C.D. A dog that is owned or co-owned by a person who has previously handled or regularly trained a dog that has won a C.D. title may not be entered in the Novice A class, nor may a dog be handled in this class by such person.

Each dog in this class must have a different handler who shall be its owner or co-owner or a member of the immediate family of the owner or co-owner, provided that such member has not previously handled or regularly trained a C.D. dog. The same person must handle the same dog in all exercises. No person may handle more than one dog in the Novice A class.

Section 2. **Novice B Class.** The Novice B class shall be for dogs not less than six months of age that have not won the title C.D. Dogs in this class may be handled by the owner or any other person. A person may handle more than one dog in this class, but each dog must have a separate handler for the Long Sit and Long Down exercises when judged in the same group. No dog may be entered in both Novice A and Novice B classes at any one trial.

Section 3. **Novice Exercises and Scores.** The exercises and maximum scores in the Novice classes are:

1. Heel on Leash .... 40 points
2. Stand for Examination .... 30 points
3. Heel Free .... 40 points
4. Recall .... 30 points
5. Long Sit .... 30 points
6. Long Down .... 30 points

Maximum Total Score .... 200 points

Section 4. **C.D. Title.** The American Kennel Club will issue a Companion Dog certificate for each registered dog, and will permit the use of the letters "C.D." after the name of each dog that has been certified by three different judges to have received qualifying scores in Novice classes at three licensed or member obedience trials, provided the sum total of dogs that actually competed in the regular Novice classes at each trial is not less than six.

Section 5. **Heel on Leash & Figure Eight.** The principal feature of this exercise is the ability of the dog and handler to work as a team.

Orders for the exercise are "Forward," "Halt," "Right turn," "Left turn," "About turn," "Slow," "Normal" and "Fast." "Fast" signifies that the handler must run, handler and dog moving forward at noticeably accelerated speed. In executing the About turn, the handler will always do a Right About turn.

The orders may be given in any sequence and may be repeated as necessary, but the judge shall attempt to standardize the heeling pattern for all dogs in any class.

The leash may be held in either hand or in both hands, provided the hands are in a natural position. However, any tightening or jerking of the leash or any act, signal or command which in the judge's opinion gives the dog assistance shall be penalized.

The handler shall enter the ring with his dog on a loose leash and stand with the dog sitting in the Heel Position. The judge shall ask if the handler is ready before giving the order, "Forward." The handler may give a command or signal to Heel, and shall walk briskly and in a natural manner with his dog on a loose leash. The dog shall walk close to the left side of the handler without swinging wide, lagging, forging or crowding. Whether heeling or sitting, the dog must not interfere with the handler's freedom of motion at any time. At each order to Halt, the handler will stop and his dog shall sit straight and promptly in the Heel Position without command or signal, and shall not move until the handler again moves forward on order from the judge. It is permissible after each Halt, before moving again, for the handler to give a command or signal to Heel. The judge shall say, "Exercise finished" after this portion of the exercise.

Before starting the Figure Eight the judge shall ask if the handler is ready. Figure Eight signifies that on specific orders from the judge to Forward and Halt, the handler and dog, from a starting position midway between two stewards and facing the judge, shall walk briskly twice completely around and between the two stewards, who shall stand 8 feet apart. The Figure Eight in the Novice classes shall be done on leash. The handler may choose to go in either direction. There shall be no About turn or Fast or Slow in the Figure Eight, but the judge must order at least one Halt during and another Halt at the end of this portion of the exercise.

Section 6. **Heel on Leash & Figure Eight Scoring.** If a dog is unmanageable, or if its handler constantly controls its performance by tugging on the leash or adapts pace to that of the dog, the dog must be scored zero.

Substantial deductions shall be made for additional commands or signals to Heel and for failure of dog or handler to change pace noticeably for Slow and Fast.

Substantial or minor deductions shall be made for such things as lagging, heeling wide, poor sits, handler failing to walk at a brisk pace, occasional guidance with leash and other imperfections in heeling.

In scoring this exercise the judge shall accompany the handler at a discreet distance so that he can observe any signals or commands given by the handler to the dog. The judge must do so without interfering with either dog or handler.

Section 7. **Stand for Examination.** The principal features of this exercise are that the dog stand in position before and during the examination, and that the dog display neither shyness nor resentment.

Orders are "Stand your dog and leave when you are ready," "Back to your dog" and "Exercise finished." There will be no further command from the judge to the handler to leave the dog.

The handler shall take his dog on leash to a place indicated by the judge, where the handler shall remove the leash and give it to a steward who shall place it on the judge's table or other designated place.

On judge's order the handler will stand and/or pose his dog off leash by the method of his choice, taking any reasonable time if he chooses to pose the dog as in the show ring. When he is ready, the handler will give his command and/or signal to the dog to Stay, walk forward about six feet in front of the dog, turn around and stand facing the dog.

The judge shall approach the dog from the front, and shall touch only the dog's head, body and hindquarters, using the fingers and palm of one hand only. He shall then order, "Back to your dog," whereupon the handler shall walk around behind his dog and return to the Heel Position. The dog must remain standing until after the judge has said, "Exercise finished."

Section 8. **Stand for Examination, Scoring.** The scoring of this exercise will not start until the handler has given the command and/or signal to Stay, except for such things as rough treatment of the dog by its handler or active resistance by the dog to its handler's attempts to make it stand. Either of these shall be penalized substantially.

A dog that displays any shyness or resentment or growls or snaps at any time shall be scored zero, as shall a dog that sits before or during the examination or a dog that moves away before or during the examination from the place where it was left.

Minor or substantial deductions, depending on the circumstance, shall be made for a dog that moves its feet at any time or sits or moves away after the examination has been completed.

Section 9. **Heel Free, Performance and Scoring.** This exercise shall be executed in the same manner as Heel on Leash & Figure Eight except that the dog shall be off leash and that there shall be no Figure Eight. Orders and scoring shall also be the same.

Section 10. **Recall.** The principal features of this exercise are that the dog stay where left until called by its handler, and that the dog respond promptly to the handler's command or signal to Come.

Orders are "Leave your dog," "Call your dog" and "Finish."

On order from the judge, the handler may give command and/or signal to the dog to Stay in the sit position while the handler walks forward about 35 feet to the other end of the ring, where he shall turn and stand in a natural manner facing his dog. On judge's order or signal, the handler will give command or signal for the dog to Come. The dog must come straight in at a brisk pace and sit straight, centered immediately in front of the handler's feet, close enough that the handler could readily touch its head without moving either foot or having to stretch forward. The dog must not touch the handler or sit between his feet.

On judge's order the handler will give command or signal to Finish and the dog must go smartly to the Heel Position and sit. The manner in which the dog finishes shall be optional with the handler provided that it is prompt and that the dog sit straight at heel.

Section 11. **Recall, Scoring.** A dog must receive a score of zero for the following: not staying without additional command or signal, failure to come on the first command or signal, moving from the place where left before being called or signalled, not sitting close enough in front that the handler could readily touch its head without moving either foot or stretching forward.

Substantial deductions shall be made for a slow response to the Come, varying with the extent of the slowness; for extra command or signal to Stay if given before the handler leaves the dog; for the dog's standing or lying down instead of waiting in the sit position; for extra command or signal to Finish and for failure to Sit or Finish.

Minor deductions shall be made for slow or poor Sits or Finishes, for touching the handler on coming in or while finishing, and for sitting between the handler's feet.

Section 12. **Group Exercises.** The principal feature of these exercises is that the dog remain in the sitting or down position, whichever is required by the particular exercise.

Orders are "Sit your dogs" or "Down your dogs," "Leave your dogs" and "Back to your dogs."

All the competing dogs in the class take these exercises together, except that if there are 12 or more dogs they shall, at the judge's option, be judged in groups of not less than 6 nor more than 15 dogs. When the same judge does both Novice A and Novice B, the two classes may be combined provided that there are not more than 15 dogs competing in the combined classes. The dogs that are in the ring shall be lined up in catalog order along one of the four sides of the ring. Handlers' armbands, weighted with leashes or other articles if necessary, shall be placed behind the dogs.

For the Long Sit the handlers shall, on order from the judge, command and/or signal their dogs to Sit if they are not already sitting. On further order from the judge to leave their dogs, the handlers shall give a command and/or signal to Stay and immediately leave their dogs. The handlers will go to the opposite side of the ring, turn and stand facing their respective dogs.

If a dog gets up and starts to roam or follows its handler, or if a dog moves so as to interfere with another dog, the judge shall promptly instruct the handler or one of the stewards to take the dog out of the ring or to keep it away from the other dogs.

After one minute from the time he has ordered the handlers to leave their dogs, the judge will give the order to return, whereupon the handlers must promptly go back to their dogs, each walking around and in back of his own dog to the Heel Position. The dogs must not move from the sitting position until after the judge has said, "Exercise finished." The judge shall not give the order "Exercise finished" until the handlers have returned to the Heel Position.

Before starting the Long Down the judge shall ask if the handlers are ready. The Long Down is done in the same manner as the Long Sit except that instead of sitting their dogs the handlers shall, on order from the judge, down their dogs without touching either the dogs or their collars, and except further that the judge will order the handlers to return after three minutes. The dogs must not move from the down position until after the judge has said, "Exercise finished."

The dogs shall not be required to sit at the end of the Down exercise.

Section 13. **Group Exercises, Scoring.** During these exercises the judge shall stand in such position that all of the dogs are in his line of vision, and where he can see all the handlers in the ring without having to turn around.

Scoring of the exercises will not start until after the judge has ordered the handlers to leave their dogs, except for such things as rough treatment of a dog by its handler or active resistance by a dog to its handler's attempts to make it Sit or lie Down. These shall be penalized substantially; in extreme cases the dog may be excused.

A score of zero is required for the following: the dog's moving at any time during either exercise a substantial distance away from the place where it was left, or going over to any other dog, or staying on the spot where it was left but not remaining in whichever position is required by the particular exercise until the handler has returned to the Heel Position, or repeatedly barking or whining.

A substantial deduction shall be made for a dog that moves even a minor distance away from the place where it was left or that barks or whines only once or twice. Depending on the circumstance, a substantial or minor deduction shall be made for touching the dog or its collar in getting the dog into the Down position.

There shall be a minor deduction if a dog changes position after the handler has returned to the Heel Position but before the judge has said, "Exercise finished." The judge shall not give the order "Exercise finished" until the handlers have returned to the Heel Position.

CHAPTER 4

OPEN

Section 1. **Open A Class.** The Open A class shall be for dogs that have won the C.D. title but have not won the title C.D.X. Obedience judges and licensed handlers may not enter or handle dogs in this class. Each dog must be handled by its owner or by a member of his immediate family. Owners may enter more than one dog in this class but the same person who handled each dog in the first five exercises must handle the same dog in the Long Sit and Long Down exercises, except that if a person has handled more than one dog in the first five exercises he must have an additional handler, who must be the owner or a member of his immediate family, for each additional dog, when more than one dog that he has handled in the first five exercises is judged in the same group for the Long Sit and Long Down.

Section 2. **Open B Class.** The Open B class will be for dogs that have won the title C.D. or C.D.X. A dog may continue to compete in this class after it has won the title U.D. Dogs in this class may be handled by the owner or any other person. Owners may enter more than one dog in this class but the same person who handled each dog in the first five exercises must handle each dog in the Long Sit and Long Down exercises, except that if a person has handled more than one dog in the first five exercises he must have an additional handler for each additional dog, when more than one dog that he has handled in the first five exercises is judged in the same group for the Long Sit and Long Down. No dog may be entered in both Open A and Open B classes at any one trial.

Section 3. **Open Exercises and Scores.** The exercises and maximum scores in the Open classes are:

1. Heel Free	40 points
2. Drop on Recall	30 points
3. Retrieve on Flat	20 points
4. Retrieve over High Jump	30 points
5. Broad Jump	20 points
6. Long Sit	30 points
7. Long Down	30 points
Maximum Total Score	200 points

Section 4. **C.D.X. Title.** The American Kennel Club will issue a Companion Dog Excellent certificate for each registered dog, and will permit the use of the letters "C.D.X." after the name of each dog that has been certified by three

different judges of obedience trials to have received qualifying scores in Open classes at three licensed or member obedience trials, provided the sum total of dogs that actually competed in the regular Open classes at each trial is not less than six.

Section 5. **Heel Free, Performance and Scoring.** This exercise shall be executed in the same manner as the Novice Heel on Leash and Figure Eight exercise, except that the dog is off leash. Orders and scoring are the same as in Heel on Leash and Figure Eight.

Section 6. **Drop on Recall.** The principal features of this exercise, in addition to those listed under the Novice Recall, are the dog's prompt response to the handler's command or signal to Drop, and the dog's remaining in the Down position until again called or signalled to Come. The dog will be judged on the promptness of its response to command or signal and not on its proximity to a designated point.

Orders for the exercise are "Leave your dog," "Call your dog," an order or signal to Drop the dog, another "Call your dog" and "Finish." The judge may designate in advance a point at which, as the dog is coming in, the handler shall give his command or signal to the dog to Drop. The judge's signal or designated point must be clear to the handler but not obvious or distracting to the dog.

On order from the judge, the handler may give command and/or signal for the dog to Stay in the sit position while the handler walks forward about 35 feet to the other end of the ring, where he shall turn and stand in a natural manner facing his dog. On judge's order or signal, the handler shall give command or signal to Come and the dog must start straight in at a brisk pace. On judge's order or signal, or at a point designated in advance by the judge, the handler shall give command or signal to Drop, and the dog must immediately drop completely to the down position, where he must remain until, on judge's order or signal, the handler again gives command or signal to Come. The dog must come straight in at a brisk pace and sit straight, centered immediately in front of the handler's feet, close enough that the handler could readily touch the dog's head without moving either foot or having to stretch forward. The dog must not touch the handler nor sit between his feet.

The Finish shall be executed as in the Novice Recall.

Section 7. **Drop on Recall, Scoring.** All applicable penalties listed under the Novice Recall as requiring a score of zero shall apply. In addition, a zero score is required for a dog that does not drop completely to the down position on a single command or signal, and for a dog that drops but does not remain down until called or signalled.

Substantial deductions, varying with the extent, shall be made for delayed or slow response to the handler's command or signal to Drop, for slow response to either of the Comes, for extra command or signal to Stay if given before the handler leaves the dog, for the dog's standing or lying down instead of waiting where left in a sit position, for extra command or signal to Finish and for failure to finish.

Minor deductions shall be made for slow or poor sits or finishes, for touching the handler on coming in or while finishing, or for sitting between the handler's feet.

Section 8. **Retrieve on the Flat.** The principal feature of this exercise is that the dog retrieve promptly.

Orders are "Throw it," "Send your dog," "Take it" and "Finish."

The handler shall stand with his dog sitting in the Heel Position in a place designated by the judge. On order, "Throw it," the handler shall give command and/or signal to Stay, which signal may not be given with the hand that is holding the dumbbell, and throw the dumbbell. On order to send his dog, the handler shall give command or signal to retrieve. The retrieve shall be executed at a fast trot or gallop, the dog going directly to the dumbbell and retrieving it without unnecessary mouthing or playing with the dumbbell. The dog must sit straight to deliver, centered immediately in front of the handler's feet, close enough that the handler can readily take the dumbbell without moving either foot or having to stretch forward. The dog must not touch the handler nor sit between his feet. On order from the judge to take it, the handler shall give command or signal and take the dumbbell.

The finish shall be executed as in the Novice Recall.

The dumbbell, which must be approved by the judge, shall be made of one or more solid pieces of one of the heavy hardwoods, which shall not be hollowed out. It may be unfinished, or coated with a clear finish, or painted white. It shall have no decorations or attachments but may bear an inconspicuous mark for identification. The size of the dumbbell shall be proportionate to the size of the dog. The judge shall require the dumbbell to be thrown again before the dog is sent if, in his opinion, it is thrown too short a distance, or too far to one side, or too close to the ringside.

Section 9. **Retrieve on the Flat, Scoring.** A dog that fails to go out on the first command or signal, or goes to retrieve before the command or signal is given, or fails to retrieve, or does not return with the dumbbell sufficiently close that the handler can easily take the dumbbell as described above, must be scored zero.

Substantial deductions, depending on the extent, shall be made for slowness in going out or returning or in picking up the dumbbell, for not going directly to the dumbbell, for mouthing or playing with or dropping the dumbbell, for reluctance or refusal to release the dumbbell to the handler, for extra command or signal to finish and for failure to sit or finish.

Substantial or minor deductions shall be made for slow or poor sits or finishes, for touching the handler on coming in or while finishing, or for sitting between the handler's feet.

Section 10. **Retrieve over High Jump.** The principal features of this exercise are that the dog go out over the jump, pick up the dumbbell and promptly return with it over the jump.

Orders are "Throw it," "Send your dog," "Take it" and "Finish."

This exercise shall be executed in the same manner as the Retrieve on the Flat, except that the dog must clear the High Jump both going and coming. The handler must stand at least eight feet, or any reasonable distance beyond

8 feet, from the jump but must remain in the same spot throughout the exercise.

The jump shall be as nearly as possible one and one-half times the height of the dog at the withers, as determined by the judge, with a minimum height of 8 inches and a maximum height of 36 inches. This applies to all breeds with the following exceptions:

The jump shall be once the height of the dog at the withers or 36 inches, whichever is less, for the following breeds—

Bloodhounds	Mastiffs
Bullmastiffs	Newfoundlands
Great Danes	St. Bernards
Great Pyrenees	

The jump shall be once the height of the dog at the withers or 8 inches, whichever is greater, for the following breeds—

Spaniels (Clumber)	Norwich Terriers
Spaniels (Sussex)	Scottish Terriers
Basset Hounds	Sealyham Terriers
Dachshunds	Skye Terriers
Welsh Corgis (Cardigan)	West Highland White Terriers
Welsh Corgis (Pembroke)	Maltese
Australian Terriers	Pekingese
Cairn Terriers	Bulldogs
Dandie Dinmont Terriers	French Bulldogs

The jumps may be preset by the stewards based on the handler's advice as to the dog's height. The judge must make certain that the jump is set at the required height for each dog. He shall verify in the ring with an ordinary folding rule or steel tape to the nearest one-half inch, the height at the withers of each dog that jumps less than 36 inches. He shall not base his decision as to the height of the jump on the handler's advice.

The side posts of the High Jump shall be 4 feet high and the jump shall be 5 feet wide and shall be so constructed as to provide adjustment for each 2 inches from 8 inches to 36 inches. It is suggested that the jump have a bottom board 8 inches wide including the space from the bottom of the board to the ground or floor, together with three other 8 inch boards, one 4 inch board, and one 2 inch board. A 6 inch board may also be provided. The jump shall be painted a flat white. The width in inches, and nothing else, shall be painted on each side of each board in black 2 inch figures, the figure on the bottom board representing the distance from the ground or floor to the top of the board.

Section 11. **Retrieve over High Jump, Scoring.** Scoring of this exercise shall be as in Retrieve on the Flat. In addition, a dog that fails, either going or returning, to go over the jump, or that climbs or uses the jump for aid in going over, must be scored zero. Touching the jump in going over is added to the substantial and minor penalties listed under Retrieve on the Flat.

Section 12. **Broad Jump.** The principal features of this exercise are that the dog stay sitting until directed to jump and that the dog clear the jump on a single command or signal.

Orders are "Leave your dog," "Send your dog" and "Finish."

The handler will stand with his dog sitting in the Heel Position in front of and at least 8 feet from the jump. On order from the judge to "Leave your dog," the handler will give his dog the command and/or signal to Stay and go to a position facing the right side of the jump, with his toes about 2 feet from the jump, and anywhere between the lowest edge of the first hurdle and the highest edge of the last hurdle.

On order from the judge the handler shall give the command or signal to jump and the dog shall clear the entire distance of the Broad Jump without touching and, without further command or signal, return to a sitting position immediately in front of the handler as in the Recall. The handler shall change his position by executing a right angle turn while the dog is in mid-air, but shall remain in the same spot. The dog must sit and finish as in the Novice Recall.

The Broad Jump shall consist of four hurdles, built to telescope for convenience, made of boards about 8 inches wide, the largest measuring about 5 feet in length and 6 inches high at the highest point, all painted a flat white. When set up they shall be arranged in order of size and shall be evenly spaced so as to cover a distance equal to twice the height of the High Jump as set for the particular dog, with the low side of each hurdle and the lowest hurdle nearest the dog. The four hurdles shall be used for a jump of 52" to 72", three for a jump of 32" to 48", and two for a jump of 16" to 28". The highest hurdles shall be removed first. It is the judge's responsibility to see that the distance jumped is that required by these Regulations for the particular dog.

Section 13. **Broad Jump, Scoring.** A dog that fails to stay until directed to jump, or refuses the jump on the first command or signal, or walks over any part of the jump, or fails to clear the full distance, with its forelegs, must be scored zero. Minor or substantial deductions, depending on the specific circumstances in each case, shall be made for a dog that touches the jump in going over or that does not return directly to the handler. All other applicable penalties listed under the Recall shall apply.

Section 14. **Open Group Exercises, Performance and Scoring.** During Long Sit and the Long Down exercises the judge shall stand in such a position that all of the dogs are in his line of vision, and where he can see all the handlers in the ring, or leaving and returning to the ring, without having to turn around.

These exercises in the Open classes are performed in the same manner as in the Novice classes except that after leaving their dogs the handlers must cross to the opposite side of the ring, and then leave the ring in single file as directed by the judge and go to a place designated by the judge, completely out of sight of their dogs, where they must remain until called by the judge after the expiration of the time limit of three minutes in the Long Sit and five minutes in the Long Down, from the time the judge gave the order to "Leave your dogs." On order from the judge the handlers shall return to the ring in single file in reverse order, lining up facing their dogs at the opposite side of the ring, and returning to their dogs on order from the judge.

Orders and scoring are the same as in the Novice Group exercises.

CHAPTER 5
UTILITY

Section 1. **Utility Class.** The Utility class shall be for dogs that have won the title C.D.X. Dogs that have won the title U.D. may continue to compete in this class. Dogs in this class may be handled by the owner or any other person. Owners may enter more than one dog in this class, but each dog must have a separate handler for the Group Examination when judged in the same group.

Section 2. **Division of Utility Class.** A club may choose to divide the Utility class into Utility A and Utility B classes, provided such division is approved by The American Kennel Club and is announced in the premium list. When this is done the Utility A class shall be for dogs which have won the title C.D.X. and have not won the title U.D. Obedience judges and licensed handlers may not enter or handle dogs in this class. Owners may enter more than one dog in this class but the same person who handled each dog in the first five exercises must handle the same dog in the Group Examination, except that if a person has handled more than one dog in the first five exercises he must have an additional handler, who must be the owner or a member of his immediate family, for each additional dog, when more than one dog he has handled in the first five exercises is judged in the same group for the Group Examination. All other dogs that are eligible for the Utility class but not eligible for the Utility A class may be entered only in the Utility B class to which the conditions listed in Chapter 5, Section 1 shall apply. No dog may be entered in both Utility A and Utility B classes at any one trial.

Section 3. **Utility Exercises and Scores.** The exercises, maximum scores and order of judging in the Utility classes are:

1. Signal Exercise .... 40 points
2. Scent Discrimination
   Article No. 1 .... 30 points
3. Scent Discrimination
   Article No. 2 .... 30 points
4. Directed Retrieve .... 30 points
5. Directed Jumping .... 40 points
6. Group Examination .... 30 points
   Maximum Total Score .... 200 points

Section 4. **U.D. Title.** The American Kennel Club will issue a Utility Dog certificate for each registered dog, and will permit the use of the letters "U.D." after the name of each dog that has been certified by three different judges of obedience trials to have received qualifying scores in Utility classes at three licensed or member obedience trials in each of which three or more dogs actually competed in the Utility class or classes.

Section 5. **Signal Exercise.** The principal features of this exercise are the ability of dog and handler to work as a team while heeling, and the dog's correct responses to the signals to Stand, Stay, Drop, Sit and Come.

Orders are the same as in Heel on Leash and Figure Eight, with the additions of "Stand your dog," which shall be given only when dog and handler are walking at normal pace, and "Leave your dog." The judge must use signals for directing the handler to signal the dog to Drop, to Sit and Come, in that sequence, and to finish.

Heeling in the Signal Exercise shall be done in the same manner as in Heel Free, except that throughout the entire exercise the handler shall use signals only and must not speak to his dog at any time. On order from the judge, "Forward," the handler may signal his dog to walk at heel, and on specific order from the judge in each case, shall execute a "Left turn," "Right turn," "About turn," "Halt," "Slow," "Normal" and "Fast." These orders may be given in any sequence and may be repeated as necessary, but the judge shall attempt to standardize the heeling pattern for all dogs in the class.

On order from the judge, and while the dog is walking at heel, the handler shall signal his dog to Stand in the heel position near one end of the ring. On further order, "Leave your dog," the handler shall signal his dog to Stay, go to the other end of the ring and turn to face his dog. On separate and specific signals from the judge, the handler shall give his signals to Drop, to Sit, to Come and to Finish as in the Recall. During the heeling part of this exercise the handler may not give any signal except when a command or signal is permitted in the Heeling exercises.

Section 6. **Signal Exercise, Scoring.** A dog that fails, on a single signal from the handler, to stand or remain standing where left, or to drop, or to sit and stay, or to come, or that receives a command or audible signal from the handler to do any of these parts of the exercise, shall be scored zero.

Minor or substantial deductions depending on the specific circumstances in each case, shall be made for a dog that walks forward on the Stand, Drop or Sit portions of the exercise.

A substantial deduction shall be made for any audible command during the Heeling or Finish portions of the exercise.

All the penalties listed under the Heel on Leash and Figure Eight and the Recall exercises shall also apply.

Section 7. **Scent Discrimination.** The principal features of these exercises are the selection of the handler's article from among the other articles by scent alone, and the prompt delivery of the right article to the handler.

Orders are "Send your dog," "Take it" and "Finish."

In each of these two exercises the dog must select by scent alone and retrieve an article which has been handled by its handler. The articles shall be provided by the handler and shall consist of two sets, each comprised of five identical objects not more than six inches in length, which may be items of everyday use. One set shall be made entirely of rigid metal, and one of leather of such design that nothing but leather is visible except for the minimum amount of thread or metal necessary to hold the object together. The articles in each set must be legibly numbered, each with a different number and must be approved by the judge.

The handler shall present all 10 articles to the judge, who shall designate one from each set and make written note of the numbers of the two articles he has selected. These two handler's articles shall be placed on a table or chair within the ring until picked up by the handler, who shall hold in his hand only one article at a time. The judge or steward will handle each of the remaining 8 articles as he places them on the floor or ground about 15 feet in front of the handler and dog, at random about 6 inches apart. The judge must make sure that the articles are properly separated before the dog is sent, so that there may be no confusion of scent between the articles.

Handler and dog shall turn around after watching the judge or steward spread the articles, and shall remain facing away from those articles until the judge has taken the handler's scented article and given the order, "Send your dog."

The handler may use either article first, but must relinquish each one immediately when ordered by the judge. The judge shall make certain that the handler imparts his scent to each article only with his hands and that, between the time the handler picks up each article and the time he gives it to the judge, the article is held continuously in the handler's hands which must remain in plain sight.

On order from the judge, the handler will immediately place his article on the judge's book or work sheet. The judge, without touching the article with his hands, will place it among those on the ground or floor.

On order from the judge to "Send your dog," the handler may give the command to Heel before turning, and will execute a Right about Turn, stopping to face the articles, the dog in the Heel Position. The handler shall then give the command or signal to retrieve. Handlers may at their discretion on orders from the judge to "Send your dog," execute with their dog a Right about Turn to face the articles, simultaneously giving the command or signal to retrieve. In this instance the dog shall not assume a sitting position, but shall go directly to the articles. The handler may give his scent to the dog by gently touching the dog's nose with the palm of one open hand, but this may only be done while the dog and handler have their backs to the articles and the arm and hand must be returned to a natural position before handler and dog turn to face the articles.

The dog shall go at a brisk pace to the articles. It may take any reasonable time to select the right article, but only provided it works continuously. After picking up the right article the dog shall return at a brisk pace and complete the exercise as in the Retrieve on the Flat.

These procedures shall be followed for both articles. Should a dog retrieve a wrong article in the first exercise, that article shall be placed on the table or chair. The correct article must be removed, and the second exercise shall be conducted with one less article on the ground or floor.

Section 8. **Scent Discrimination, Scoring.** Deductions shall be the same as in the Retrieve on the Flat. In addition, a dog that fails to go out to the group of articles, or retrieves a wrong article, or fails to bring the right article to the handler, must be scored zero for the particular exercise.

Substantial deductions shall be made for a dog that picks up a wrong article, even though he puts it down again immediately, for any roughness by the handler in imparting his scent to the dog, and for any excessive motions by the handler in turning to face the articles.

Minor or substantial deductions, depending on the circumstance in each case, shall be made for a dog that is slow or inattentive, or that does not work continuously. There shall be no penalty for a dog that takes a reasonably long time examining the articles provided the dog works smartly and continuously.

Section 9. **Directed Retrieve.** The principal features of the exercise are that the dog stay until directed to retrieve, that it go directly to the designated glove, and that it retrieve promptly. The orders for the exercise are "One," "Two" or "Three," "Take it" and "Finish." In this exercise the handler will provide three predominantly white, cotton work gloves, which must be open and must be approved by the judge. The handler will stand with his back to the unobstructed end of the ring with his dog sitting in the Heel Position midway between and in line with the two jumps. The judge or steward will then drop the three gloves across the end of the ring, while the handler and dog are facing the opposite direction, one glove in each corner and one in the center, about 3 feet from the end of the ring and for the corner gloves about 3 feet from the side of the ring. All three gloves will be clearly visible to the dog and handler, when the handler turns to face the glove designated by the judge. There shall be no table or chair at this end of the ring.

The gloves shall be designated "One," "Two" or "Three" reading from left to right when the handler turns and faces the gloves. The judge will give the order "One," or "Two," or "Three." The handler then must give the command to Heel and turn in place, right or left to face the designated glove. The handler will come to a halt with the dog sitting in the Heel Position. The handler shall not touch the dog to get it in position. The handler will then give his dog the direction to the designated glove with a single motion of his left hand and arm along the right side of the dog, and will give the command to retrieve either simultaneously with or immediately following the giving of the direction. The dog shall then go directly to the glove at a brisk pace and retrieve it without unnecessary mouthing or playing with it, completing the exercise as in the Retrieve on the Flat.

The handler may bend his knees and body in giving the direction to the dog, after which the handler will stand erect in a natural position with his arms at his sides.

The exercise shall consist of a single retrieve, but the judge shall designate different glove numbers for successive dogs.

Section 10. **Directed Retrieve, Scoring.** A dog must receive a score of zero for the following: not going out on a single command, not going directly to the designated glove, not retrieving the glove, anticipating the handler's command to retrieve, not returning promptly and sufficiently close so that the handler can readily take the glove without moving either foot or stretching forward.

Depending on the extent, substantial or minor deductions shall be made for a handler who over-turns, or touches the dog or uses excessive motions to get the dog in position.

All other deductions listed under Retrieve on the Flat shall also apply.

Section 11. **Directed Jumping.** The principal features of this exercise are that the dog go away from the handler in the direction indicated, stop when commanded, jump as directed and return as in the Recall.

The orders are "Send your dog," the designation of which jump is to be taken, and "Finish."

The jumps shall be placed midway in the ring at right angles to the sides of the ring and 18 to 20 feet apart, the Bar Jump on one side, the High Jump on the other. The judge must make certain that the jumps are set at the required height for each dog by following the procedure described in Retrieve over the High Jump.

The handler, from a position on the center line of the ring and about 20 feet from the line of the jumps, shall stand with his dog sitting in the Heel Position and on order from the judge shall command and/or signal his dog to go forward at a brisk pace to a point about 20 feet beyond the jumps and in the approximate center. When the dog has reached this point the handler shall give a command to Sit; the dog must stop and sit with his attention on the handler but need not sit squarely.

The judge will designate which jump is to be taken first by the dog, and the handler shall command and/or signal the dog to return to him over the designated jump. While the dog is in mid-air the handler may turn so as to be facing the dog as it returns. The dog shall sit in front of the handler and, on order from the judge, finish as in the Recall. The judge will say "Exercise finished" after the dog has returned to the Heel Position.

When the dog is again sitting in the Heel Position the judge shall ask, "Are you ready?" before giving the order to send the dog for the second part of the exercise. The same procedure shall be followed for the second jump.

It is optional with the judge which jump is taken first, but both jumps must be taken to complete the exercise and the judge must not designate the jump until the dog is at the far end of the ring. The dog shall clear the jumps without touching them.

The height of the jumps shall be the same as required in the Open classes. The High Jump shall be the same as that used in the Open classes, and the Bar Jump shall consist of a bar between 2 and 2½ inches square with the four edges rounded sufficiently to remove any sharpness. The bar shall be painted a flat black and white in alternate sections of about 3 inches each. The bar shall be supported by two unconnected 4 foot upright posts about 5 feet apart. The bar shall be adjustable for each 2 inches of height from 8 inches to 36 inches, and the jump shall be so constructed and positioned that the bar can be knocked off without disturbing the uprights.

Section 12. **Directed Jumping, Scoring.** A dog must receive a score of zero for the following: anticipating the handler's command and/or signal to go out, not leaving the handler, not going out between the jumps, not going at least 10 feet beyond the jumps, not stopping on command, anticipating the handler's command and/or signal to jump, not jumping as directed, knocking the bar off the uprights, climbing or using the top of the High Jump for aid in going over.

Substantial deductions shall be made for a dog that does not stop in the approximate center of the ring; for a dog that turns, stops or sits before the handler's command to Sit, and for a dog that fails to sit.

Substantial or minor deductions, depending on the extent, shall be made for slowness in going out or for touching the jumps. All of the penalties listed under Recall shall also apply.

Section 13. **Group Examination.** The principal features of this exercise are that the dog stand and stay, and show no shyness or resentment.

All the competing dogs take this exercise together, except that if there are 12 or more dogs, they shall be judged in groups of not less than 6 nor more than 15 dogs, at the judge's option. The handlers and dogs that are in the ring shall line up in catalog order, side by side down the center of the ring, with the dogs sitting in the Heel Position. Each handler shall place his armband, weighted with leash or other article if necessary, behind his dog. The judge must instruct one or more stewards to watch the other dogs while he conducts the individual examinations, and to call any faults to his attention.

On order from the judge, "Stand your dogs," all the handlers will stand or pose their dogs and on further order, "Leave your dogs," will give command and/or signal to Stay and walk forward to the side of the ring where they shall turn and stand facing their respective dogs. The judge will approach each dog in turn from the front and examine it, going over the dog with his hands as in dog show judging except that under no circumstance shall the examination include the dog's mouth or testicles.

When all dogs have been examined and after the handlers have been away from their dogs for at least three minutes, the judge will promptly order the handlers, "Back to your dogs," and the handlers will return, each walking around and in back of his own dog to the Heel Position, after which the judge will say, "Exercise finished." Each dog must remain standing at its position in the line from the time its handler leaves it until the end of the exercise, and must show no shyness or resentment. The dogs are not required to sit at the end of this exercise.

Section 14. **Group Examination, Scoring.** There should be no attempt to judge the dogs or handlers on the manner in which the dogs are made to stand. The scoring will not start until after the judge has given the order to leave the dogs, except for such general things as rough treatment of a dog by its handler, or active resistance by a dog to its handler's attempts to make it stand. Immediately after examining each dog the judge must make a written record of any necessary deductions, subject to further deductions for subsequent faults.

A dog must be scored zero for the following: displaying shyness or resentment, moving a minor distance from the place where it was left, going over to any other dog, sitting or lying down before the handler has returned to the Heel Position, growling or snapping at any time during the exercise, repeatedly barking or whining.

Substantial or minor deductions, depending on the circumstance, must be made for a dog that moves its feet at any time during the exercise, or sits or lies down after the handler has returned to the Heel Position.

CHAPTER 6

TRACKING

Section 1. **Tracking Test.** This test shall be for dogs not less than six months of age, and must be judged by two judges. With each entry form for a licensed or member tracking test for a dog that has not passed an AKC tracking test there must be filed an original written statement, dated within six months of the date the test is to be held, signed by a person who has been approved by The American Kennel Club to judge tracking tests, certifying that the dog is considered by him to be ready for such a test. These original statements cannot be used again and must be submitted to The American Kennel Club with the entry forms. Written permission to waive or modify this requirement may be granted by The American Kennel Club in unusual circumstances. Tracking tests are open to all dogs that are otherwise eligible under these Regulations.

This test cannot be given at a dog show or obedience trial. The duration of this test may be one day or more within a 15 day period after the original date in the event of an unusually large entry or other unforeseen emergency, provided that the change of date is satisfactory to the exhibitors affected.

Section 2. **T.D. Title.** The American Kennel Club will issue a Tracking Dog certificate to a registered dog, and will permit the use of the letters "T.D." after the name of each dog which has been certified by the two judges to have passed a licensed or member tracking test in which at least three dogs actually participated.

The owner of a dog holding both the U.D. and T.D. titles may use the letters "U.D.T." after the name of the dog, signifying "Utility Dog Tracker."

Section 3. **Tracking.** The tracking test must be performed with the dog on leash, the length of the track to be not less than 440 yards nor more than 500 yards, the scent to be not less than one half hour nor more than two hours old and that of a stranger who will leave an inconspicuous glove or wallet, dark in color, at the end of the track where it must be found by the dog and picked up by the dog or handler. The article must be approved in advance by the judges. The tracklayer will follow the track which has been staked out with flags a day or more earlier, collecting all the flags on the way with the exception of one flag at the start of the track and one flag about 30 yards from the start of the track to indicate the direction of the track; then deposit the article at the end of the track and leave the course, proceeding straight ahead at least 50 feet. The tracklayer must wear his own shoes which, if not having leather soles, must have uppers of fabric or leather. The dog shall wear a harness to which is attached a leash between 20 and 40 feet in length. The handler shall follow the dog at a distance of not less than 20 feet, and the dog shall not be guided by the handler. The dog may be restrained by the handler, but any leading or guiding of the dog constitutes grounds for calling the handler off and marking the dog "Failed." A dog may, at the handler's option, be given one, and only one, second chance to take the scent between the two flags, provided it has not passed the second flag.

Section 4. **Tracking Tests.** A person who is qualified to judge Obedience Trials is not necessarily capable of judging a tracking test. Tracking judges must be familiar with the various conditions that may exist when a dog is required to work a scent trail. Scent conditions, weather, lay of the land, ground cover, and wind, must be taken into consideration, and a thorough knowledge of this work is necessary.

One or both of the judges must personally lay out each track, a day or so before the test, so as to be completely familiar with the location of the track, landmarks and ground conditions. At least two of the right angle turns shall be well out in the open where there are no fences or other boundaries to guide the dog. No part of any track shall follow along any fence or boundary within 15 yards of such boundary. The track shall include at least two right angle turns and should include more than two such turns so that the dog may be observed working in different wind directions. Acute angle turns should be avoided whenever possible. No conflicting tracks shall be laid. No track shall cross any body of water. No part of any track shall be laid within 75 yards of any other track. In the case of two tracks going in opposite directions, however, the first flags of these tracks may be as close as 50 yards from each other. The judges shall make sure that the track is no less than 440 yards nor more than 500 yards and that the tracklayer is a stranger to the dog in each case. It is the judges' responsibility to instruct the tracklayer to insure that each track is properly laid and that each tracklayer carries a copy of the chart with him in laying the track. The judges must approve the article to be left at the end of each track, must make sure that it is thoroughly impregnated with the tracklayer's scent, and must see that the tracklayer's shoes meet the requirements of these regulations.

There is no time limit provided the dog is working, but a dog that is off the track and is clearly not working should not be given any minimum time, but should be marked Failed. The handler may not be given any assistance by the judges or anyone else. If a dog is not tracking it shall not be marked Passed even though it may have found the article. In case of unforseen circumstances, the judges may in rare cases, at their own discretion, give a handler and his dog a second chance on a new track. A track for each dog entered shall be plotted on the ground by one or both judges not less than one day before the test, the track being marked by flags which the tracklayer can follow readily on the day of the test. A chart of each track shall be made up in duplicate, showing the approximate length in yards of each leg, and major landmarks and boundaries, if any. Both of these charts shall be marked at the time the dog is tracking, one by each of the judges, so as to show the approximate course followed by the dog. The judges shall sign their charts and show on each whether the dog "Passed" or "Failed," the time the tracklayer started, the time the dog started and finished tracking, a brief description of ground, wind and weather conditions, the wind direction, and a note of any steep hills or valleys.

The Club or Tracking Test Secretary, after a licensed or member tracking test, shall forward the two copies of the judges' marked charts, the entry forms with certifications attached, and a marked and certified copy of the catalog pages or sheets listing the dogs entered in the tracking test, to The American

Kennel Club so as to reach its office within seven days after the close of the test.

CHAPTER 7
NONREGULAR CLASSES

Section 1. **Graduate Novice Class.** The Graduate Novice class shall be for C.D. dogs that have not been certified by a judge to have received a qualifying score toward a C.D.X. title prior to the closing of entries. Dogs in this class may be handled by the owner or any other person. A person may handle more than one dog in this class, but each dog must have a separate handler for the Long Sit and Long Down exercises when judged in the same group. Dogs entered in Graduate Novice may also be entered in one of the Open classes.

Performances and judging shall be as in the Regular classes, except that the Figure 8 is omitted from the Heel on Leash exercise. The exercises, maximum scores and order of judging in the Graduate Novice class are:

1. Heel on Leash (no Figure 8) 30
2. Stand for Eaxmination 30
3. Open Heel Free 40
4. Open Drop on Recall 40
5. Open Long Sit 30
6. Open Long Down 30
   Maximum Total Score 200

Section 2. **Brace Class.** The Brace class shall be for braces of dogs of the same breed that are eligible under these Regulations and capable of performing the Novice exercises. The dogs need not be owned by the same person, but must be handled by one handler. Dogs may be shown unattached or coupled, the coupling device to be not less than six inches over-all length; whichever method is used must be continued throughout all exercises. A separate Official Entry Form must be completed in full for each dog entered.

Exercises, performances and judging shall be as in the Novice class. The brace should work in unison at all times. Either or both dogs in a brace may be entered in another class or classes at the same trial.

Section 3. **Veterans Class.** The Veterans class shall be for dogs that have an obedience title and are eight or more years old prior to the closing of entries. The exercises shall be performed and judged as in the Novice class. Dogs entered in the Veterans class may not be entered in any Regular class.

Section 4. **Versatility Class.** The Versatility class shall be for dogs that are eligible under these Regulations and capable of performing the Utility exercises. Owners may enter more than one dog. Dogs in this class may be handled by the owner or any other person, and may be entered in another class or classes at the same trial.

Six exercises will be performed, two each from the Novice, Open and Utility classes, except that there will be no Group exercises. The exercises will be performed and judged as in the Regular classes. The exercises to be performed by each dog will be determined by the handlers drawing one of a set of cards listing combinations of the six exercises totaling 200 points. These cards will be furnished by the trial-giving clubs. Each handler shall provide a dumbbell, Scent Discrimination articles and Directed Retrieve gloves.

Novice	exercise No. 1.	25
Novice	exercise No. 2.	25
Open	exercise No. 1.	35
Open	exercise No. 2.	35
Utility	exercise No. 1.	40
Utility	exercise No. 2.	40
Maximum Total Score		200

Section 5. **Team Class.** The Team Class shall be for teams of any four dogs that are eligible under these Regulations. Five dogs may be entered, one to be considered an alternate for which no entry fee shall be required. However, the same four dogs must perform all exercises. Dogs need not be owner-handled, need not be entered in another class at the same trial, and need not have obedience titles. A separate Official Entry Form must be completed in full for each dog entered.

There shall be two judges, one of whom will call commands while the other scores the teams' performances. The teams will be judged one at a time, except for the Long Sit and Long Down exercises which shall be done with no more than four teams (16 dogs) in the ring.

The dogs on a team will perform the exercises simultaneously and will be judged as specified for the Novice class, except that a Drop on Recall will be used in place of the Recall exercise. In all exercises except the Drop on Recall, the teams have the option of executing the judge's commands on the team captain's repeat of the command.

In the Figure Eight portion of the Heel on Leash exercise, five stewards will be used. The stewards shall stand eight feet apart in a straight line. One dog and his handler shall stand between two stewards, all members of the team facing in the same direction. On orders from the judge, the team shall perform the Figure Eight, each handler starting around the steward on his left and circling only the two stewards between whom he had been standing.

In the Drop on Recall exercise, the handlers will leave their dogs simultaneously on command of the judge. The dogs shall be called or signalled in one at a time on a separate command from the judge to each handler. The handler shall, without any additional command from the judge, command or signal his dog to drop at a spot mid-way between the line of dogs and the handlers. Each dog shall remain in the Down position until all four have been called and dropped, whereupon the judge shall give the command to call the dogs, which shall be called or signalled simultaneously. The finish shall be done in unison on command from the judge.

Section 6. **Team Class, Scoring.** Scoring of the Team class shall be based on the performance of the dogs and handlers individually plus team precision and coordination. Each dog and handler will be scored against the customary maximum, for a team total of 800 maximum available points. Individual dog's scores need not be recorded. The exercises and maximum scores are:

1. Heel on Leash 160
2. Stand for Examination 120
3. Heel Free 160
4. Drop on Recall 120
5. Long Sit 120
6. Long Down 120
   Maximum Total Score 800

SUGGESTED CONSTRUCTION
OF HIGH JUMP

FRONT VIEW OF HIGH JUMP

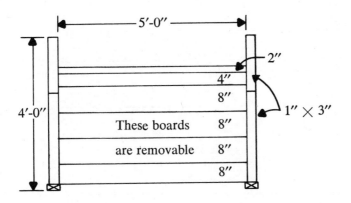

SIDE VIEW OF HIGH JUMP

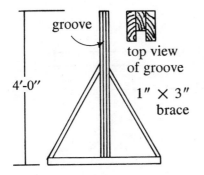

This upright consists of two pieces of $1'' \times 3''$ and one piece $1'' \times 2''$, nailed together, with the $1'' \times 2''$ forming the groove for the boards to slide in.

The high jump must be painted a flat white.

SUGGESTED CONSTRUCTION OF BROAD JUMP

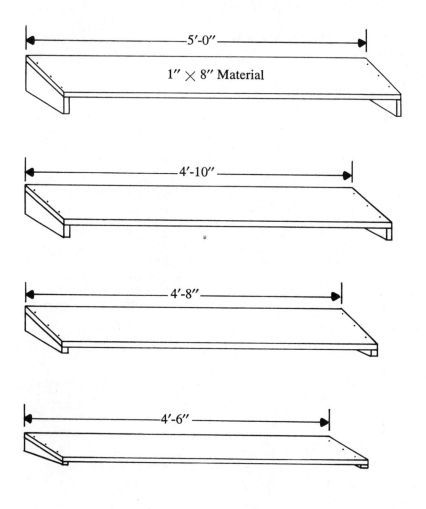

|←————————— 5'-0" —————————→|

1″ × 8″ Material

|←————————— 4'-10" —————————→|

|←————————— 4'-8" —————————→|

|←————————— 4'-6" —————————→|

END VIEW OF FOUR HURDLES

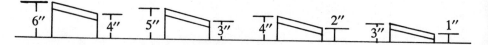

6″   4″   5″   3″   4″   2″   3″   1″

This jump must be painted a flat white.

INDEX